BEYOND THE BATTLEFIELD

Spirituality as an Enabler of Indian Military Leadership

BEYOND THE BATTLEFIELD

SPIRITUALITY AS AN ENABLER OF INDIAN MILITARY LEADERSHIP

Lt Gen Ajai Kumar Singh

PVSM, AVSM, YSM, SM, VSM, PhD (Retd)

Foreword by

Gen Anil Chauhan PVSM, UYSM, AVSM, SM, VSM

CDS & Secretary DMA

PENTAGON PRESS LLP

First published in 2025 by
PENTAGON PRESS LLP
206, Peacock Lane, Shahpur Jat
New Delhi-110049, India
Contact: 011-26490600

Typeset in Adobe Garamond, 11.5 Point
Printed by Aegean Offset Printers, Greater Noida

ISBN 978-81-982857-6-8 (HB)

www.pentagonpress.in

To Shalini, my inspiration, who, despite suffering from an acute medical condition and pain, plodded steadily ahead and smilingly endured every suffering for a higher purpose. Her attitude and positive approach during her fight against numerous medical ailments made me realise our higher purpose for life.

Contents

FOREWORD

1. The Indian civilisation is among the oldest in the world. India's rich cultural and spiritual heritage has been a guiding force in sharing its ethos and values. It has consistently sought excellence with its strategic thoughts shaped by various factors such as geography, historical experiences and its connect with spirituality.

2. Ancient Indian stratagems, detailed in the texts like the Ramayana, Mahabharata, Bhagavad Gita, Arthashastra, Nitisara, Panchatantra, Thirukural and numerous others, encapsulate several pearls of ancient wisdom that serve as repositories of knowledge. These ancient texts also feature intricate narratives of warfare and delve deep into broader themes such as ethics, morality, spirituality and the consequences of war.

3. War and Warfare, today, are evolving rapidly, marked by technological advancements and shifting geo-political dynamics. Despite the changing contours, I firmly believe that the broad stratagems on 'Principles of Warfare' and 'Connect of Spirituality with Leadership' contained in our ancient texts remain perennially relevant, as they provide timeless lessons in statecraft, good governance, military decision-making and conflict resolution whilst maintaining a high moral ground.

4. It fills me with contentment and pride to note that senior military leaders like General Ajai Kumar Singh are utilizing their vast experience and military acumen to underscore the critical role of India's rich spiritual and cultural heritage. His brilliant articulation "Beyond The Battlefield – Spirituality as an Enabler of Indian Military Leadership" is a seminal work that masterfully bridges the gap between theoretical insights and practical application as it seeks to highlight the enduring connect between Indian spirituality and military leadership.

Contd 2/-

5. The book serves as a testament to the timeless relevance of India's philosophical traditions and their role in shaping leaders who are not only tactically astute but also morally grounded. The integration of spirituality in military leadership also fosters a sense of purpose and inner strength, enabling leaders to navigate complex challenges with composure. It encourages decision-making rooted in principles rather than impulses, ensuring that actions align with long-term goals and ethical standards.

6. As Vishnu Purana states "सा विद्या या विमुक्तये" (True knowledge is the one that liberates), I am sanguine that this book will instantaneously connect with all its readers as it stands out for its relevance beyond the battlefield. I am also certain that the concepts, dextrously iterated in the book, will further invoke ideation by future generations of Indian military leaders and strategists on a topic that would only gain importance in the foreseeable future.

Jai Hind!

(Anil Chauhan)
General
Chief of Defence Staff

Preface

रथः शरीरं पुरुषस्य राजत्रात्मा नियन्तेन्द्रियाण्यस्य चाश्चाः ।
तैरप्रमत्तः कुशली सदश्वैर्दान्तैः सुखं याति रथीव धीरः ।।

The human-body is the chariot, the soul (intellect) is its charioteer, the senses are its horses. The person who holds them carefully, cleverly and wisely travels happily in the world like a superior Rrathwan.

– *Kathopanishad* (1.3.3-4) [v21]

The Indian military leadership that leads the Indian Army is engaged in one of the most significant and critical tasks to ensure the security of our beloved nation. Undertaking this task involves making well-considered decisions in the most challenging environments with time and information criticality adding to the degree of difficulty. Motivating the command beyond tangibles, making them disregard personal safety and transcend into the zone where lines separating life and death get blurred, are critical towards achieving this important and critical task. While presently the Indian military leadership is undertaking the said task admirably, there is always scope to strengthen it in a way that allows it to do so in a better manner. This research examines the feasibility of spirituality being that enabler of Indian military leadership whereby it makes it more efficient and effective in today's challenging environment.

Most people believe that there is no place for spirituality in the military leadership. In fact, they believe that it is a domain for the saints and the non-fighters. Nothing can be farther from the truth! Spirituality has been the single and most potent source of strength and inspiration that has shaped and changed many lives. Thus, this researcher strongly believes that spirituality is an elixir, the imbibing of which can be a game changer for the Indian military.

With this in mind, I have undertaken this cherished research in which I have initially studied military leadership and spirituality independently and then gone on to understand the interplay between them. By doing so I have understood ways in which spirituality can improve Indian military leadership. Based on this understanding, I have offered workable recommendations for institutionalising the inculcation of spirituality in the Indian defence forces.

I am aware that the road to institutionalising spirituality in the Indian defence forces will be long and winding. Notwithstanding this, I am confident that spirituality would enable the Indian military leadership in more ways than one. The need of the hour therefore is to embrace this concept so that tomorrow's military leadership is well evolved and capable of leading the Indian armed forces effectively through all kinds of challenges and situations that India may face in the ongoing Amrit Kaal.

I also wish to deeply acknowledge the selfless work of my fellow officers who actively assisted me in this research, notably Maj Gen Ashish Sirsikar, Maj Gen Raman R Tiwari, Brig Sushil Chandwani, Col JS Chouhan, Col HS Kohli, Col Sanju Mathew, Maj Abhay Joshi and Hav Nagendra Kumar.

Lt Gen Ajai Kumar Singh, PVSM, AVSM, YSM, SM, VSM, PhD (Retd)

Acknowledgements

This research work has been a period of immense learning for me and I have grown both individually and professionally. While the research bears my name, I am just the front as I have been constantly helped and supported by two important pillars and I would be failing in my duty if I did not acknowledge their contribution towards the successful conduct and conclusion of this research.

I commence by thanking the first pillar and its members, namely, Chaudhary Charan Singh University, Meerut and Meerut College, Meerut. I wish to thank the University for having the faith in allowing me to undertake this research and sincerely hope that this work of mine matches up to the high standards of this esteemed university. I am grateful to the gracious and knowledgeable Vice-Chancellor, Prof. Sangeeta Shukla, whose valuable inputs have helped me refine my research. I am thankful to Prof. Anjali Mittal, Principal, Meerut College for her invaluable guidance. I am grateful to Prof. Hemant Kumar Pandey, HoD, Department of Defence Studies, Meerut College, for his support. I remain eternally grateful to Prof. Anurag Jaiswal, Department of Defence Studies, Meerut College, my supervisor, who with his vast knowledge on the subject and years of experience has been able to give me continuous and nuanced guidance that has resulted in this research being what it is today. I am grateful to the Late Prof. Sanjay Kumar, Prof. Mohd. Rizwan and Prof. Naveen Verma and all the staff of the Department of Defence Studies who, with their continued support, helped me in the conduct and finalisation of my research.

The second pillar that I wish to acknowledge is my family, Shalini, my very gracious wife who has always been my guiding light and source of inspiration and Sanjana, Sukriti, Abhinav and Akshat, my lovely children. All of them have given me unstinted and unending love and support during the period of this research without which this work wouldn't be half of what it is today!

I conclude with the humble hope that this effort of mine is of value to the strategic community and serves as a source of knowledge on this contemporary topic. I also hope that my research will awaken the interest and curiosity of academia towards exploring this important subject further and help in enabling and strengthening the organisation because of whom I am what I am today, namely, the Indian Army.

Jai Hind !

Lt Gen Ajai Kumar Singh, PVSM, AVSM, YSM, SM, VSM, PhD (Retd)

Introduction

हतो वा प्राप्स्यसि स्वर्गं जित्वा वा भोक्ष्यसे महीम् ।
तस्मादुत्तिष्ठ कौन्तेय युद्धाय कृतनिश्चयः ।।

"If you die in battle you will attain heaven. If you win, you will attain the Earth. So, get up and fight. Treat joy and sorrow, victory and defeat, gain and loss alike and prepare yourself for battle."

Lord Krishna to Arjun
Bhagavad Gita, Chapter 2, Verse 37

The Problem Statement

India, over the last few decades, has emerged as a regional power and major world player in the international arena. Along with recognition have come some vulnerabilities – internal and external. Consequently, the Indian armed forces have to be in a constant state of battlefield readiness to handle the persistent threat of a two-and a half-front war as well as be the last bastion for assistance in resolution of internal security threats. Besides, soldiers today have high aspirations on account of the prevailing socio-economic conditions in the country and are highly vulnerable to combat stress, which is an outcome of operational vulnerabilities, situational uncertainties and fatigue due to long tenures in combat/combat-like military operations. Amidst such a demanding environment, the prime responsibility of military commanders is to control combat stress and motivate their men to be able to successfully execute their tasks when called upon to do so. Thus, military leadership emerges as the most crucial factor in deciding and/or Victor or Vanquished, Life or Death, Honour or Humiliation, as in the profession of arms there is no reward for the runners-up.

Existing research on leadership has attributed personal traits of a leader as a determining factor over other parameters while evaluating the performance of a unit or subunit in adverse situations. However, it has also been seen that some leaders despite possessing the above-mentioned traits and applying all doctrinal leadership techniques have failed to achieve the desired results. It is felt that there are some intangible qualities in a leader that allow him to lead his men to success in the fog of war. What then are these qualities?

Motivation, beyond the advocated management principles, complemented by personal traits entering into the realms of self-actualisation could give the soldier confidence, peace and the required balance to act in the desired manner. Leadership should mobilise them by creating a context and culture that influences them to aspire and struggle for the shared vision. It involves a higher sense of calling to fight for something larger than themselves. A common vision created, a value congruence achieved and a higher level of commitments made that inspire both the leader and the led to develop hope, faith, and a sense of bigger purpose detached from immediate tangible gains, that is, transcend into equanimity. An example of this is seen in the *Mahabharata*, where Shree Krishna advises Arjun:

सुखदुःखे समे कृत्वा लाभालाभौ जयाजयौ ।
ततो युद्धाय युज्यस्व नैवं पापमवाप्स्यसि ॥

—*Bhagavad Gita, Chapter 2, Verse 38*

which translates as:

> "*Fight for the sake of duty, treating alike happiness and distress, loss and gain, victory and defeat. Fulfilling your responsibility in this way, you will never incur sin.*"

Soldiers whom military leaders command have to be taken to this level of superior being where they can relate to an existential perspective on life, death and the nature of reality. The question at hand therefore is: *What can enable a military leader to inspire his men to achieve this exalted form of life?* Spirituality which encapsulates these dimensions may be that enabling factor. My research seeks an answer to this specific question. My research will attempt to identify the role of spirituality and look at the ways in which it can enable military leadership, thereby making it more effective and efficient, both in critical operational peacetime environments.

Literature Review

There is a large corpus of literature on topics of leadership and quite a few on varying domains of spiritualism but very few of them attempt to establish the spiritual dimension in military leadership. Most of these attempts have been made in foreign armies. Extant literature on the subject is elucidated upon in the following paragraphs.

Maj. M.S. Torchinsky in his paper 'Strengthening the Military by way of the Soul' has delved into the increased influx of diverse cultures and religious traditions into the Canadian armed forces (CAF). According to him, the younger lot in the CAF reflect a generational change and the challenge is how the military should consider matters of religion and spirituality. He accepts that a co-relation exists between spirituality and productivity but there is a lack of consensus on aspects of religion and secularist beliefs in the CAF. However, the Chaplain Branch in the CAF holds the view that spirituality can coexist with and independent of religion. It considers spirituality to be that part of an individual that connects one to the state of mind, being and place, and gives one a sense of belonging and purpose. Of late, in the Canadian armed forces, spiritual well-being and resilience is emerging as an important cohesive factor within a unit with spiritual leadership falling in the domain of the commanding officer.

Carroll Connelly and Paolo Tripodi in their book, 'Aspects of Leadership; Ethics, Law and Spirituality', have tried to establish an insightful connect between leadership and spirituality. The book, through essays written by Marine Corps officers, academia, legal luminaries and chaplains, highlights the importance of ethics, law and spirituality in counter insurgency warfare. In its section on spirituality, it deals with measures to limit the impact of stress and spiritual disorders. The role of leadership and chaplains in enabling spirituality has been indicated; however, its modalities have not been adequately researched.

Jay Conger, Professor of Leadership and Administration, University of San Diego, CA, along with his associates in his book, 'Spirit at Work: Discovering Spirituality in Leadership' has given a perceptive exploration into the role of spirituality in leadership. Though his focus has been largely on leaders in business, public administration and non-profit organisations, the writers have emphasised the gains of applying spiritual qualities such as justice, fortitude and prudence in enhancing personal aspirations and organisational objectives. The book provides some practical examples on putting the spirit to work in workplaces but falls a little short on delving deep into the intrinsic aspects of spirituality that can be related to leadership.

Another paper that researches into the role of spirituality in bringing about a transformation in army is 'Spiritual leadership and Army transformation: Theory, measurement, and establishing baseline'. Three writers, Louis W. Fry, Steve Vitucci and Mari Cedilo have attempted to establish the role of spiritual leadership in bringing about an organisational transformation. Drawing examples from an attack helicopter squadron in Texas, they have researched the efficacy of spiritual training in influencing responses to visions, altruistic love, hope and faith among soldiers. They state that the purpose of spiritual leadership is to tap into the fundamental needs of both leader and followers for spiritual survival and developing a vision that puts them on a journey which, when undertaken, will give a sense of calling and that life has a meaning and makes a difference. *They found that those practising spiritual leadership at the personal level will score high on life satisfaction in terms of joy, peace and serenity.* Their research *conclusively establishes the relevance of spiritual leadership in transformation of the army and recommends further research on outcomes of spiritual leadership on individuals and organisational effectiveness before it is widely applied.*

In the Indian context too, spirituality has evoked interest among new thinkers who have drawn a definite co-relation between leadership and spirituality. Soni Agarwal (2015) through the research paper, 'Spirituality and Effective Leadership' in the *International Research Journal* and Abhinav Pradhan bring out a clear consistency between spiritual values, its practice and effective leadership. India is known for its rich tradition of ancient wisdom. These include the Vedas, Upanishads, Puranas, *Bhagavad Gita* and the two great epics, the *Mahabharata* and the *Ramayana*. These scriptures contain certain principles for warfare which are essentially applicable even in today's context. According to the paper mentioned above, there are two types of spirituality, 'intrinsic and extrinsic'. While the intrinsic is related to individuals, the extrinsic deals with spiritualism at the place of work. Spirituality encompasses a number of dimensions and lessons from the *Bhagavad Gita*, which when understood illustrate that spirituality is a must for military leadership.

Another relevant evidence of a unique leadership was portrayed by Guru Gobind Singhji, the tenth Sikh Guru. A research paper in *International Journal of Trends in Scientific Research and Development* (IJTSRDO, volume-2, Jan-Feb 2018), clearly states that Guru Gobind Singh was a saint as well as a soldier for his followers, who were inspired by him to fight injustice and persecution in order to reinstate justice, peace and righteousness.

Research Gap

As separate subjects, both spirituality and military leadership have been studied in detail and depth. In fact, it would be fair to say that reams and reams of paper have been written on them. It is though surprising to note that only limited literature is available on the effect of spirituality on military leadership. Further, of that which is available, most of it has been written from a Western perspective. This aspect is clearly evident from the literature review that has elucidated upon certain Western writings on the subject at hand but none so at all from an Indian perspective. The same is extremely surprising as India, since time immemorial, has always had brilliant military leaders who have been deeply guided by spirituality. Instances of this are seen in the epics, namely, the *Ramayana* and the *Mahabharata* and other military leaders down the ages such as Samudra Gupta (Indian Napoleon), Harshavardhan, Prithviraj Chauhan, Shivaji, Lt. Gen. Hanut Singh and Maj. Gen. S.C. Gupta. *There, therefore, exists an interesting research gap on the possible connect between spirituality and military leadership.* As an Indian military leader who is spiritually inclined, I feel that this research gap needs to be analysed and bridged to the maximum extent possible. In doing so, I hope to be able to harness the unending ocean of spirituality and utilize it to further strengthen the Indian military leadership.

Objectives of the Research

The research would enable the following objectives to be achieved:

(a) Study and examine leadership and its types. Trace the evolution of Indian military leadership over the years so as to understand its strengths, weaknesses (if any) and the challenges that it faces in today's dynamic and uncertain geo-strategic environment.

(b) Understand spirituality and the benefits that it brings to the world at large and India in particular. Special emphasis would also be laid on understanding the distinction between spirituality and religion.

(c) Decipher whether spirituality and military leadership can mutually coexist and look at ways by which spirituality would enable Indian military leadership to make it more efficient and effective.

(d) Recommend measures to institutionalise the development of spirituality as an enabler of military leadership of the Indian armed forces.

Research Questions

To achieve the above-stated research objectives, this research would seek to find answers to the following research questions:

(a) What is leadership and what are its types? How has Indian military leadership evolved? Have there been instances of brilliant military leaders who have been spiritually inclined? (The same will be studied through examples).

(b) What is spirituality and what is its essence? What are its benefits?

(c) What is the difference between spirituality and religion? Are they one and the same or are they different in many ways?

(d) Is there a connect between spirituality and Indian military leadership? How can spirituality enable Indian military leadership? Can a theory for a spiritual Indian military be developed? If so, what is it?

(e) How can the inculcation of spirituality in Indian military leadership be institutionalised? What are the structures, methods, processes and timelines for it?

Hypothesis

My research will test the under-mentioned hypothesis:

> "Spirituality will enable the Indian military leadership to make it more effective and efficient in today's challenging environment."

Research Methodology

Universe of the Study. Keeping in mind the vastness of the subject, the universe of the study will be confined to an Indian context. In doing so, spirituality in an Indian context and the ways it can enable Indian military leadership will be studied.

Mixed Method – Qualitative and Quantitative. This being an important part of my research, I would like to elucidate upon my research methodology in detail. The research methodology that I have utilised to undertake my research is 'Mixed method of Qualitative and Quantitative'. While doing so, I have investigated human experience and behaviour through non-numerical data collection and interpreted it in a descriptive and analytical form and have also undertaken a survey for collection and interpretation of numerical data. For my qualitative research, I have used data collection methods of 'Focus Group, 'One on One Interaction' and 'Observation'. A brief elaboration of each is as under:

(a) *Focus Group:* I constituted a 'Southern Command Spiritual Military Leadership Focus Group". This group comprised volunteer middle- and senior-level military leaders who are spiritually inclined. This group along with me brainstormed the research subject and assisted me in arriving at the recommendations of the research.

(b) *One on One Interaction:* Being spiritually inclined, I have had numerous one on one interactions with similarly spiritually inclined individuals. The inputs from these interactions have assisted me in the development of my research immensely and have been utilised by me at relevant portions of the research.

(c) As I am spiritually inclined, I have been able to utilise my personal experiences and observations of all those that I have interacted with during the period of the research towards analysing and arriving at a better understanding of my research topic.

(d) The subject of spirituality has not been introduced in the Indian military as of now. Thus, while there were no specific case studies related to the subject, I studied instances wherein military leadership has been spiritually inclined in an Indian context. These have been included in my research at relevant places. I have also utilised my spiritual learning to conceptualise, formulate and develop the 'Southern Command Spiritual Military Leadership Model'. This can be an important case study for the future.

While undertaking my qualitative research, I have first attempted to understand 'Military Leadership' and 'Spirituality' as separate systems/entities. Information for this has been taken from secondary sources such as books, journals, official reports, newspapers, magazines, articles, and monographs. I have also extensively used the internet to gather data from various websites regarding these systems. I have then tried to understand the ways in which both of them could interact and affect each other and thus provide for ways by which spirituality can enable Indian military leadership. While attempting to collect information on this aspect, I saw that limited information on it was available. Thus, I have then gone on to utilise the quantitative research methodology to undertake a research survey through a detailed questionnaire, and utilised the data to arrive at an understanding of ways by which spirituality would enable Indian military leadership. Having done this, I then worked out recommendations in terms of organisations and implementation strategies by which spirituality could be institutionalised in the Indian armed forces. This was done by formulating the Southern Command Spiritual Military Leadership Focus Group.

Sources of Information

Primary Data. As stated earlier, limited data is available from prevalent research done by other scholars on the theme of this paper. Thus, the researcher has undertaken a research survey through a detailed questionnaire. Brief details of it are as under:

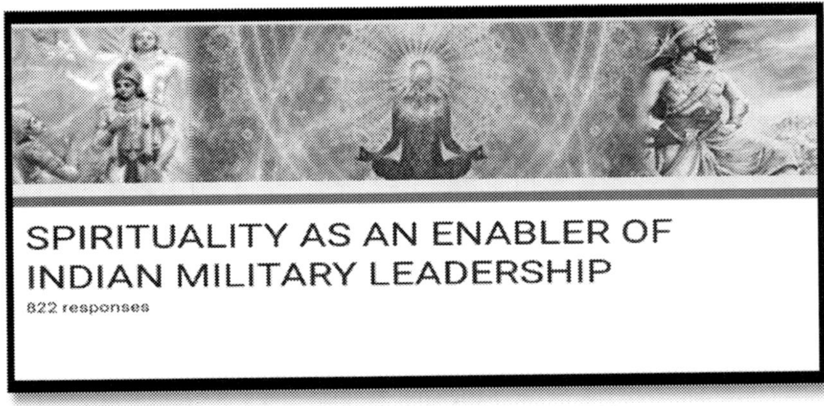

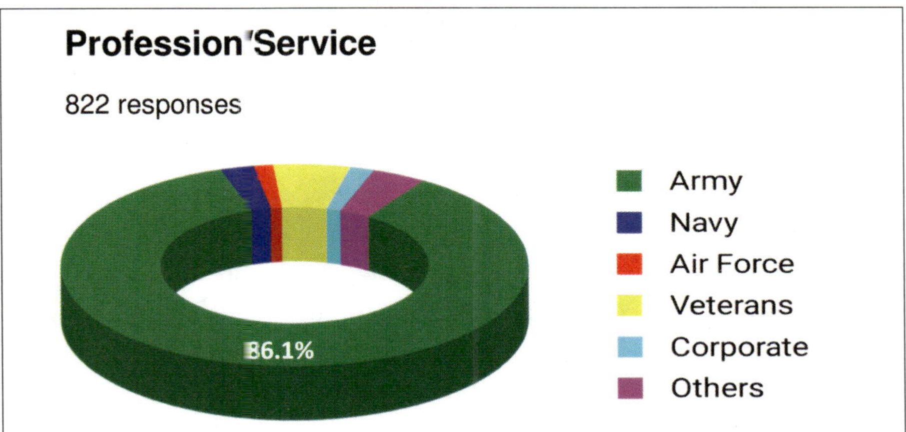
Profession'Service
822 responses
86.1%
Army
Navy
Air Force
Veterans
Corporate
Others

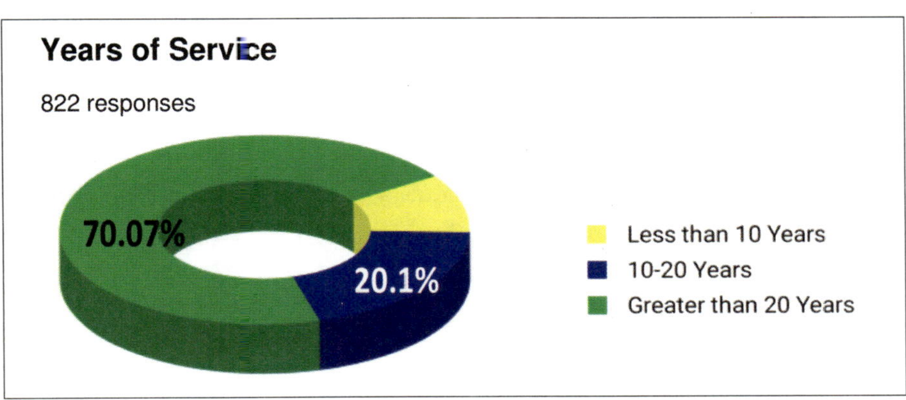
Years of Service
822 responses
70.07%
20.1%
Less than 10 Years
10-20 Years
Greater than 20 Years

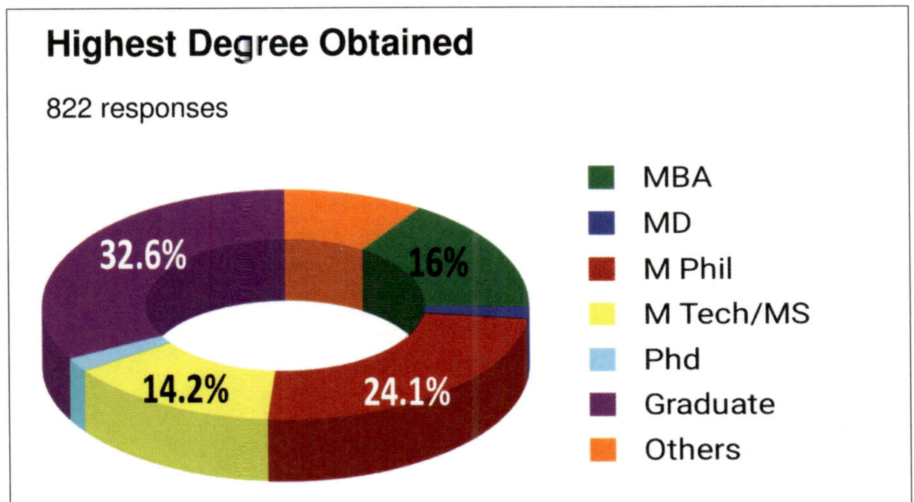
Highest Degree Obtained
822 responses
32.6%
16%
14.2%
24.1%
MBA
MD
M Phil
M Tech/MS
Phd
Graduate
Others

Basic Information related to Quantitative Research Survey. My quantitative research survey was undertaken through a detailed questionnaire compiled through Google forms and circulated by me online. The research survey sought questions under six heads, namely, 'Military Leadership', 'Evolution of Indian Military Leadership', 'Spirituality and its Relevance', 'Spirituality and Indian Military Leadership', 'Present levels of Spirituality in the Indian Armed Forces' and 'Institutionalising Spirituality as an Enabler in the Indian Armed Forces'. The research then utilised descriptive analysis through Google forms analytics and the findings have been utilised in relevant portions of this thesis to strengthen the hypothesis of this research. Post the conduct of this survey, I found that the range and spread of the survey were adequate. The respondents were from diverse backgrounds. The majority of the respondents (71%) had service of more than 20 years and were from a defence background and thus could relate to the subject and give relevant inputs on the subject. That said, respondents from other backgrounds gave an alternate view on the subject too. With about 90 per cent of the respondents having minimum educational qualifications of being graduates, they could give a considered opinion on the subject. Thus, the data set was a good fit for the research.

Secondary Data. I have utilised secondary data/information that exists on the subject from various sources. Secondary data has been used to collect necessary information regarding the theoretical and historical background. This secondary information has been sourced from various books, journals, official reports, newspapers, magazines, articles, and monographs available. I have also extensively utilised the internet to gather data from various websites dealing with the subject. Internet search engines such as Google Scholar have been utilised. In addition, existing interviews and documentaries on the research subject available on YouTube have also been accessed by me to gather data.

Organisation of the Study. The study is proposed to be carried out as under:

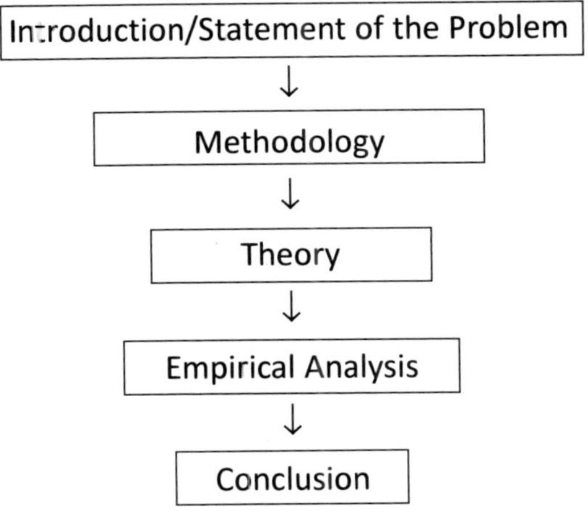

(a) *Introduction.* This part will attempt to highlight the importance of spirituality and military leadership.

(b) *Statement of the Problem.* Today's Indian military leader is saddled with myriad responsibilities and challenges. While he continues to perform in an admirable manner, is there a case where spirituality can be utilised to make him more effective and efficient?

(c) *Methodology.* This part will lay out the 'Mixed methodology of Qualitative and Quantitative' being followed to undertake this research.

(d) *Theory.* This part will study Indian military leadership, spirituality and the interplay between them.

(e) *Empirical Analysis.* Based on empirical data collected through a detailed questionnaire and other sources, the researcher will attempt to lay out ways in which spirituality could enable Indian military leadership and develop structures/processes to institutionalise it.

(f) *Conclusion.* I hope that this work will add quality to the extant literature on the subject. More importantly, I earnestly believe that this work will be the starting point towards developing spiritual Indian military leaders.

Chapterisation

The research will be presented through the following chapters:

Introduction. This will introduce the topic of research and present before the reader the importance and necessity of this research. It will include the background of the research, statement of the problem, the objectives and significance of the study, assumptions and a review of literature, research methodology and outline of the study.

Chapter 1: Military Leadership. This chapter will cover the following:

(i) Leadership – What is leadership and the essence of being a good leader.

(ii) Business leadership vs. military leadership: commonalities and differences. What makes military leadership special?

(iii) Essentials of military leadership.

Chapter 2: Evolution of Indian Military Leadership. This chapter will attempt to study Indian military leadership by tracing it down the ages. It will trace the evolution of Indian military leadership from the Vedic era to the modern-day battlefield. It will look at the stellar leadership qualities that were displayed by some of the prominent military leaders of the epics, the *Ramayana* and the *Mahabharata,* and study the contribution of Indian scriptures towards spirituality and military leadership. It will then fast forward to the post-independence period where it will attempt to critically examine the leadership qualities displayed during the wars and operations fought by India. It will also look at the contemporary leadership being displayed in the ongoing insurgency in J&K. With the above analysis, it will attempt to draw out an understanding of the Indian military leadership.

Chapter 3: Spirituality and its Relevance. This chapter will cover the following:

(i) What is spirituality and what is its essence?

(ii) What does spirituality offer to society, organisation and individual?

(iii) Spirituality and Religion – Are they one and the same? How is spirituality above all religions? Look at spirituality in an Indian context.

Chapter 4: Spirituality & Indian Military Leadership. This chapter will cover the following:

(i) Is spirituality an enabler or inhibitor of Indian military leadership?

(ii) What is the desired end-state and essentials of a spiritual Indian military leader.

(iii) Propose a spiritual leadership theory model for Indian military leadership.

Chapter 5: Present Levels of Spirituality in the Indian Armed Forces. This chapter will cover the following:

(i) Existing models for institutionalising spirituality in the armed forces over the world.

(ii) Present level and structures of spirituality in the Indian armed forces.

Chapter 6: Institutionalising Spirituality as an Enabler in the Indian Armed Forces. This chapter will cover the following:

(i) Suggest structural and organizational reforms/methodology/ processes for institutionalizing spirituality in the Indian armed forces.

(ii) Adopt timelines and mechanisms to include training.

Methodologies

In today's geo-strategic context, the role of Indian military leadership is critical as regards the dynamic geo-political situation and need for safeguarding the country from both internal and external threats. Thus, contemporary Indian military leaders need qualities that enhance their functioning and improves their ability to motivate their troops to follow them in letter and spirit by having unflinching faith in their leadership. This research aims to study ways in which spirituality can enable military leadership. A lot has been researched on military leadership; however, my research on utilising spirituality for enabling Indian military leadership is one of its kind and I hope that it will be a trendsetter for the future.

Chapter One

Military Leadership

As brought out earlier, questions from the survey relevant to this chapter are covered here. In this section, the following questions from the questionnaire are covered: *Are there differences between business leadership and military leadership? Who is a better leader: transactional or transformational? What is the best way to lead men and rate the qualities of leadership in their order of priority?*

Q 1. In your view, are there differences between the Business Leadership and Indian Military Leadership?

822 Responses

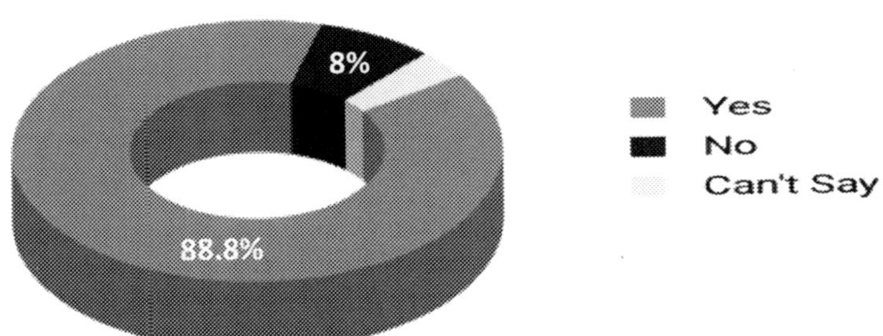

Q 2. In the current world order, a Transformational leader with Charismatic Leadership, Intellectual Stimulation and Individual Consideration will be better poised to handle various aspects of warfare as compared to a Transactional leader who operates from a perspective of Contingent Reward.

822 Responses

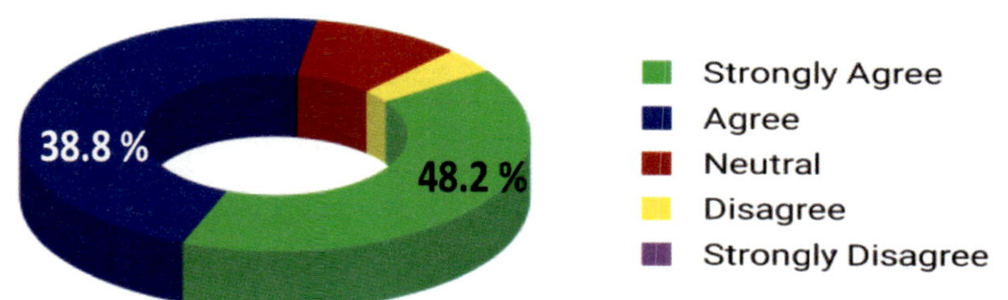

Q 3. The best way to lead a man is by (rate from '1 to 5' with '1' being the best and '5' being the least) (Pan to the left for viewing all options): 822 Responses

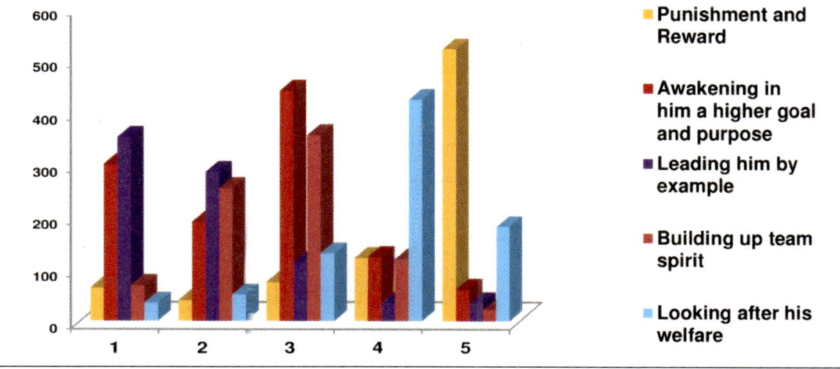

Q 4. Rate in the order of importance the qualities that a military leader should possess ('1' being the most important and '10' being the least)(Pan to the left for viewing all options) 822 Responses

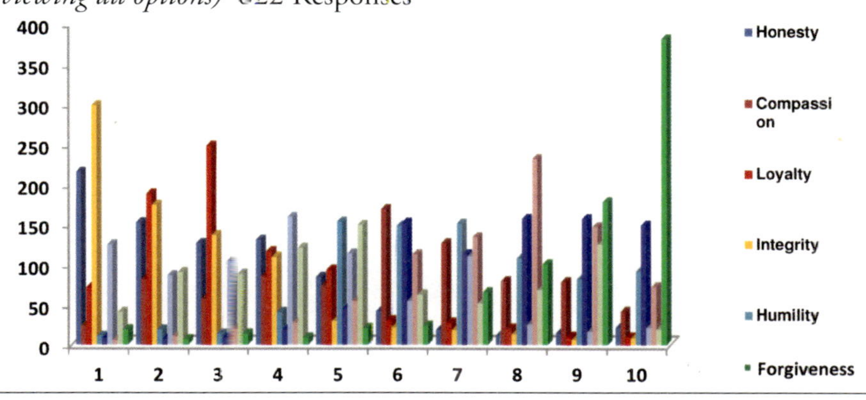

A brief analysis of the responses received to questions posed in this section is as under:

(a) A sizeable majority of 89 per cent agreed that there are significant differences between business and military leadership.

(b) A clear majority (81%) also agreed that transformational leadership was better than transactional leadership.

(c) The majority agreed that the best way to lead a man is by awakening in him to a higher purpose and looking after his welfare rather than punishing/rewarding him.

(d) As regards the qualities that a military leader should possess, the top three qualities were integrity (45%), humility (25%), and professional competence (22%).

Having seen the analysis of the survey, in this section let us understand leadership and its forms to include military leadership.

What is Leadership?

> "*I have got it, but I'll be damned if I could define it.*"
>
> – ***General George S. Patton***

Leadership is a subject that has been researched and studied extensively across ages and countries. This is supported by the fact that leadership study finds its place in all the annals of history of mankind ranging from the '*Arthashastra*' written by Chanakya in the 4th century BC, in which he describes Swami (the king)[1] to present times in which Susan Mazza in her article 'The best definition of Leadership' mentions that there are 316,641 results returned on Google while searching for leadership.[2]

In the history of warfare, weapons, equipment, tactics, and strategy may have changed over a period of time but primacy of leadership remains constant. The Indian Army's Army Training Command (ARTRAC) defines military leadership as "*the art of influencing and directing men so as to win their willing obedience, confidence, respect, and loyal cooperation to carry out the mission.*" It may seem simplistic; however, it is one of the most difficult terms to define. Many great leaders and academicians have given their own version of leadership according to circumstances and environment prevalent in their time. According to Field Marshal Montgomery, being a leader involves having the capacity and desire to bring men and women together for a similar goal and to exhibit morality that instils confidence."[3] On the other hand, it was described as 'the projection of personality' by Field Marshal Slim. The three aspects of coercion, persuasion, and leadership by example gets people to do what you want them to[4]. Notwithstanding the terminology used in each of the above definitions, leadership involves the art of handling men. It is practised by inspiring confidence in them towards their leader. Only those who can inspire their men can really be called true leaders. From the family to the community, to the country, leadership is a continuum. One of the most crucial facets of human behaviour is that it directs the best use of human resources and brings out the best in a man. Leadership is an elusive quality. No weapon or no impersonal machine ever designed can take its place. Leadership is the deciding factor in winning a war.

A leader should be capable of transforming individuals into active, responsible, and enthusiastic participants in a mission – inspiring a sense of espirit de corps. Military leadership is an art of achieving results by synergetic deployment of the led (followers), resources, time, and space. A competent military leader can change defeat into victory while an inefficient commander can change possible victory into sure defeat. In the armed forces leadership is exercised at three levels, that is, tactical, operational, and strategic. Tactical leaders are the ones who deal at the functional level wherein, the emphasis is on physical attributes, raw courage, and personal character. The other two levels of leadership require vision, wisdom, conceptual clarity of thought, clarity of war waging-cum-avoidance techniques, superior management of changing the battlefield milieu including technology and understanding the interface between politico-economic-military activities. President J.F. Kennedy in 1961, while addressing a military academy, had succinctly stated how the demands of military leadership keep changing: "You must comprehend not only this nation but other countries. You need to have some knowledge of economics, politics, diplomacy, history, reasoning, strategy, tactics, and logistics. You need to be as knowledgeable as possible about military force and aware of its limitations."

Definitions and Common Perceptions

As is evident from the opening quote, to understand military leadership is a complex proposition. For a leader, it can only be experienced. Expressing it as a concept would probably require continuous iteration both in its tangible and intangible space. Leadership has been defined, analysed, and interpreted in numerous ways by different writers. Some of these are highlighted below:

(a) 'A person who leads or commands a group, organisation or country' and 'a person who is followed by others' – New Oxford Dictionary

(b) 'The process of influencing the activities of an organised group in the efforts towards goal setting and goal achievement.' – Stodgill

(c) 'The ability to create successful plans and the ability to convince people to implement them despite all obstacles, including death.' – Anonymous

(d) 'Leadership is the art of achieving more than what the science of management says is possible.' – Colin Powell, former US Secretary of State

However, the most relevant reason for defining leadership is to have a guide for one's own development. Some definitions which further strengthen the understanding of leadership are:

(a) The ability of an individual or organisation to 'lead' or guide other people, groups, or entire companies.

(b) The act of leading a team or organisation, or having the capacity to do so.[5]

(c) The capacity and will to rally men and women for a common purpose, and a character that will inspire confidence.[6]

(d) The process of influencing the activities of an organised group in its efforts towards goal-setting and goal achievement.[7]

(e) The skill of persuading and leading others so as to win their trust, respect, and devoted cooperation in order to complete a task.[8]

(f) Leadership is the ability to create successful ideas and the ability to convince others to implement them against all obstacles, including death.[9]

(g) The exercise of leadership entails appreciation of the situation that the group is in and utilise the skills available within the group to transform the situation in favour of the group.[10]

The first five meanings emphasise the relationship between the leader and the followers as well as the leader's capacity to persuade the followers to work towards specific objectives. The last two meanings expand on the leadership quality of having the capacity to make plans.

A good leader is expected to have the ability to foresee, plan, motivate, inspire, lead, and guide. All of the above-mentioned definitions bring out various aspects related to good leadership. A thorough analysis of these definitions superimposed on our environmental realities assist us in coining a comprehensive and relevant leadership definition in the Indian context which can be "*the ability to identify and plan organizational missions and to lead the followers in their accomplishment by providing them direction and motivation.*"[11]

Leadership as an Art

The debate over whether leadership is a science or an art has divided the globe. This paradox is introduced and resolved by Keith Grint in his work '*The Arts of Leadership*.' He writes, "Despite my best efforts to analyse the data (about leadership) as objectively as possible and to run the numbers through as many sophisticated statistical models as I could manipulate, the results refused to regurgitate any meaningful pattern other than one cliché: successful leaders are successful."[12] He goes on to state that "The moment I switched from seeking information to seeking comprehension, a light of some kind started to appear."[13] The author brings out the fact that after objectively studying leadership for a decade in trying to decipher the code of this universal query, he realised that more than knowledge, the understanding of leadership is important. The author discusses three approaches to leadership that remain popular in conventional literature and amplifies a fourth approach which would be important in understanding military leadership. These are as follows:

(a) **Trait Approach.** The essence of the individual leader is critical but the context is not.[14] This approach believes that a leader has certain traits; therefore, the organisation should select a leader rather than identify. Field Manual 22-100 of the American Army lists 14 traits that appeared consistently. These include poise, fortitude, decisiveness, reliability, persistence, zeal, initiative, integrity, judgement, justice, knowledge, loyalty, tact, and selflessness.

(b) **Contingency Approach.** Knowing and understanding the background as well as the essence of the person is crucial.[15] The strategy emphasises the significance of situational analysis and self-awareness as the two growth domains. It means both the individual and the context have to align with each other.

(c) **Situational Approach.** It replicates the essentialist stance with respect to the context, which necessitates a particular style of leadership, so we do need to be very clear about where we are.[16] It further means that a leader's behaviour changes as per the situation.

(d) **Constitutive Approach.** It suggests that 'conditions' are as contentious as any other element and questions the consequence of the ostensibly objective circumstances that surround leaders.[17] It implies that leaders decide the challenges, goals, competition and tactics; and persuade the followers to believe that their understanding is the actual truth. In short, it means that followers are persuaded to achieve the objective wilfully.

This constitutive approach further strengthens the thought process that leadership is not about followers and their persuasion but the ability to identify the environment and lay down the objectives. Grint points out that "We are less likely to comprehend leadership as our analytical tools get more scientific since it is not amenable to such procedures."[18] The author goes about comparing leadership with a picture, the value of which can only be measured by non-scientific ways like popularity, price, or liking by others or one's own self. It is thus important at this juncture to define leadership as an art.

The Art of Leadership and Interpreting Military Leadership

Keith Grint further goes on to divide leadership into four central features which can be mirrored by four arts, namely, Philosophical, Fine, Martial and

Performing.[19] These features highlight a method of looking at leadership from the arts perspective so as to understand it better. This understanding will enable the research to quantify the complexities of military leadership in a simplistic way. The author summarises that leadership is critically concerned with establishing and coordinating the relationships amongst four things; the who, the what, the how and the why. The explanation of these aspects by the author has been simplified with the help of Figure 1.

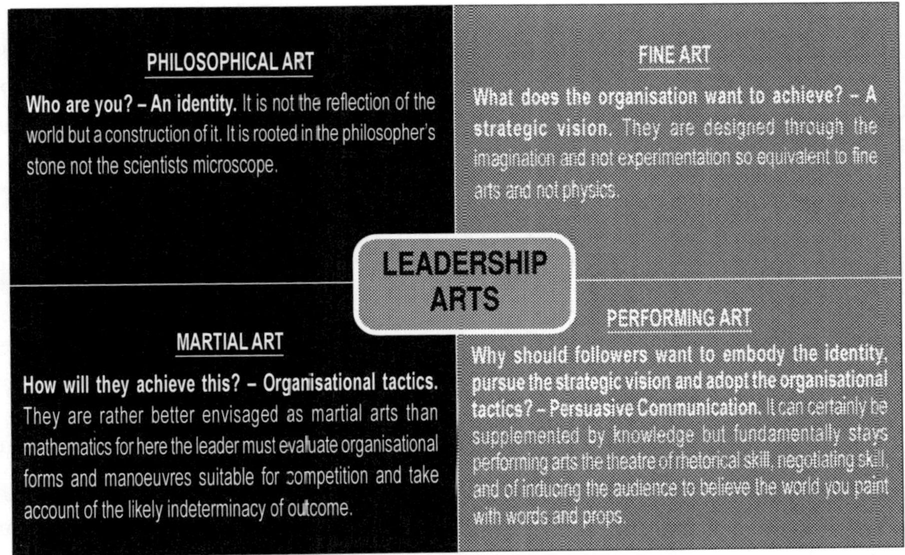

Figure 1: Understanding Leadership Arts[20]

The relevance of knowing these arts is to understand how and what influence will the various realms of challenges posed by the environment have on leadership. These arts of leadership can be honed with practice and experience backed by substantial knowledge of all spheres of leadership. Leaders can use tools of scientific study to enhance the art skill to meet an objective. These resources may include psychology, interpersonal relationships, job analysis, leadership strategies, and statistics. A leader in the midst of combat must cope with far too many unforeseen and unpredictable circumstances. As a result, the trend in military leadership has been to approach it like an art form and develop the traits and skills necessary to perfect it. This proves a point that leadership is an art that can be refined by continuous training.

Contemporary Concepts on Leadership[21]

The general principles of leadership apply regardless of time, and there are different approaches to the study of leadership, namely, the Traits Approach, Contingency Approach, Situational Approach, and Constitutive Approach. Some modern ideas have become more widely accepted as a result of growing industrialisation, a growing population, rising desire for a better quality of life, increased workplace stress, and the ongoing requirement for change management. Since the dawn of time, effective leaders have used these principles; what is new is how they are now understood. It can even be stated that it is a re-discovery of age-old tenets of leadership, which got buried in twentieth century 'corporate consumerist leadership', mainly because of the lack of spiritual intelligence among leaders. Some of these concepts that are relevant to military leadership are:

(a) Transactional Leadership

(b) Transformational Leadership

(c) Principle Centred Leadership

(d) Servant Leadership

Transactional Leadership.[22] A transactional leader views the relationship between him and his subordinates as a transaction on a contractual basis, merely part of a job, and hence temporary in nature. Any leadership based on this philosophy would at best be transactional in nature – in which the subordinates' needs are met if their performance meets the objectives laid down by the leader with heavy dependence on a quid pro quo. Bass & Avolio, 1990, defined the Dimensions of Transactional Leaders as under:

(a) *Contingent Reward (CR).* Here, the leader makes it clear what is anticipated of them and what rewards they will receive if they perform to expectations.[23]

(b) *Active Management by Exception.* The task manager focuses on monitoring task completion for any possible problems and resolving them to maintain current performance levels.

(c) *Passive Avoidant Leadership.* Here, the leader frequently defers making any choices and typically reacts only after issues have become serious enough to warrant corrective action.

Transformational Leadership.[24] Unlike a transactional leader, a transformational leader uses intrinsic rather than extrinsic rewards to inspire his team. Therefore, a leadership strategy that strives to fully integrate the person with the broader purpose through a strong belief in the cause while placing self-interest at second place is what is required at this time. At first sight, this may appear to be a utopian pipe dream or chimera, but a closer look at history may suggest otherwise. When we recall Alexander the Great refusing water in the desert to share the tribulations of his troops, Hannibal leading his army with elephants over the Alps, and Winston Churchill offering nothing more than 'blood, sweat, tears and toil,' we are indeed looking at elements of this very form of leadership. A shining example is that of Mahatma Gandhi who moved the masses to struggle towards the super-ordinate goal of freedom on the strength of morality, intense belief, and commitment to the cause in the face of impossible odds. The search, then, is not for a new form of leadership, but in identifying the ingredients of an existing style that have always been the hallmark of effective leaders through the ages. James McGregor Burns has called it 'Transformational Leadership' in his work on leadership. The main dimensions of transformational leaders as defined by Bass & Avolio, 1990, are:

(a) *Charismatic Leadership (CL).* The ability to instil trust in the subordinate and make them feel good about themselves when they are associated with the leader is what defines charismatic leadership (Idealised Influence).

(b) *Intellectual Stimulation (IS).* This component is demonstrated by the leader's capacity to inspire others to consider novel approaches to problem-solving and new ways of carrying out their tasks.[25]

(c) *Individual Consideration (IC).* This aspect is determined by how well the leader supports personal growth, how much input the leader believes he or she provides to subordinates, and how well the leader invests time in integrating new members into the team or group.[26]

Qualities of a Transformational Leader.[27] Some of the qualities of a transformational leader are enumerated below:

(a) *Definition.* According to Burns, transformational leadership "ultimately becomes moral in that it raises the level of human conduct and ethical aspirations of both leader and led and thus it has a transforming effect." This occurs when "one or more persons engage with others in such a way that leaders and followers raise one another to higher levels of motivation and morality – power bases are linked not as counter-weights, but as mutual support for a common purpose."

(b) *Situational Sensitivity and Style Flexibility*. A balanced combination of rational and emotional elements forms the foundation of a transformational leader's working style. He is aware that the worst form of oppression is a highly programmed way of functioning. There is little opportunity to work in a motivated way. As a result, when creating the job schedule, he leaves enough room for managing the emotions of subordinates.

(c) *Change in Need Levels*. This form of leadership attempts to bring about a transformation both at an organisational as well as individual level. In the armed forces context, it must be viewed as a process of culture change, with values of duty, honour and country as the core. Heavy emphasis on a strong work ethic is also necessary. At an individual level, transformational leadership must bring about a change in the basic orientation of the subordinate – a shift in focus from the self to the organisation goals and raising needs from the low order to the high order needs of self-esteem and self-actualisation as suggested by Abraham Maslow. Since organisations are aggregates of individuals, changes at both the organisation and individual level would have an influence on one another, leading to enhanced effectiveness.

(d) *Discerning Qualities*. The transformational leader is actually a change agent. The unique characteristics about transformational leaders that emerge from one of the surveys of Burns are as follows:

  (i) *Charismatic Leadership*. Unshakeable character, setting an example, encouraging mutual trust and confidence, a firm conviction in the greater good, and an unrelenting pursuit of excellence on a personal level are all components of charisma. Without these attributes, a leader cannot hope to exercise any significant influence on subordinates, much less transform them.

  (ii) *Individualised Consideration*. A transformational leader must not only place self-interest below that of subordinates and the organisation, but also provide evidence to that effect. This aspect must not only appear to be, but actually be genuine. He should be able to identify growth needs in subordinates. Actually, he must be in a position to create these very needs in subordinates as a foundation for intense motivation.

(iii) *Intellectual Stimulation.* Leaders should improve the ability of their team members to solve problems. Sometimes, subordinates are unaware of their own potential. A transformational leader makes them aware of this hidden potential. In doing so, the transformational leader facilitates a fundamental change in subordinates, making them work towards fulfilling these needs.

Principle-Centred Leadership.[28] Dr. Stephen R. Covey argues in his book '*Principle-Centred Leadership*' that some ineffective habits have their roots in societal conditioning that favours quick fixes and short-term thinking. In school, students frequently put off studying for tests before effectively cramming for them. Covey questions whether such an approach would work on a farm. Whether one could forget to milk a cow for two weeks and then milk the yield in one go? Whether one could forget to plant in spring and hope to harvest in the autumn? He is emphatic that such an approach would not work, because there are natural laws governing them. Likewise, he asserts that the only thing that endures over time is the law of the farm – going through the full cycle like preparing the ground, planting the seed, weeding, watering, and gradually nurturing it till development, before one can harvest. The inference is that natural laws and principles, like the law of the farm, operate in all aspects of our lives. There are no short cuts to them; therefore, if we want to be truly effective, we must put these concepts at the core of our individual and interpersonal interactions as well as our business operations.

Covey stresses on two important aspects which are enumerated below:

(a) *The Inner Compass.* Right beliefs are like compasses; they show the way. They ensure that we do not become lost, perplexed, or duped by conflicting voices and ideals if they are read properly. Natural rules are self-evident and self-validating principles. They don't alter or move. They serve as a true north compass when navigating the streams of existence. The foundation of Covey's approach to principle-centred leadership is the understanding that natural rules, such as those governing agriculture, cannot be broken. He claims that throughout the course of human history, these laws have consistently been successful. When individuals and organisations are led and governed by these tried-and-tested concepts, they are more productive and empowered. They are by no means quick fixes, but rather fundamental ideas that, when constantly practiced, develop into behavioural habits that allow for fundamental changes in people, relationships, and organisations.

(b) *Principles and Values.* Covey makes a distinction between principles and values. Values are private and subjective, whereas principles are external and objective. Regardless of circumstances, principles follow the rules of nature. Values are similar to maps, which are arbitrary efforts to depict or describe a place. The principle-centred compass provides priceless vision and direction, while the value-based map offers a good description. While a precise map is a useful management tool, a compass based on the concepts of 'true north' is an instrument for empowerment and leadership. The secret to building strong internal power is to centre lives on the right principles. Whatever occupies the centre of our existence serves as the main energy source for maintaining it. Life becomes more evenly distributed, cohesive, organised, anchored, and rooted when it is centred on the right ideals. It offers a stewardship to everything in life, including time, talents, money, possessions, relationships, families, and one's own body. It serves as the foundation for all activities, relationships, and choices.

Some distinguishing characteristics of principle-centred leaders, which differentiate them from others, are:

(a) *Energy.* They radiate positive energy, are happy, cheerful, positive, optimistic and upbeat. They thereby dispel negative energy fields of others and magnify smaller positive energy fields.

(b) *Trust.* They do not over-react to the negative behaviour of others. They do not negatively judge others, label others, or see others as their competitors. They work in an environment of abundance. They create a climate of growth and opportunity.

(c) *Balanced Personality*. They have many friends. They are active, healthy, and energising. They are open in communication and take a holistic view of life. Their behaviour and attitudes are appropriate, given the circumstances. They possess harmony, moderation, patience, and wisdom. They can feel their own self-worth, which is manifested in their courage and integrity. They are not workaholics. They do not condemn themselves for foolish actions of others. They feel genuinely happy at the success of others. They take the blame and praise proportionately without overreaction.

(d) *Growth*. They educate themselves with their own experiences as also from the experience from others. They do not remain stagnant but learn and grow. They do not break promises as they lower one's self-esteem. They work in an environment of abundance. They create a climate of growth and opportunity.

(e) *Synergy*. In a team, they compensate their own weaknesses with the strength of others and compensate the weakness of others by their own strength, thus synergising the whole system. Thus, they are catalysts of change.

(f) *Service Orientation*. They are service oriented, serving life as a mission and not a career.

(g) *Exercising All Dimensions*. They exercise the physical, mental, emotional, and spiritual facets of personality.

Principle centred leaders achieve primary rather than secondary greatness. Primary greatness comes from within; it is all-encompassing and lasts long. It does not depend upon recognition, rewards, and praise. As opposed to this, secondary greatness aims at immediate gratification, is short term, and is transitory in nature. Principle centred leaders are thus poised for success – not only for themselves, but also for their counterparts, competitors and for the organisation as a whole.

Servant Leadership.[29] Robert K. Greenleaf coined the term 'Servant-Leader,' in his book, '*Servant as Leader*' (1970). His definition of servant leadership is that it is "a useful ideology that encourages people to lead by serving first as a means of extending service to both individuals and institutions." Having official leadership positions is not a requirement for servant-leaders. Collaboration, trust, foresight, listening, and the moral exercise of authority are all fostered through servant leadership.

According to Greenleaf, "Leaders who put others first are servants. It starts with the instinctive desire to serve first and foremost. The desire to lead is then brought about by conscious choice. The difference between that person and a leader initially is obvious. The distinction can be seen in the servant's concern for seeing to it that other people's needs are met in the order of importance."

Servant leadership is not a specific leadership approach; rather, it refers to the motivations behind a leader's ideas, statements, and deeds. A leader can adhere to any of the six leadership philosophies developed in response to McClelland's 'three needs' and still be a servant leader. Servant leaders instead lead in accordance with their calling, vision, and principles rather than their post or leadership role. It can be difficult for servant leaders to make sure that their beliefs and guiding principles are shared by others in their organisation, so it is crucial for them to collaborate with others to create a shared mission and a set of principles.

Qualities of a Servant Leader.[30] Larry Spears, CEO of the Greenleaf Centre, has identified ten qualities that, in his opinion, are crucial for the development of servant-leaders after carefully reading Greenleaf's original writings. This is true even though various servant leadership proponents may place slightly different emphases on particular aspects of the practice. The following ten qualities are not all-inclusive by any means. However, they serve to convey the strength and potential of this idea:

(a) *Listening*. In the past, leaders have been praised for their ability to communicate and make decisions. Servant-leaders must make a strong commitment to pay close attention to what others are saying in order to acquire these crucial skills. The group's will should be recognised and communicated by servant leaders. They make an effort to listen intently to 'what is said' (and 'not said'). Connecting with one's inner voice and striving to interpret the signals being sent by one's body, soul, and intellect are also parts of the listening process. The growth and well-being of the servant-leader depends on their ability to listen and take time for reflection.

(b) *Empathy*. Servant-leaders try to comprehend and relate with others. People require acceptance and appreciation for their distinctive and special spirit. Even when forced to disapprove of a co-worker's behaviour or performance, one must presume that they have the best of motives and refrain from disliking them as a person. The most effective servant-leaders are those who have honed their ability to listen empathically.

(c) *Healing*. A strong factor for transformation and integration is learning to heal. Healing oneself and others is one of the greatest benefits of compassionate leadership. Many individuals have been emotionally wounded in various ways and have a broken spirit. Although this is a trait of humanity, servant leaders are aware of the opportunity they have to aid in the healing of individuals who come into contact with them. According to Greenleaf in "The Servant as Leader," there is a subliminal message sent to the one being served and led if implicit in the relationship between the servant-leader and the led is the awareness that the search for completeness is something that they have."

(d) *Awareness*. The servant-leader is strengthened by consciousness in general and awareness of oneself. Understanding ethical, political, and moral problems can be accomplished through awareness. It makes it easier to see most circumstances from a more comprehensive, integrated perspective. It can be frightening to devote to promoting awareness because you never know what you might learn! "Awareness is not a giver of solace – it is just the opposite," said Greenleaf. It's upsetting. They don't look for comfort. They are secure within themselves.

(e) *Persuasion*. Servant leaders rely on persuasion rather than positional authority when making decisions. Instead of imposing their will on others, servant leaders try to persuade them. This specific aspect makes one of the most obvious distinctions between the servant leadership model and the conventional authoritarian model. The servant leader is good at fostering group agreement.

(f) *Conceptualisation*. Servant leaders work to develop their capacity for big goals. One needs to think out of the box to be able to approach a problem or organisation from a conceptual viewpoint. This trait calls for dedication and practice for many leaders. The pressure to meet immediate operational objectives consumes the traditional leader. The leader must broaden his/her thinking to include more expansive mental thinking if they also want to be a servant-leader. A delicate balance between conceptual thinking and a day-to-day operational strategy must be struck by servant leaders.

(g) *Foresight.* Servant leaders with foresight are able to understand the consequences of their decisions in the future as well as the lessons learned from the past and the reality of the present. Its base is firmly planted in the perceptive mind. The ability to foresee the situation's most likely result is hard to define but easier to recognise. This and conceptualisation are intimately related. One may tell when they have a premonition. Even though it merits careful analysis, the subject of foresight has received little attention in leadership studies.

(h) *Stewardship.* According to Robert Greenleaf, all institutions should be held in trust for the greater benefit of society, and CEOs, employees, directors, and trustees all have important roles to play in this process. Like stewardship, servant-leadership presupposes a dedication to meeting the requirements of others. Additionally, it places a focus on using openness and persuasion rather than dominance.

(i) *Commitment to the Growth of People.* People have an intrinsic worth that goes beyond their observable accomplishments as employees, according to servant leaders. They have a strong commitment to the development of each and every person within the organisation, including their personal, professional, and spiritual progress.

(j) *Building Community.* Servant leaders feel that much has been lost in recent human history as the primary impact on people's lives has shifted from small groups to large institutions. Because of this insight, the servant leader starts to consider how to encourage a sense of belonging among individuals who work for a particular institution. Servant leadership holds that people who work for organisations and other institutions can develop a true community. To rebuild a community as a viable way of life for many people, Greenleaf maintains that "all that is needed is for enough servant leaders to show the way, not through mass movements, but by each servant leader demonstrating his or her unlimited liability for a particular community-related group."

Core Values of Leadership and Interpreting Military Leadership

Military leadership has frequently been based on moral principles, and it has progressed from being wholly autocratic to democratic, leading to participative leadership. Directive leadership, which involves the decentralisation of control and the distribution of authority, has grown in popularity more lately. The common threads running through all its expressions have been professionalism, camaraderie, esprit de corps, bravery, courage, discipline, and faith. These ideas have led to the development of the military's culture of integrity, loyalty, duty, respect, and honour.

It is largely understood that ethos shape values and values drive behaviour. It is the core values that form the basis or foundation of our society and also influence the art of leadership. The core values, namely, character, courage, and competence,[31] which are the drivers of military leadership in our Armed Forces, are discussed in the following paragraphs:

(a) *Character.* The act of leading during pivotal moments and crisis circumstances is a representation of psychological fortitude and human positivism and is linked to the leader's character, which is the most crucial and necessary quality that a leader must have. Character is the collective term for a person's noble, ethically upholding inner qualities. Additionally, it connotes honour, devotion, impartiality, moral rectitude, truthfulness, and dedication. It can be characterised as an interpersonal strength that includes caring for and forming relationships with others as well as the virtues of respect, kindness, and social intelligence. In simple words, a leader must abide by the prevailing moral codes of society and the armed forces and place the interests of his men above that of his own. As Gen. Norman Schwarzkopf puts it, "*Leadership is a potent combination of strategy and character. But if you must be without one, be without strategy.*"

(b) *Courage.* The character traits of bravery, persistence, integrity, and vitality are what define courage as an emotional strength that includes exerting one's will to achieve goals in the face of opposition. Leaders who are courageous often show courage in crucial situations and do not back down from threats, challenges, or difficulties. They are willing to take a stance for what they believe to be right despite the consequences and persist in completing difficult tasks. Courage manifests itself in three interrelated but separate dimensions, that are moral, physical, and psychological. The same are elucidated below:

(i) *Moral Courage.* Moral courage is the capacity to uphold one's beliefs and ideals in the face of all challenges. This value serves as the foundation for all other values and serves as the spark for their realisation.

(ii) *Physical Courage.* On the other hand, physical courage denotes fortitude, valour, and intrepidity. Tenacity, self-control, the desire to succeed, and the resilience to withstand prolonged peril, adversity, and privation are at the core of physical bravery. In combat, fear is unavoidable, and leaders must conquer it while taking into account how it affects each of their subordinates individually.

(iii) *Psychological Courage.* It contains the capacity to handle a difficult circumstance. It is the courage that comes from confronting one's inner demons and encompasses qualities like self-awareness, evaluation, respect, control, and confidence. It is a crucial component of charismatic leadership.

(c) *Competence.* Competence has two ingredients – knowledge and its productive application. A leader must always strive for improvement through professional reading, military training, and practical experience.

Other Values. The other important values that a leader must possess are as under:

(a) Power of Perception.

(b) Commitment to the organisation.

(c) Dynamism.

(d) Perseverance.

(e) Tenacity.

(f) Decisiveness.

(g) Initiative.
(h) Humour.
(j) Integrity and loyalty.
(k) Justice.
(l) Humility.
(m) Self-appraisal.
(n) Pride and confidence.
(o) Resolve.

Functions of Leadership

The act of 'leading men into combat' will always remain the paramount function of a military leader. All the desired functions of a military leader constitute two facets which are to fulfil his charter of duties and shoulder the responsibilities assigned to him. These duties can be further categorised as directed, specified or implied while the responsibility of the leader is both individual and collective. The four vital functions which a leader must execute continuously to influence his command are discussed in the following paragraphs.

Combat Leadership. Leadership and training have a considerable influence on the behaviour of men under conditions of stress and strain. A leader therefore must develop the strength of his command through realistic training simulating the actual combat conditions. The following must remain the guiding principles:[32]

(a) Develop, coordinate, and control the combat power of all the elements of his command.
(b) Promptly restore any part of the potential combat power that may have been reduced or destroyed.
(c) Recognise those battlefield conditions that have a bearing on the combat potential of his command.
(d) Combat fear and isolation through regular visits to isolated posts, informal interaction, and dissemination of accurate information to maintain high morale and motivation.

Training. A good military leader must always lay emphasis on object-oriented training of his men to ensure they deliver when it is required. Training is one of the most indispensable functions of a leader during peace. In reality, training is the place where a variety of foundations are built, including the organisation's culture, creative approaches, and professional competence. A leader must expect high standards from his team. However, he must at the same time show tolerance to mistakes in order to provide a conducive learning environment.

Administration. The part of command known as administration is responsible for troop and equipment supply, maintenance, and movement as well as the organisation, discipline, and welfare of its members. In order to successfully handle the job at hand, administrative arrangements must ensure that the maximum value is obtained from all resources, including men, and that these are properly prepared and balanced. A sound and effective administration goes a long way in ensuring that the troops are always motivated and prepared to undertake any task and successfully accomplish it.

Welfare. Welfare has often been misconstrued by some as paternalistic generosity or pampering. 'Welfare' as explained in the Oxford Thesaurus highlights two very basic yet important attributes – well-being and social security. These are covered as under:

(a) *Well Being.* It includes health, comfort, security, safety, protection, prosperity, and success. In practical terms, this would translate provision of adequate and hygienic living conditions, hot and sumptuous meals, and timely rotation on isolated posts, adequate rest and recreation facilities, security, opportunities for career progression, timely and accurate documentation, and leave as per a leave plan. All leaders must ensure that these amenities are made available at all times and no dilution in standards occurs at any point in time. Regular feedback should also be obtained from the troops.

(b) *Social Security.* Social security would include the rightful status of a soldier in society, supporting a soldier in civil litigations, ensuring that the men get their rightful pension on retirement and also post-retirement assistance to ensure their safety and well-being. The well-being of soldier is related more to the day-to-day provision of a safe, productive, and flourishing functional environment while social security deals with a more complex and long-term welfare which has a bearing on the very image of the Armed Forces in society.

The relevance of military leadership requires no further elaboration. Therefore, it is pertinent to continuously strive to keep pace with the social, economic, and cultural environment as also the revolution in military affairs and understand, analyse and continuously evolve to suit the requirements posed by the environment. Good leaders should, therefore, continuously aim at enhancing their knowledge, build up on their core values, and understand the societal changes and their impact on the soldiers to derive effective ways to lead their men.

Characteristics of Military Leadership. Air Commodore Jasjit Singh (retired) in his book '*Military Leadership for Tomorrow*' states that "The raison d'être of a military force, of course, is to apply sanctioned violence in pursuits of national interests and win the nation's wars for it. Clearly the primary business of a soldier is to fight; and that of his military leader is to ensure that he fights with maximum capability and effect, with minimum costs."[33] The author puts into perspective very simplistically the requirements of a military leader. Behind this simplistic statement lies the complexity of warfare which makes military leadership distinct from the rest. The characteristics for a better understanding of military leadership in an objective manner are as follows:

(a) A military commander must have confidence in his troops and also have their support; he must be able to motivate them to risk their lives for a cause they may only vaguely understand and must possess the courage to demand that they do so.[34] This is what makes military leadership different from the normal, wherein the blind faith of a subordinate tests the character of a military leader. This highlights the importance of the 'performing art' of a military leader, wherein, he requires persuasive communication (see Figure 1).

(b) The military profession has another distinct feature: a wrong decision or failure may jeopardise national security and sometimes national survival. The immediate penalty is paid by the men under the command of the leader who may lose their lives or honour or both. The stakes are indeed very high. What makes the task of a military leader all the more formidable is that he often has to take crucial, long-term decisions in a very short time with inadequate inputs, and even persist with a faulty plan if various constraints do not permit a course correction.[35] Thus, knowingly going towards or leading troops in a way fraught with extreme risks and uncertainties can be a routine job of a military leader making it even more challenging.

(c) One more characteristic that makes military leadership unique is "the way it demands and taps even the last ounce of an individual's physical and psychic resources on the battlefield."[36]

(d) Another complex characteristic of military leadership is that it requires followers to act against their basic human instincts of avoidance of hardship, safety from injury, placid living among the family and preservation of life. Here, followers are not enticed by material gain; rather they have everything to lose except their sense of self-realisation, self-esteem, and a sublime urge for honour; soldiering is a spiritual journey which a normally selfish human being cannot fully appreciate.[37] This is one factor that brings the importance of the art of leadership in understanding the nuances of military leadership.

Dissonance in Conceptual Leadership and Desired Essential Attributes

Symptoms of Dissonance. Notwithstanding, the devastating degradation in the service environment, the tenets of leadership and leadership wisdom of earlier eras are still valid. The concepts emerging in the current environment are useful in expanding the conceptual base of leadership values and enabling a clear comprehension of leadership dynamics. The major disturbing dissonances, which have a long-term implication relating to the leadership culture and ethos, are enumerated in the following paragraphs.[38]

(a) *Credibility and Cynicism.* Progressive erosion of credibility of the system and lack of faith in the senior leadership has resulted in growing cynicism among middle and junior level leadership, both towards the organisation and towards senior leaders.

(b) *Careerism.* 'Self before Service' and 'cut-throatism' have emerged as core values, due to the highly competitive and materialistic environment. This cuts across leadership at all levels, but when manifested at senior levels, results in a cascading effect, which has a serious implication for the organisation.

(c) *Crunch.* Ineffective management and a lackadaisical attitude towards the job is sought to be covered up in the omnipresent excuse of a resource crunch. When displayed by senior leadership, it gives rise to cynicism at junior levels leading to lack of adequate effort in job accomplishment. This results in stagnation in the environment.

(d) *Creativity and Conceptual Skills.* Both are in short supply. Creativity is often stifled by senior leaders due to professional insecurity and lack of vision resulting in poorly motivated and ill-trained subordinates, incapable of handling responsibility and carrying out independent actions.

(e) *Accountability and Result Orientation.* Existing systems are not conducive to result orientation except in battle. Accountability is often diffused or undifferentiated.

Causes of Dissonance.[39] Various reasons for dissonance in conceptual leadership as highlighted above are elaborated below:

(a) *Credibility and Cynicism.* In the Indian context, leadership without a moral base can have little credibility due to the concept of *dharma* (righteousness) being so deeply ingrained in our collective consciousness. Though the scope of morality is all inclusive, yet expectations from senior leaders are quite realistic and down to earth. These are primarily concerned with the leader's professional morality. Credibility is extremely important at the top, as moral bankruptcy flows from the top to down. It is the role model at the top who can either correct or corrupt the system. A leader is expected to be fair, just, caring, compassionate, and always possessed of good faith in his dealings. This is not expecting too much of senior leaders, yet, so often this faith is squandered due to the following aberrations:

(i) *Favouritism and Whimsical Policies.* Numerous instances exist of senior leaders rewarding their favourites with undeserved decorations and promotions. Personal staff officers have been given high rewards for carrying out petty tasks. Such patronage is usual in human nature but when it becomes blatant and visibly unjust, it hurts the very fabric of fair play and even-handed justice. This hurts the moral authority of senior leaders and damages the credibility of the system as a whole. Such examples in the Army are far and few, but it takes only a few malignant cells to destroy a healthy body.

(ii) *Manipulative Leaders*. Manipulative leadership values have spawned a culture of unprincipled power play. A manipulative tendency in senior leaders gives rise to a culture of favouritism in which merit becomes the first casualty. Only those who toe the line make it to the top, with others, despite their unquestionable professional competence, falling by the wayside, which in the long run has ominous portents for the organisation.

(iii) *Professional Duplicity*. This is a malignancy of senior and middle level officers. These officers master the art of stage-managed presentations, visits, cover-ups, and double standards. Such diplomatic skills combined with professional competence are a sure recipe for assured advancement in one's career. The younger generation has these very officers as its role model. As a result, it reacts to these hypocritical values with disgusted cynicism and loses faith in such officers or itself gets corrupted at a nascent stage in service and emulates its role models. Both these have a debilitating effect on organisational morale.

(iv) *Sycophancy and Servility*. This is a spinoff of rampant careerism and a flawed appraisal system, wherein even a single act becomes a proverbial kiss of professional death. Senior officers further use this as the proverbial 'Sword of Damocles'. With the pyramid becoming very narrow as it approaches the top, this threat reduces many a middle ranking officer to a 'spineless wonder'. By the time these servile officers reach the top, the damage to the system in the form of corrupting many junior officers has been done. Many senior officers also use the lure of a medal as an instrument of exploitation.

(b) *Careerism*. While ambition is a legitimate aspiration and can indeed be a driving force behind a man, yet when it starts placing self before service, it becomes an aberration of military values. Many senior leaders having risen to the top by pursuing these very means fail to grasp the difference between legitimate aspirations and cut-throatism. This makes the identification of the problem difficult, let alone tackling it. It is indeed a by-product of prevailing social values, but it is the job of the senior leadership to insulate the organisation against undesirable influences of the outside world. Materialistic values have existed in the Western world for a much longer period and yet they have sustained a healthy military ethos. It is the responsibility of the leadership at the top to restructure personal policies suitably to ensure that rampant careerism is arrested.

(c) *Resource Crunch.* Resource crunch is an inescapable reality and should act as a spur for innovative management, sensible prioritisation, and optimal utilisation. It should not be allowed to become an excuse and an escape from reality, primarily due to a shackled military mind. In the context of the Indian Army, it required General B.C. Joshi, the late Chief of the Army Staff, to show the way to deal with resource crunch in a dynamic fashion.

(d) *Creativity and Conceptual Ability.* The premium on conformity and discipline curbs creativity and encourages mediocrity at the middle level. This perpetuates itself in the form of lack of innovativeness and reluctance to tread off the beaten path in dealing with real-life problems emerging due to changing social values and technological challenges being presented to the modern military leadership. The problem emerges due to the failure of senior leaders to recognise the need for change due to their relative insulation from ground level situations and inability to encourage radical thoughts or ideas due to strict doses of conformity they had been expected to follow during their long and illustrious careers. The need of the times is visionary and innovative leadership at the conceptual level, which can take the lead in encouraging the above changes for the common good of the organisation. To recognise the need for change and then identify, encourage and exploit the creative and conceptual potential of middle and junior level leadership, through suitable selection and placement policies, is thus the need of the hour for conceptual level leaders.

(e) *Conflict Management.* Organisational politics and power play are inherent in all organisations and the Army is no exception. This is mostly due to shackled military minds that are incapable of rising to the occasion, resulting in petty ego clashes. Military egos tend to be overly sensitive especially with the passage of time and increase in service levels. Thus, conflict management assumes great importance in the Army and requires structural reforms to be initiated, which can only be done by the senior leadership.

(f) *Accountability and Result Orientation.* The greatest strength of the Armed Forces is their result orientation in battle or crisis situations. This is also their Achilles' heel in non-combat areas. The systems and products are not cost- or time-sensitive with the military bureaucracy having less accountability than their civilian counterparts. This is reflected in time and cost overruns in various projects, inordinately delayed investigations, and legal and disciplinary cases which all point towards diffused responsibility. These weaknesses are due to poor management information systems, absence of result-oriented systems and flawed personnel policies mainly inherited from the colonial set-up and some that originated thereafter. The responsibility of the senior level leadership is to recognise these problems and initiate systemic and policy reforms to overcome them.

Essential Attributes of Conceptual Leadership

After analysing the battlefield of the future, and the key issues for future leadership, symptoms, and causes of discord and disharmony, it is now possible to spell out the essential attribute of conceptual leadership, which will meet the requirements of the future battlefield milieu. The list is not an exhaustive compendium of all leadership values, but only those which are considered absolutely mandatory for conceptual leaders.

Intellective Aspects of Conceptual Leadership.[40] These include aspects such as:

(a) *Imaginative Intellect.* It is a very important aspect requisite in a conceptual leader and includes his ability to innovate. War is a matter of wits and an imaginative leader can force an enemy commander out of his wits, prompting him to commit a fatal mistake, which may result in a decisive, battle-winning advantage. Perfect knowledge is very important in enhancing imaginative intellect. It provides a breath of perspective and independence of the mind and is directly related to creativity. Clausewitz noted the need for an independent or imaginative intellect, especially in senior leaders. According to him, problems only get worse as one's position rises, peaking at the supreme commander."[41] Nearly all solutions at this level must be left to the creative mind. Leaders must remember that friction and the fog of war will govern the battlefield. Knowledge not only provides stability and lowers stress and anxiety but also acts as a catalyst towards improving the imaginative intellect. In World War I, when it was found that machine guns were taking a heavy toll of troops, the tank was invented. Later, in World War II, when it was found that tanks were playing havoc, anti-tank guns and missiles were invented. Similarly, air power was developed as a third dimension to deal effectively with targets beyond the range of surface weapons. These require a great deal of imagination and, hence, become a very important pre-requisite for conceptual leaders.

(b) *Cognitive Complexity*. Connected with the intellect aspect is cognitive complexity. It can be characterised as the scope and complexity of the world that a person can pattern and build, taking into account the volume and complexity of the information being digested. It serves as a gauge of one's capacity to hold opposing viewpoints, weigh numerous variables, and still arrive at sensible solutions. In the future battlefield milieu, the amount of information available to senior commanders will be colossal, resulting in an information overload. Under such circumstances, the commander's ability to sift through the mass of data and extract useful information will result in sound and timely decisions, making cognitive complexity a battle-winning factor.

(c) *Vision*. Another important attribute in a conceptual leader is 'vision'. According to Clausewitz, 'War cannot be waged with distinction except by men of outstanding vision'.[42] Vision is the ability to project oneself into the future and visualise the scenario, or courses of events or developments that are likely to take place and cater for them. The standard rises with every step. A higher intellect is needed for military genius in order to develop a sense of unity and a capacity for judging what is magnified to an astounding degree. Senior leadership in future conflicts will be required to make accurate operational and strategic decisions and that too in the midst of confusion and uncertainty of battle. A fine example of display of great vision is that of Sardar Vallabh Bhai Patel, whose vision of a strong nation made him work speedily, energetically and with considerable political finesse to integrate the erstwhile princely states into India.

Character Aspect of Conceptual Leadership.[43] Desirable traits related to this aspect include:

(a) *Willpower.* It is the foremost quality for any military leader and is manifested in a fierce desire to achieve success despite all odds. Willpower or lack of it displayed by leaders is infectious and can either raise or destroy the morale of the forces. In the implementation of any plan, programme, or project, difficulties will arise. Failures will occur on the part of people who have to execute the plans, which could either be due to natural causes, lack of natural resources, or the frailties of human nature. A good leader must have the ability to persist in spite of setbacks and difficulties that may arise. While this may be true of leadership at all levels, it assumes critical importance at senior levels, as the hurdles encountered in implementing any programme would increase manifold. Sir Winston Churchill, Prime Minister of UK during World War II, articulated the value of dogged perseverance in a most dramatic manner. On being invited to a school to deliver the keynote address to students on leadership values, Churchill just said "NEVER, NEVER, NEVER, NEVER AND NEVER."[44] In just five words, he distilled the great secret of success and leadership. It has been said that as long as soldiers battle with enthusiasm, a significant amount of willpower is not required. However, when the going gets tough and extraordinary results are required, combatants start to lose the traits of a well-oiled machine. As friction starts to emerge, the leadership must be incredibly resolute to surmount it. The collective effort of dwindling strength – both physical and moral – and the wrenching sight of life being sacrificed, must be fought by a leader, first in himself and then in everyone else. As soon as individual power begins to fade and can no longer be encouraged by the leader's will, the responsibility of overcoming mass inertia shifts more and more to the leader. By the fire in his own soul and the tenacity of his purpose, he must rekindle enthusiasm and renew hope in everyone. Every rise in a leader's position must be accompanied by a commensurate increase in strength because this burden grows with the size of one's command.[45]

(b) *Decisiveness.* This is yet another important aspect of conceptual leadership. It implies the ability to take sound and timely decisions. Any leader who is indecisive would give the impression of being professionally incompetent and weak on willpower. This in turn would lower of the morale of junior leaders and reduce their resolve for mission accomplishment. An excellent example of decisiveness is the decision taken by General Eisenhower to launch 'Operation Overload' as planned on 6 June 1944, in spite of predictions of inclement weather with only a partial break.

(c) *Courage.* In every society, bravery is the most respected human quality. Being a man implies having courage. At a lower level, success in action depends on physical courage. At a higher level, a commander needs moral courage. Moral courage can only come through selflessness. A leader must have the courage of his convictions and should be prepared to sacrifice his career or reputation for them in larger interest of the organisation.

(d) *Character.* Character is really a combination of the positive personal qualities of a leader, which manifest in his functioning. Good character implies selflessness, dedication, a positive outlook, and self-discipline. It is manifestation of sound moral values that a leader must possess. Military leadership is the art of leading men into war even in the face of certain death. A man is not going to be led to his death for any amount of salary. Peer pressure drives an individual to fight, but group effectiveness is dictated by the character and moral values of the leader, which places him on a higher- and larger-than-life pedestal. The potential for leadership is directly proportional to a leader's character. In order to grow greater, 'I' in a leader must become smaller.

(e) *Equanimity.* Equanimity is a very important requisite in a higher commander. It implies composure, coolness under stress, imperturbability, and unflappability, which are all vital for a higher commander to be able to think calmly, irrespective of the circumstances. This enables a commander to take sound decisions and pursue his aim to its logical conclusion. Such a quality will generate greater confidence in subordinates towards the ability of their commander, raise their morale, and assist in mission accomplishment.

(f) *Tolerance for Ambiguity.* It will be an essential attribute for future conceptual leaders. In a future battlefield scenario, information about the enemy would always be incomplete. It would require greater tolerance for ambiguity for a leader to able to effectively comprehend a larger picture in spite of gaps. People with low tolerance for ambiguity have a high level of authoritarianism and are aggressive, and tough-minded with preoccupied dominance. Such leaders will not tolerate criticism, if it suggests inadequacies in their leadership or policies. Such leaders will also be unable to comprehend the overall picture, which will result in faulty decision making. On the contrary, leaders with a high tolerance for ambiguity are individualistic, tolerant, democratic, unprejudiced, and egalitarian.

Knowledge Aspect of High Command.[46] The knowledge aspect of high command basically concerns the following issues:

(a) *Professional Acumen.* This is one quality without which no leader can hope to reach the highest rung of leadership. It implies a continuous study of the profession as well as practical experience in the field. It also entails a thorough study of the enemy and understanding his strategy and tactics to be able to defeat him. the professional incompetence of a leader will be discovered sooner or later by his subordinates, leading to a loss of confidence in his ability. A professionally incompetent leader can enforce but never enthuse his command, leading to a failure in optimally achieving the desired goals.

(b) *Strategy.* Future leaders will have to understand the relationship between grand strategy and military strategy. They will then be required to establish a correct relationship between economics, logistics, and strategy. From a military point of view, economic factors exert their influence on both strategy and military operations through the working of the armed forces. The Gulf War clearly brought out the significance of the above statement. Future leaders will have to understand that the logistic process is the military element in its military operations. Economic strength limits the combat forces one can apply. Senior leadership with knowledge of the above issues will be able to create a force, sustain the same, and restructure it when required.

(c) *Management and Command Relationship*. Senior leadership will have to manage both, that is, the organisation and the environment. Leading, managing and synchronising the resources is not easy. Our organisations are becoming complex and unmanageable. In order to perceive their own roles within the context of a thorough understanding of the organisation, senior leaders must work to keep a broad perspective of the entire organisation. Such all-encompassing methods take time to create. Senior leaders undoubtedly fall under the biblical maxim that we should "run with patience that is set before us." They need the perseverance to fully understand how their company operates as well as the diligence, intelligence, and analytical skills needed to tackle challenging organisational issues and set the organisation on new paths. The Armed Forces are entering one of the most challenging periods since their existence; the challenges being resource crunch, communal forces and the unipolar world syndrome. These challenges will test our nation, our organisation, and our leaders.

(d) *Politico-Military Interface*. Understanding the politico-military interface is essential at the highest military levels. Von Clausewitz propounded that war is but an extension of policy by other means. Some people might even entertain the idea that the opposite is true in the current international context and that diplomatic policy is merely an outward manifestation of conflict. According to the initial hypothesis, conflict ultimately resolves the problems that diplomacy was unable to address. The second puts forth the idea that diplomacy is the ultimate arbiter and addresses the problems that conflict has been unable to resolve. Both ideas are completely acceptable expressions of the relationship between diplomacy and military action and do not necessarily clash with one another. This relationship is more pronounced in today's environment. The senior leadership, in particular those who are at the decision-making level, must clearly comprehend that using military force does not serve any purpose as an end in itself and only obtains 'legitimacy' in the context of the political goal it intends to accomplish.

Skills. Certain skills required for a leader can be further divided under four heads as follows.[47]

(a) *Technical Skills.* It is the capacity to apply information, procedures, methods, and tools to the accomplishment of particular duties. Technical expertise is gained through education, training, execution of particular tasks, and experience.

(b) *Human Relations Skills.* It is the capacity and discretion in working with and managing people, including knowledge of what motivates them and the use of effective leadership. These skills can be further categorised as emotional skills, spiritual and moral skills, social skills and a combination of all of them as extension skills.

(c) *Conceptual Skills.* This can be explained as having the capacity to comprehend the organisational complexity as a whole and how one's own operation factors into it. This information enables one to act in accordance with the organisation's goals rather than based only on the needs and goals of their own immediate group.

(d) *Communication.* The word 'communication' comes from the Latin word 'cummuris' meaning common. Thus, for successful communication, people try to meet on common ground at least momentarily to share information, attitudes, ideas, and understanding. Communication is the process by which a mind influences another. In a future battlefield, ambiguity, mobility and agility will dominate the proceedings and under such circumstances the importance of communication needs no further emphasis. It is in peace time that such attributes of command are developed, both at the junior and senior levels of leadership.

More than at any other time, one needs to be vigilant and create future leadership, which will cater to the needs of our country. It is now that we will be required to concentrate on leadership virtues at the senior level. War begins in the minds of men. Strategies for warfare also begin in the minds of men. In order to be effective in war, it is imperative that senior commanders are more decisive. Minds can be effective only if they are freed from the chains that prevent the complete intelligence of an individual from operating at full capacity. These chains are formed by feelings and emotions which are self-centred and consume psychic energy, which otherwise would have been available for decisive decision-making. In order to reduce this wasteful psychic energy consumption, conceptual leaders should be selfless, which implies that their personal interests should be subordinate to the interests of the service.

Irrespective of the type of war, that is, conventional, nuclear, or low-intensity conflict, the qualities desirable in a leader remain the same. A leader should be able to decide a course of action based purely on facts and information and not on desires and hope. No amount of external training can make a man an effective decision-maker, especially under stress. The only way is through internal means by achieving self-actualisation, having high moral values, which would reduce selfishness, which, in turn, would lead to better decision-making capability. This is the main reason as to why military services throughout the world insist on high moral values in their commanders. The possession of high moral values in a senior commander is more important than having better military hardware and more men. After all, history is replete with examples of commanders who turned the outcome in war even when the odds were stacked against them.

Motivation, beyond the advocated management principles, complemented by personal traits entering into the realms of self-actualisation, could give the soldier confidence, peace and the required balance to act in the desired manner. By fostering an environment and culture that encourages aspiration and to fight for a common goal, leadership should mobilise them. It entails a stronger feeling of calling to fight for a cause greater than oneself. it is the common vision created, a value congruence achieved and a higher level of commitment made that inspires both the leader and the led to develop hope, faith, and a sense of higher purpose detached from immediate tangible gains, that is, transcend into equanimity. The question at hand therefore is: "*What can enable a military leader to inspire his men to achieve this exalted form of life? Is spirituality, which encapsulates these dimensions, that enabling factor?*"

NOTES

1. Pillai, Radhakrishnan and Sivanandhan, D. *Chanakya's 7 secrets of leadership*, Jaico Publishing House, Mumbai 2016, p. 5.
2. Mazza Suzane. 'The Best definition of leadership', accessed from <http://leadchangegroup.com/ best-definition-leadership, on 6 October 2018.
3. General K.V. Krishna Rao Param Vishista Seva Medal (retired), 'Leadership Challenges at

Conceptual Level;'. *Defence Management*, volume 27, May 2000, p. 2.

4. Ibid.
5. Definition of Leadership, accessed from <http://www.businessdictionary.com/definition/leadership.html>, on 6 October 2018.
6. Kala, PVSM, AVSM, SC, Lt. Gen. H.B.. *Demystifying Military leadership*, Manas Publications, New Delhi, 2003, p. 25.
7. Robert L. and Rosenbach William E. Military Leadership in pursuit for excellence, in *'Ethics of Leadership'* by Colonel Malham M Wakin, Jupiter Boulder, Westview Press (published in India by L D. Dewan, ,Jupiter Publications, Pathankot, p. 98.
8. Kala. loc cit.
9. Ibid., p. 26..
10. Chacko, Gp. Capt. Johnson. Chapter 23, 'Nurturing strategic leadership' in, *A Campaign called Victory India*, edited by Col. Vinay B. Dalvi (retd.), Pentagon Press, New Delhi 2016, p 159.
11. Lt. Gen. H.B. Kala, PVSM, AVSM, SC. *Demystifying Military Leadership*. New Delhi. Manas Publications, 2005, p. 26.
12. Grint, Keith. *The Arts of Leadership*, Oxford University Press, New York, 2000, p. 1.
13. Ibid.
14. Ibid., pp. 2-5.
15. Ibid.
16. Ibid.
17. Ibid.
18. Ibid.
19. Ibid., pp 27-28.
20. Ibid.
21. Precis on Organisational Behaviour, pp. 27–56.
22. Ibid.
23. Bass, Bernard M. loc. cit.
24. Precis on Organisational Behaviour, op. cit.
25. Bass, Bernard M, et al. Re-examining the components of transformational and transactional leadership, *Journal of Occupational and Organizational Psychology*, 1999, p. 444.
26. Ibid., p. 445.
27. Precis on Organisational Behaviour, op. Cit.
28. Ibid.
29. Ibid.
30. Ibid.
31. Lt. Gen. H.B. Kala, PVSM, AVSM, SC. *Demystifying Military Leadership*, New Delhi, Manas Publications, 2005. p. 57.
32. GS pamphlet on Leadership and Military Command, Controller of Publications, Delhi, 1976,. p. 48.
33. Singh Jasjit. *Military Leadership for tomorrow, An article on 'Military Leadership: An Introductory essay*, KW Publishers, New Delhi, 2009, p. ix.
34. Taylor, Robert L and Rosenbach, William E. 'Military leadership in pursuit for excellence,' in *'Leadership as an art'* by Colonel Malham M. Wakin, Jupiter Boulder, Westview Press, published in India by L.D. Dewan, ,Jupiter Publications, Pathankot, p. 17.
35. Kala. op cit., p. 58.
36. Dalvi, Col. Vinay B. *Victory India: A way to quality military leadership*, Pentagon Press, New Delhi 2013, cover theme, p. xv.

37. Ibid., p. 284.
38. Lieutenant General Y.N. Sharma, Param Vishisht Seva Medal, Ati Vishisht Seva Medal, Vishisht Seva Medal, (retired). '*Military Leadership: Contemporary Challenges*'. *Defence Management*, October 2095, p. 2.
39. Ibid.
40. Brigadier I.J. Singh, 'Leadership Challenges', Trishul, vol. X, no. 2, p. 70.
41. Ibid.
42. Ibid.
43. General K.V. Krishna Rao, Param Vishisht Seva Medal (retired). 'Leadership Challenges at Conceptual Level,' *Defence Management*, vol. 27, May 2000, pp. 2-7.
44. ARTRAC, Leadership, 1999, p. 81.
45. Brigadier I.J. Singh. op. cit. p. 70.
46. Brigadier I.J. Singh. loc. cit.
47. Brigadier I.J. Singh. op. cit., p. 73.

Chapter Two

Evolution of Indian Military Leadership from the Vedic Era to the Modern-Day Battlefield

"A person who is expert in the knowledge of appropriate action, weaponry, tactical deployment of troops, ways of humiliating the enemy, who is not a boy but is mature, brave, trained in soldiery, able-bodied and who is intent on performing his duty, is always loyal to his sovereign master and is an enemy of his sovereign's enemy – such a person, from whatever caste or parentage, may be appointed commander-in-chief of the army or an officer in the army by a sovereign desirous of victory."

— ***Shukraniti II, pp. 138-140***

In the section 'Evolution of Indian Military Leadership' of the questionnaire, questions related to this subject were posed to the respondents. They were: Relevance of ancient Indian scriptures? Need for reviewing SSB selection procedure? State of Indian military leadership to lead today's informed soldier? Importance of traits listed in Indian mythology such as motivation, sacrifice, and empathy? The response to these questions is presented through the following pie charts:

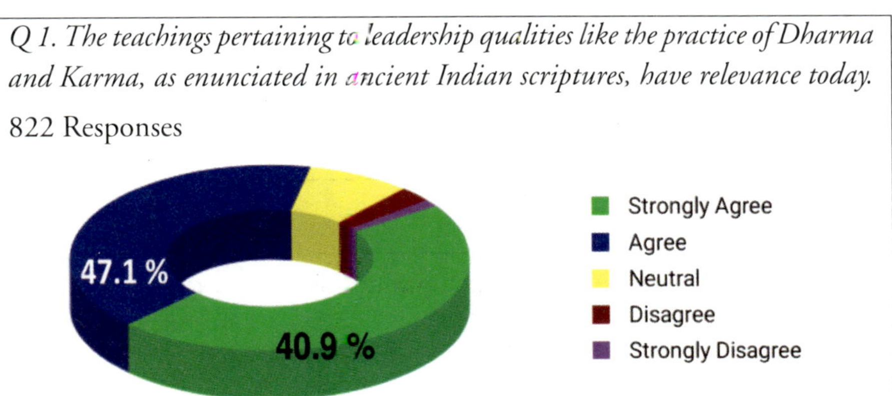

Q 1. The teachings pertaining to leadership qualities like the practice of Dharma and Karma, as enunciated in ancient Indian scriptures, have relevance today.

822 Responses

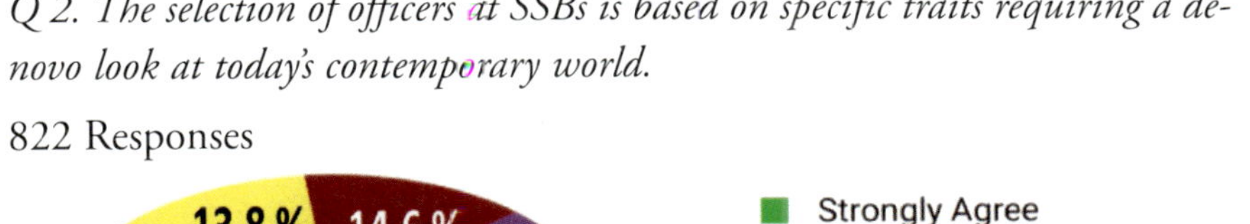

Q 2. The selection of officers at SSBs is based on specific traits requiring a de-novo look at today's contemporary world.

822 Responses

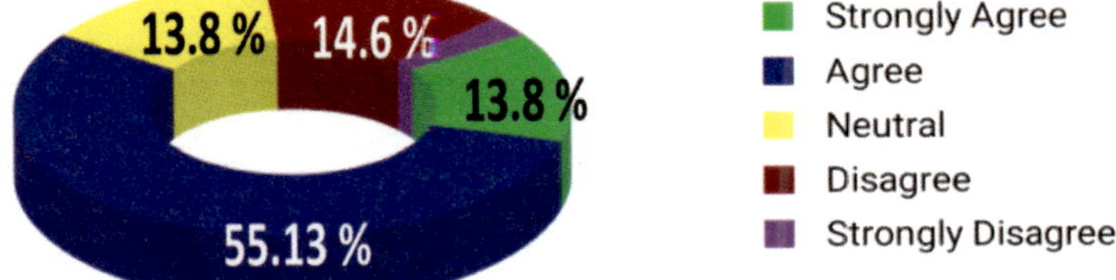

Q 3. The soldier of today is more educated and informed. He has far greater requirements. To lead such a soldier, our existing form of military leadership needs to be better equipped.

822 Responses

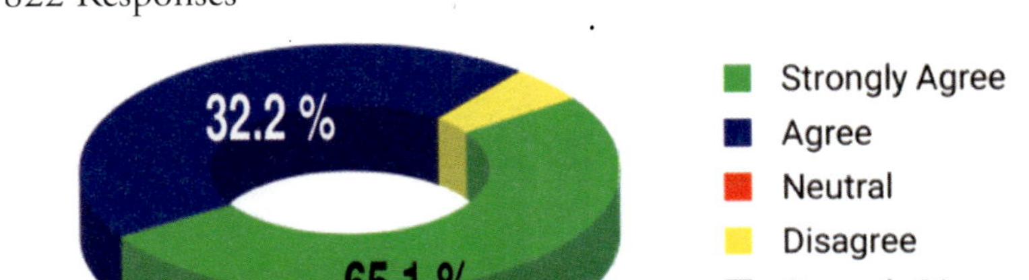

Q 4. In your view, will leadership traits such as motivation, sacrifice, and empathy listed in Indian mythology, find resonance with the troops of Indian Army?

822 Responses

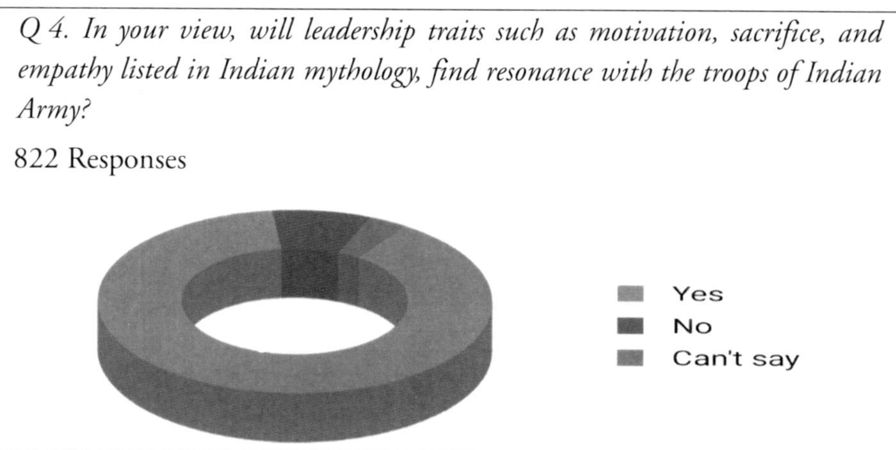

A brief analysis of the responses received to the questions posed in this section is as under:

(a) A complete majority of 88 per cent feel that the practice of '*Dharma* and *Karma*' mentioned in the ancient Indian scriptures are relevant today.

(b) A reasonable majority of 74 per cent feel that the SSB selection procedure needs to be reviewed.

(c) A resounding 88 per cent majority feel that contemporary military leaders need to be better equipped to lead today's educated and informed soldier.

(d) Also, 87 per cent of the respondents feel that leadership traits such as motivation, sacrifice, and empathy, as enunciated in the ancient Indian scriptures, will find resonance with Indian army troops.

Indian Scriptures: Contribution to Spirituality& Military Leadership

It is said that nearly 5,000 years ago, there evolved the blessed land of Aryavarta, a unique civilisation, a land of plenty, a veritable utopia on Earth which came to be known as a 'golden bird' for it had an abundance of mineral wealth and resources. This later came to be known as Bharat and subsequently, India. It would be fair to say that this land hosted the world's most ancient and well-educated society, was home to a plural culture and gave birth to intellectual giants, philosophers, seers, and prophets.

Vedic Literature

The Vedic period extends from the date of the origin of the Vedas (1500 B.C.) to the time of the *Bhagavad Gita*[1] (5 B.C.). Vedism, indigenously named to mean 'eternal religion' (Sanatan Dharma), has no beginning but a history of infinity and is in fact a 'way of life'. Over the centuries, Vedic culture grew, took shape, developed, and spread far and wide within, as well as outside India. The fountainhead of this culture lies in the Vedas, which contain all the concepts that dominate an individual and social life of the Vedic people. Satyavrata Siddhantalankar (1986) provides a fascinating account of the evolution of Vedic literature in his book, '*Heritage of Vedic Culture*.'[2] The constituents of Vedic literature are as follows:

(a) *Vedas*. Four in number:

- (i) The *Rigveda* primarily deals with *Jnana* (knowledge).
- (ii) The *Yajurveda* deals with *Karma* (action).
- (iii) The *Samaveda* deals with *Upasana* (worship).
- (iv) The *Atharvaveda* deals with miscellaneous subjects.

The first three form the mental triad of 'Knowing', 'Willing' and 'Feeling' which are the three principles of the mind. The *Stiha-veda* comprises the Puranas, Strivritta (history), Akhyaa (tales), Udharanas (illustrative stories); the Samahita has a specific ideology of its own.

Brahma Granthas

Nine in number, they contain various rules for the employment or incantations of hymns of various *yagnas* (sacrifices). These are explanations of the Vedas.

Upanishads

'Upa-ni-shad' means to "sit near another person" and it was passed on by a preceptor to his disciples by word of mouth down the generations. Upanishadic literature contains lucid expositions of all essential ideas like spiritual unity, knowing oneself, philosophy of life, arts, science, and economics. There are eleven principal Upanishads, namely, Isa, Kena, Katha, Prashna, Manduka, Mandukya, Taittiriya, Aithareye, Chandogya, Brihadarankya and Shvetashvatara.

Solidarity of existence and spiritual unity can be found in the Isa, while the external character of self and universe and nature of knowledge is seen in the Kena. The Katha presents a blend of profound philosophy, deep mysticism and poetry. The Mundaka describes economics, politics, sciences and art/literature. Moving on, philosophical import and spiritual upliftment can be found in the Chandogya.

The Brihadaranyaka is the longest Upanishad and, as its name implies, is a 'big (brihat)' + 'forest (aranya)' of spiritual inspiration and philosophical thought. The roles of a wife, husband, and Brahmin have been put across in a philosophical debate in this treatise.

The Upanishads are a storehouse of provable and proven spiritual thoughts that are presented along with myths/legends and speculation (cosmological) associated with the origin of the universe and nature.

Swami Ranganathananda[3] says that the Upanishads should be thought of as a 'reading of the book within' which contains a list of suggested 'Do's and Don'ts' that enable and assist individual and collective behaviour and the conduct of their followers. The Upanishads are seen as one of the few holy books that address primarily the discovery of essential spiritual truths with the aim of leading man (irrespective of caste and creed) to self-realization. It is therefore referred to as Sruti (body of super-sensual knowledge) par excellence while all other scriptures like the *Ramayana*, *Gita* and *Mahabharata* are referred to as 'Smritis'.

The Upanishads seek 'Satya-Truth'; on the other hand, the Samhitas lay great emphasis on 'Rita', morality. They bring out three essential qualities for a leader: physical (vigour and health); mental (adaptability, vigour, judgement and ability to understand and learn) and moral (initiative, dignity, energy, loyalty, firmness, trust and willingness to accept responsibilities).

Faith in oneself and in one's ability, *Tat Tvam Asi* (that art thou) is the basic teaching of the Upanishads. The roots of India are deep and strong, and have immeasurable potentialities. Anyone can mould himself to be what he wants. Each one can be inspired to imbibe knowledge and reach the peak of human endeavour. The Upanishads are traditional means of knowledge, accumulated over years by the sages. It is therefore referred to as 'Anadi', that is, without beginning akin to gravity which was present irrespective of the existence of human life. *The moral, ethical and spiritual paths therefore existed as guiding lamps for the human race.*

The Vedangas. They are six in number and have been evolved as part of Vedic literature. 'Veda' means 'scripture' and 'Anga' means 'limb'. These are utilized for the correct interpretation of the main Vedic texts. These are:

(a) Shiksha - Science of pronunciation.
(b) Chhanda - Science of prosody.
(c) Vyakarna - Science of grammar.
(d) Nirukta - Etymological explanation of difficult Vedic words.
(e) Jyotisha - Astronomy.
(f) Kalpa - Rituals for individuals and society.

Upa Vedas. These represent distinct branches of knowledge:

(a) Ayurveda - Medicine
(b) Dhanurveda - Military Science
(c) Gandharveda - Music
(d) Sthaptyaveda - Architecture

Darshanas. Six in number, the Darshanas basically evolved as systems of philosophy. They dealt with aspects regarding the origin of the universe. These are:

(a) Vaishesika - Atomic theory
(b) Nyaya - Theory of matter
(c) Sankhya - Theory of matter and soul
(d) Yoga - Discipline of body and mind
(e) Vedanta - Philosophy
(f) Mimansa - Rituals of the Vedas

From the above, it is evident that Vedic literature was not the product of the imagination of a single individual, but evolved with time by the fusion of the intellect of a number of enlightened minds. It can also be well understood that an imbibing of relevant aspects of Vedic literature would be of great value to any leadership, including military leadership.

Arthashastra. Kautilya's *Arthashastra* is a profound anthology on politics. It dissects the administration of a state, the duties of a king towards his subjects and its precise precepts of management that are relevant even to modern-day management theories.

The Ramayana and Mahabharata. An important facet of Indian philosophy that affects lives is the theory of transmigration of souls and the Law of *Karma* (deeds). The doctrine is based on the theory of deeds or retribution, for which a man is rewarded or punished as per the deeds done in a previous life. The *Ramayana* covers facets on human aspects in idealism, commitment, honour moderation and the likes in simple prose. It is an encyclopaedia of Hindu life and culture. On the other hand, the *Mahabharata* looks at the power struggle between the Pandavas and Kauravas and explores the importance of human ethics and values. While it is revered by Hindus, it actually lays down in elaborate detail a path that should be followed by all to lead an ideal life. It has therefore been rightfully said of the *Mahabharata* that *"what is in it can be found elsewhere too, what is not in it is nowhere".*

The Bhagavad Gita. Of the 18 Puranas, the Gita is considered the culmination of the wisdom of the entire mosaic of Vedic literature. It exhaustively covers all fields of knowledge including, religion, philosophy, moral and social codes, human values and history. The knowledge of its teachings leads to the realization of all human aspirations. The invaluable aspect of 'Nishkama Karma', devotion to duty above all, and importance of 'Jnana' (knowledge) are perhaps its most profound tenets. The *Bhagavad Gita,* 'The Song Celestial' as Edwin Arnold has called it, is of profound wisdom and timeless knowledge, and serves as an inspiration and an exhortation for selflessness, courage, righteousness, duty before self and noble activity. One of its greatest ontological contributions is that it has corrected the view of total renunciation and abandonment of action to attain emancipation. It has highlighted the importance of duty. It lays great emphasis on its doctrine of Karma Yoga which is the performance of duty in a selfless manner by cultivating self-control. The objectives of *Gita* are threefold:

(a) Self-realisation that comes from knowledge.

(b) Devotion to God and performance of right actions.

(c) Detachment from desire of rewards, which results from control of the lower self.

Besides the *Bhagavad Gita*, the *Mahabharata* too has made other contributions towards the development of mankind. Some of the important ones are:

(a) *Nitishastra*. Which deals with management of human affairs.

(b) *Shantiparva*. An excellent treatise, which amplifies the qualities, duties and styles of functioning of a leader.

Strength of Indian Philosophy

India is a major confluence of a number of religions and cultures, each of them contributing to the enrichment of the 'Indian Thought Process'. Although Vedic literature had consolidated its position as a fountainhead of philosophical thought having evolved over a number of centuries, yet it did not hinder or inhibit the development of other philosophies propounded by subsequent saints and gurus. It is interesting to see the salient aspects of each of these religions and philosophies. Vested interests have always tried to drive a wedge between various Indian philosophical schools of thought, but they have not succeeded. On the contrary, other philosophies have been able to merge smoothly with the native Indian thought process. Three main reasons may be attributed to the inner strength of Indian philosophy:

(a) The foundations of Vedic literature are built on philosophical concepts and not on religions. This has provided Indian culture the flexibility to absorb other philosophies with an open mind not very common in other parts of the world.

(b) Religions and philosophies that have influenced later generations have themselves been influenced by the basic Indian ethos.

(c) Religions that came to India from abroad found several common threads with indigenous philosophy, thus making their fusion with cultures and philosophies easy.

Review of Epics and Scriptures

From the vast spectrum of Indian philosophy, some specific literature has been reviewed critically to determine the influence of spirituality on military leadership.

The Ramayana

The portrayal of the character of Rama is utopian. He was an ideal son, brother, father, husband, and king. He blended *Artha* and *Dharma* beautifully. He demonstrated the latter aspect of *Dharma* by accepting the command of exile from his father. He upheld the moral principles by not accepting the crown, and proved that moral principles are the soul of a kingdom, a binding factor.

Rama was a balanced man who was never jealous or devious, neither over-depressed nor ecstatic in victory. His act of slaying Vali was not an act of cowardice, albeit a lesson taught to the immoral king who had treacherously banished Sugriva to the jungles and lusted for his wife. It was paying him back in the same coin.

Known for his *Dama* (sense control), *Shama* (mind control), *Kshama* (forgiveness) and *Satya* (speaking the truth), he won over many indifferent kings by the purity of his actions. He had control over anger and desperation in adversity and calamities.

Rama was a brave, non-malicious, serene and soft-spoken energetic man, who was devoted to duty. He eschewed frivolity and was a master in the skills of warfare, *Dharma* and *Artha*.

He honoured Brahmins (learned people), was concerned for the needy, humble about his prowess, and loved his subjects. He never rebuked when maligned, forgave a hundred petty incidents, was pleased with small kindnesses and was a clear judge of character.

An important takeaway from the *Ramayana* is that it clearly brings out weaknesses or undesirable traits that a king must avoid:

(a) Atheism
(b) Failure to fight foes
(c) Laziness
(d) Procrastination
(e) Inability to keep a secret
(f) Anger
(g) Hypocrisy
(h) Fondness for foolish friends
(j) Omission of auspicious rituals

In the Ayodhya Kand of Valmiki's *Ramayana*, Rama categorically inquires from Bharat the quality of ministers/leaders running the state. *He says they should be strong willed with a high emotional quotient. The emphasis is on commitment, compassion, competence and confidentiality. In taking complex decisions, an effective group should be consulted. Never do it unilaterally, nor have too many people.*

He further explains to Bharat that grievance redressal should be done with promptitude, and to prefer one wise man against a thousand fools, as one is enough to see through crisis and ensure prosperity.

Rama was a great proponent of *Dharma. Adharma* (rule of the bad) in a city or village corrupts the kingdom. He said that Dharmatma is obeyed unquestionably. He was called 'Maryada Purushottam' (a man of principles who respected limits in all fields of behaviour).

The Mahabharata

The *Mahabharata* is one of the most comprehensive works that elucidates on human travails, strengths and weaknesses, social and ethical relations and thoughts on human problems; in fact, it is an unrivalled code of life. It contains conversations between Man and God. Some invaluable lessons that can be drawn from it are discussed in the following paragraphs.

Path of Dharma. It advocates a ruthless following of the Righteous Path known as the Path of *Dharma.* An individual should not sway from the path of *dharma* come what may. Only selfless duty is required to be done.

On Duty. The foremost duty of a king is to remain steadfast and never lose hope even if everything fails around him. The welfare of his subjects should be the highest concern. Manu, the lawgiver, also reiterates the point that a king who neglects his subjects should be avoided. A king should work at all times. Vigilance should never be relaxed. He should perform his duty with devotion and cultivate self-restraint.

Truth and *Dharma*. War can be conducted without violating *dharma.* The strategy applied for the conduct of war can be crooked or straight wisdom. Be straight when you attack and crooked if attacked first. Speaking the truth goes hand in hand with *dharma.* Nothing is higher than the truth. However, never speak a truth if it covers a lie. Speak a lie if the lie spoken is actually a cover for the truth. Truth is duty, penance, yoga and Brahman.

On Being Insulted. A learned person must behave with restraint in public. One should not allow hate to control him.

On Desires and Wrongdoing. Desire is the root of wrongdoing. It leads to the birth of other vices such as greed and lust. These in turn lead to the mind being led astray and results in doing wrong. Thus, the control of desires is essential.

On Vices. These are:

(a) Wrath
(b) Pride
(c) Jealousy
(d) Fear
(e) Malice
(f) Loss of Judgment
(g) Cruelty
(h) Evil Intention
(j) Lust
(k) Slander
(l) Sorrow
(m) Mistrust

On Selecting a Friend. A leader will have a lot of friends. The company that a man keeps defines him and thus a leader should be extremely careful in selection of his friends and associates. If a leader is surrounded by friends with vices, he will be affected by them as they would offer him incorrect advice as also lead to affecting his personality in a negative manner.

Behaviour of Leader/King in Daily Life. A leader must treat all his subordinates equally and in a fair manner. He must be spiritually inclined and be able to pull in his desires like a tortoise pulls in its head and feet.

The Bhagavad Gita

कर्मण्येवाधिकारस्ते मा फलेषु कदाचन ।
मा कर्मफलहेतुर्भूर्मा ते सङ्गोऽस्त्वकर्मणि ।।

—*Bhagavad Gita, Chapter 2, Verse 47*

Action alone is thy province, never the fruit thereof, let not thy motive
Be the fruit of action, nor shouldest there be desire to avoid action.

Naib (1980) says that the *Gita* conveys for soldiers a message of detachment or selfless action, 'Nishkama Karma' performed skilfully and courageously in a spirit of sacrifice. The *Gita* has a positive attitude towards life. It exhorts people to live a full life practising moderation and shunning excessive indulgence. *The Gita emphasizes various aspects for a leader to follow in Jnana,*

Karma and Dhyan Yoga, dealing with three important precepts of knowledge, action and mind.

As a Karma Yogi, a leader has to fight a battle considering happiness and misery with equanimity and equally so consider victory and defeat (Chapter II, Verse 37).

हतोवाप्राप्स्य सिस्वर्गं जित्वावाभोक्ष्यसेमहीम् ।
तस्मादुत्तिष्ठ कौन्तेय युद्धायकृत निश्चयः ।।

– *Bhagavad Gita, Chapter 2, Verse 37*

If you are killed in this battle, you will go to heaven and if you win in battle, you will enjoy the kingdom of earth. "So Rise, O son of Kunti! Gather courage and get into battle with resolve"

Krishna advises human beings to "live in this world but do not live in it." By this is meant that one must live in this world and undertake his duties without any attachment. Towards this, adoption of Jnana Yoga would enable the way of discrimination and knowledge (Sankhya), while undertaking Karma Yoga, and would lead us on the path of right action, meditation and spiritualism. Besides, there is a rare wise man who can go down the path of discrimination while most will be constrained to the combined path of activity and meditation.

Naib (1980) says, "Generally, Yoga is understood as a Vedic ritual like Havan (sacrificial fire) and the like. But with time, it has evolved into a world full of beauty and power. It applies to any act of sacrifice or selfless service. Some essentials of Jnana Yoga are:

(a) *Even Mindedness.* In pleasure and pain, and success and failure, enduring opposites with equanimity is critical. This is the hallmark of a Yoga practitioner.

(b) *Skill in Action.* That is proficiency in the use of weapons and science of warfare. In chapter II, verse 50, the Lord lays down three conditions for acquisition of knowledge. These are *Daya* (humility), repeated questioning and service (seva).

(c) *Steadfast Concentration.* This is to be achieved in battle noise and din. This can be achieved through a practice of meditation.

It is extremely important to understand that one cannot attain moksha by not taking any actions. It is incorrectly believed and understood that renunciation and living in seclusion would lead to the divine while achieving wisdom is better than activity. However, the highest levels of knowledge would be achieved through activity only. Towards this end, spiritual activities such as being meditative, religious, social and moral are extremely important and necessary. Thus, as per the *Gita*, a sincere, hardworking and honest man is far better than the recluse who leads an idle life of non-existence.

The *Gita* advises all humans to cleanse their souls through the activities of service, devotion, morality and meditation as a life of materialism is one of ignorance and would lead to nothing but suffering.

The most important precepts of the three Yogas are evenness and tranquillity of the mind, control of the senses and desires, avoiding brooding on thoughts thereof, specially of the past and futile dreaming, as also selfless action without yearning of fruits thereof. Jnana and Karma Yoga are not different. Both are closely interrelated. Jnana Yoga is the inspiration and basis of Karma Yoga. A good Karma Yogi has to have good Jnana. While the two essential ingredients of Jnana Yoga are evenness of mind and skill in action, finding their practical application is Karma Yoga.

The *Gita* advises all humans to continue to fight their desires and not give in to them else they would be enmeshed in the cycle of never-ending reincarnation. Man's desire to live a life of sensory temptation is called Karma and when this is not achieved it leads to anger also known as Krodha. These lead to individuals being tied up in the material world. This is encapsulated in the following shloka:

क्रोधाद्भवति सम्मोहः सम्मोहात्स्मृतिविभ्रमः।
स्मृतिभ्रंशाद् बुद्धिनाशो बुद्धिनाशात्प्रणश्यति।

—*Bhagavad Gita, Chapter 2, Verse 63*

When a man thinks of objects, attachments for them arise, from attachments desire is born: from desires arise anger. From anger comes delusion; from delusion loss of memory; from loss of memory destruction of reason or discrimination and with this he perishes.

Morarji Desai (1978) said that intense desire, anger and greed are the triple gates to hell which destroys the soul. A person who practises Kriya Yoga goes beyond the state of physical perceptions and experiences divine bliss.

जितात्मनः प्रशान्तस्य परमात्मा समाहितः ।
शीतोष्णसुखदुःखेषु तथा मानापमानयोः ।।

—*Bhagavad Gita, Chapter 6, Verse 7*

When one has conquered one's (lower) self by one's higher self and has attained self-control and peace, he is balanced in cold and heat, in pleasure and pain, in honour and dishonour.

Arthashastra

Kautilya was one of the greatest teachers of statecraft. He has given to the world his masterful treatise titled *Arthashastra*. Some important aspects from it are enumerated in the following paragraphs.

Society was broadly divided into four classes. The Brahmins, who were the 'intellectual class'; Kshatriyas the 'protectors of land'; the Vaishyas or 'traders' and Shudras, 'the craftsmen and artisans'. Emphasis on relationship was there, and ascetics, sages were respected.

The Kautilyan Economy. The state economy was well run and managed. All resources were state property and the treasury was ever flowing.

Welfare. Both animal and human welfare was well looked after.

प्रजासुखे सुखं राज्ञः प्रजानां च हिते हितम् ।
नात्मप्रियं हितं राज्ञः प्रजानां तु प्रियं हितम् ।।

"*In the happiness of his subject lies the king's happiness, in their welfare his welfare. He shall not consider as good only that which pleases him but treat as beneficial to him whatever pleases his subjects.*"

– *Kautilya (1.19.34)*

A king was to have high ideals, intellect, energy, and behave like a sage, a monarch, a rajarishi, that is, he undertakes yogakshema of his subordinates in that he enriches and does good for his people wherein Yoga implies achievement of the goal and Kshema implies enjoying the same peacefully. Thus, the welfare of the people is as important as doing dharma.

Adherence to Dharma. Kautilya believed that the king should allow his subjects dharma as he follows his. Thus, Kautilya preferred to have an ignorant 'dharmi' king rather than an intelligent 'adharmi' prince. A king should not tax unjustly, since impoverished and discontented people can be provoked to revolt. So, self-preservation is important.

Maintenance of Law and Order. It is important that the good of the people is not construed as their open-ended welfare. It also has to include the maintenance of law and order by meting out punishments if required. This is a very important aspect of the science of government. However, extremities in this regard of being too strict or too lenient are to be avoided. Thus, being fair and giving a well-considered judgement is critical. Towards the same, any of the following can be utilised as per the situation at hand:

(a) *Saam* (making peace).

(b) *Dama* (buying out with material gifts).

(c) *Bheda* (causing dissension).

(d) *Danda* (handling with force).

Attributes of a King

Kautilya enunciated some important aspects regarding a king. An ideal king is one who has good personal attributes, high leadership ability, intellect, energy, respect for elders, truthful and resolute, disciplined and a high level of gratitude. An elaboration on qualities that are desirable are in the following paragraphs:

(a) *Intellect*

  (i) Never ending desire to learn.

  (ii) Listen, grasp, retain and understand through reflection.

(b) *Enthusiastic and Energetic King.* Brave, dexterous and full of spirit to achieve.

(c) *Personal Attributes.* The following personal attributes are essential for an ideal king:

  (i) Eloquent, sweet to talk, not frown, look into the eyes.

  (ii) Sharp intellect and bold.

  (iii) Keen mind and strong memory.

  (iv) Listens to guidance.

(v) Fair and transparent in his dealings.

(vi) Endowed with a foresight to utilise opportunities.

(vii) Handle with equanimity normal times and crises.

(viii) Be aware of when to make peace and when to fight.

(ix) Conduct himself with dignity at all times.

On Vices. Vices such as anger and greed are to be avoided at all cost. While anger makes one lose control and make wrong decisions, greed leads to humiliation and lowering of stature. Making enemies is worse than losing wealth. While anger makes enemies, greed leads to loss of wealth. However, while wealth can be made again, an enemy once made can cause long-term harm. Thus, anger is the worst and has to be avoided.

Self-Control. Self-control is the essence of all forms of growth and is an essential attribute. It is important to live in accordance with the shastras and this involves avoiding over-indulgence in anything. History has numerous examples of illustrious kings like Ravana and Duryodhana who perished on account of the above deficit.

Thus, an ideal king should be a Rajarishi and one who has a high level of self-control, respect for elders, no vices, with moderate habits, observes dharma and enables observance of the same by his subordinates, enriches and looks after the welfare of his people and be capable of self-discipline at all times.

Takeaways from Indian Scriptures

Kautilyan society of the Varna system was an endogamic one – Aryans and non-Aryans. The Aryans had the four Varnas, namely, Brahmin, Kshatriya, Vaishnav and Shudra, while Krishna had clearly brought out that all humans are born Shudras; it is their deeds, actions and education that makes them Brahmins, or learned ones, and it is not hierarchical. Even in the present day, this Varna system is being followed, though the lines of distinction are merging, but still the hierarchy can be established. Theoretically, Kshatriyas are the mainstay as the military leaders with a sprinkling of the other Varnas.

Whether, the *Gita* or the *Upanishad*, the message of 'Nishkama Karma' is loud and clear. In coming to grips with life, Shankaracharya explained one of its verses thus:

बालस्तावत्क्रीडासक्तः
तरुणस्तावत्तरुणीसक्तः
वृद्धस्तावच्चिन्तासक्तः
परमे ब्रह्मणि कोऽपि न सक्तः ।।

—*Bhaja Govindam, Shlok 7*

"*Childhood is attached to play,*
Youth is attached to sex
Old age immersed in anxieties,
There is none attracted to the 'Supreme Brahman'."

The *Upanishads* address themselves to the question of harmonising the internal and the external, that is, the subjective and inner world of man with the objective universe.

Yagya or sacrifices also lead to purification of mind. A purified mind is necessary for distilling the discriminative intelligence so that perceptions can get finer and finer.

The *Upanishads* talk about the intuitive mind, Vigyana, which is covered by the surface mind, Manas. For the former to function, it is important that the latter is pacified and made calm, something like calming the turbulence of the surface of a lake to see its bottom. The intuitive mind comes into operation only in a pure being, devoid of desire. The intuitive mind which is nearest to the sheath of bliss has the capability to function without using the gross sense organs, since it has access to the subtler and much more powerful controllers of these organs, namely, the internal organs attached to it.

The Vedic view lays down that a man must pass through normal life conscientiously and with knowledge, live its values, and accept its enjoyments (karma). Artha or material well-being is equally important to sustain and enrich life. However, dharma (or the art of ethical living) is what gives coherence and direction to the different activities of life. Finally, the pursuit of liberation, 'Moksha', helps to develop a spiritual mentality and to seek higher knowledge. This is the ultimate, the rest are instrumental, being preparatory to the knowledge of truth, which alone makes man free.

Happiness is essentially an emotional or spiritual experience of the individual, though influenced by external circumstances. Ethics, on the other hand, is normative and deals with conduct. To Vedic sages, happiness and peace were closely interlinked. One was not attainable without the other. The sages modelled the societal structure on triune aspect of the one, the '**Sachidananda**' (Existence – Consciousness – Beatitude). Thus, heavenly happiness or beatitude is the ultimate happiness, and all other forms of happiness are temporary and volatile. As the *Isha Upanishad* says, "enjoyment through renunciation of desires and regarding all material wealth as belonging to Lord is the right dictum for happiness."

The eight-fold path of Nirvana given by Buddha or the practice of the eight limbs of the *Patanjali Yoga Sutra*, which the *Gita* also recommends, provides an ethical code of conduct. Yoga requires the cultivation of truth, the practice of loving all beings and an adjustable social life. The ethical ideals of non-violence, non-covetousness, non-stealing, and steadfast commitment to truth, makes the life of a yogi a social one. Thus, a yogic life is both spiritually oriented, as well as conveying a message of social unity as displayed by Gobind Singh. He has to live a harmonious life and maintain a balance of spiritual and social life. It teaches a philosophy of moderation – as is evident in the *Gita* (6, 17) – "Yoga, which is regulated in diet and recreation, regulated in performing actions, regulated in sleeping and waking."

In the *Gita*, Sri Krishna is the 'Sarathi', the chariot driver of Arjun. He does not bear weapons or fight directly but assists Arjun through his vision, skill and ability to manoeuvre him through the battlefield to take the best advantage of various opportunities. The warrior is the soldier; when glory comes, the credit goes to the warrior and not the Sarathi. It is this non-appropriation of credit that leads to success. As Lao Tze points out, "Those who do not claim credit always get that credit," an issue, often forgotten.

Knowledge for a leader is equally important. Tipu Sultan and Gobind Singh were all highly proficient in various arts and sciences beside military knowledge. In the *Gita*, knowledge is of two types. One that is derived from experience of others, that is, 'gyana', and the second 'vigyana', is the intuitive knowledge that comes out of the depths of the human being. This is the capacity for abstract thinking. To develop this ability, which is absolutely essential for a leader, it is necessary to create an environment where concentration and reflection are encouraged. One has to steadfastly overcome the mental barriers of emotions like pride, ego and heart to be able to reflect on the past, logically and scientifically.

Integrating the intuitive mind with the rational in thought and action is a precondition to developing an ability to take a macro view of situations and take appropriately correct decisions.

According to the *Gita*, everything has to be integrated. The main principle flowing from this is to be impartial, not to favour any one goal, any one mode, or group of persons. A leader has not to be swayed by happiness or sorrow, ego or nepotism, greed or desire. His impartiality ensures the success of his mission and he is the true 'sthitapragya' the one who is steadfast in enlightenment. To be liberated is not only to develop detachment from material acquisitions but also to be able to control anger, unhappiness on its non-achievement.

In the last verse of the *Gita*, Sanjay, the minister of Dhritrashtra, has said, "Where there is Krishna, the master of Yoga, and Arjuna, the wielder of the bow, there in that society shall be found, wealth, victory, general welfare, unwavering justice and ethical sense – this is my conviction." The verse in fact refers to the confluence, in each person, of two energies needed to achieve total human welfare, namely, the *first energy of vision, yoga, calmness and spirituality (as represented by Krishna) and that of action and implementation (as represented by Arjun). This amalgamation of energies is referred to in the Gita and Chinese philosophy of Taoism as the state of "sagely within and kingly without."* This, in essence is what spirituality would offer to the Indian military leadership and the fourfold benefit of the same are: 'Shri,' (economic prosperity), 'Vijaya' (victory), 'Bhutih' (general welfare) and 'Dhruvanitih' (constant justice and ethical sense).

It is therefore safe to state on the basis of the above that spirituality has a lot to offer to the Indian military leadership and should actually be the core or essence of it. Having established the fact that spirituality would enable the Indian military leadership significantly, let us now move to developing a theory for the interplay between spirituality and Indian military leadership.

Military Leadership Traits in the *Ramayana* and the *Mahabharata*

Dharma serves as the defining idea in Indian culture. Dharma appears to be associated with morality, ethics, and virtue in nearly all post-Vedic contexts. The behaviour of the idealised epic characters in the *Mahabharata* and the *Ramayana*, however, indirectly allude to Hindu notions about common dharma. In Hinduism, as well as in the broader South and Southeast Asian cultural landscape, the aforementioned epics serve as the primary lexicon. Constant exposure to them in varied idioms yields moral teaching. Finally, one desires to actively recreate or graft the epic narrative onto one's own unique life rather than merely imitating epic characters. Instead of prioritising personal ambitions as one is accustomed to doing in everyday modern Western life, the *Ramayana* teaches that one should sacrifice their own interests for the benefit of their nuclear family. The interests of one's nuclear family should be put aside for the benefit of a larger definition of family. Finally, one should surrender the interests of all restrictive family ideals in favour of more inclusive family ideals, or for dharma. The credo of the Indian armed forces fits in perfectly with this concept.

Early in India's history, the worth and significance of the army were recognised, and, as a result, a permanent military presence was maintained to quell internal rebellion or external aggression. This led to the creation of a warrior class within India and to serve the country by means of warfare became its *dharma*. The Dharmayuddha and the Kutayuddha are two types of warfare recognised by Hindu military science. Dharma, or the law of kings and warriors, is the basis for the Dharmayuddha conflict. In other words, society approved of war because it was just and moral. Kutayuddha, on the other hand, was an unjust war that involved covert fighting. The Niti and Saurya, or moral principles and bravery, are both highly valued in Hindu warfare. Therefore, it became clear that fighting without respect for moral principles had reduced the institution to nothing more than animal savagery. A king who seeks dharma vijaya should follow the moral guidelines given to soldiers. The principles regulating the two kinds of warfare are elaborately described in the *Dharmasutras*, the epics (*Ramayana* and *Mahabharata*), the treatises of *Kautilya*, *Kamandaka* and *Sukra*.[4]

Ramayana Period and *Hanuman* as a Leader

The Epic. A Sanskrit epic poem by Sage Valmiki is called the *Ramayana*. It is one of the two most important pieces of Indian literature, along with the *Mahabharata*. The *Ramayana* is a crucial component of Hinduism, Hindu life, and Hindu culture. The *Ramayana* story has persisted over time in a variety of forms, including epics, Upanishads, Puranas, legends, and folklore.

Photo 1: Hanuman with Lord Rama and Laxman

The Ramayana depicts the duties of relationships, portrays ideal life characters and narrates a storyline exploring the human values and the concept of dharma (see photo 1). The characters of the *Ramayana* display a wide range of human emotions and persona. The leadership traits of various characters can also be identified based on the events that unfold in the storyline thus highlighting various leadership lessons.[5]

Introduction to the Character. *Hanuman*, son of *Anjani*, a female *apsara,* and *Kesari* is one of the central characters in the story of the *Ramayana.* He is renowned for his courage, power, selflessness and faithfulness. In addition, he is mentioned in a number of other literatures, like the *Mahabharata*, the *Puranas*, and several Jain writings. Hanuman took part in Rama's conflict with Ravana, the evil king. Hanuman was endowed with miraculous powers and strength but is described as mischievous and naughty in his early years. On finding his antics unbearable and also realising that he was a child, a mild curse was placed on him by a sage due to which he was unable to realise his real powers unless reminded of it by someone. This curse becomes a boon to this unrelenting child and after the wealth of knowledge which he obtains from the Lord Surya (Sun), he later transforms into an self-less and loyal follower of Lord Rama in his battle against King Ravana. This curse was later removed by the end of the *Kishkindha Kanda* when Jambavantha reminded him of his abilities and inspired him to join the search for Sita, the abducted wife of Lord *Rama.*

Leadership Qualities. Hanuman led the charge of the Vanar Sena against the mighty Ravana. His adventures are best described in the *Sundar Kand* which is the fifth chapter in the *Ramayana.* Some of the important incidents narrated in the epic are reproduced below to understand the character of Hanuman as a leader:

(a) *Communication Skills.* During Rama's fourteen-year exile, Hanuman encounters Rama in the foothills of Mount Rishyamuka while posing as a beggar at Sugriva's request. As mentioned in the epic, his mastery of language, knowledge, gestures, diction, expressions, clarity and behaviour impresses Rama so much that he accepts his request to help Sugriva against Bali who was his more powerful elder brother forcing him into exile. Also, he decided against speaking Sanskrit while interacting with Sita in the Ashok vatika so that she does not get scared.

(b) *Wisdom and Remorse.* He accidentally enters Ravana's harem while looking for Sita, and immediately feels guilty for having invaded their privacy. In his speech to Ravana in the latter's court, he demonstrates both his spiritual knowledge and diplomatic abilities.[6]

(c) *Humaneness and Compassion.* In the Ashoka Vatika, when he discovers Sita in agony because of Ravana's threat and the presence of demons as security guards, his emphatic response to pain on the one hand and his consideration of the advantages and disadvantages of the next course of action on the other, highlight both his humanity and his capacity for making decisions.

(d) *Resolve and Perseverance.* One of the most famous incidents of the *Ramayana* is when Lakshman, the younger brother of Lord Rama, is mortally wounded and can be saved only by a specific herb found only on the Gandhamadana mountain. Hanuman volunteers for the task of fetching that herb and while executing this task he defeats an army of protective demigods, uproots the entire mountain as he is unsure of the identification of herb and swiftly returns before it's too late. This shows the resolve and determination of Hanuman for accomplishment of the task at hand.[7]

(e) *Integrity and Skills.* In the entire epic, Hanuman proves his capabilities time and again. On his way to find Sita, he displays extraordinary power by crossing the ocean. He outwits the demon *Sursa* with his intelligence and proves his integrity when he chooses not to rest on *Mandara* mountain.

(f) *Quick Thinking.* While going to Lanka in search of Sita, he comes across Sampati, a giant vulture, who wanted to eat him up. Showing presence of mind, Hanuman starts talking about an even bigger vulture, Jatayu, brother of Sampati, who laid down his life to defend Sita against Ravana. Thus, not only was a crisis averted but Sampati also assisted him in finding Sita with the help of his distant sight.[8]

(g) *Crisis Handling and Initiative.* The brilliance of Hanuman as a crisis manager can be visualised by the fact that not only did he always resolve a crisis but went much beyond it. He not only located Sita, which was his primary task, he also collected information about Lanka, judged the strength of Ravana and demoralised the Lankans by burning down the city when his tail had been set on fire by Ravana (see photos 2 & 3). This incident made Lankans feel that Ravana had done a great mistake in abducting Sita for his pleasure.

Photo 2: Hanuman with Sita

(h) *Tact and Foresight.* When Ravana captured Hanuman and asked him who he was, showing wisdom and foresight, he replies that he is an ambassador of King Sugriva, and thus escaped a death sentence. As a result, he was able to diffuse imminent danger to a lower level.

(j) *Sense of Self.* When Hanuman returned to Lord Rama after a successful completion of his task of getting information of Sita, Rama praises him a lot. On this, instead of being arrogant, the joyous Hanuman fell at Rama's feet and asked Lord Rama to save him from the tentacles of egoism.

(k) *Humility.* Hanuman is much adored by people because of his unmatched strength and simplicity as he chooses to sit at the feet of Rama, while at Ravana's court, he claims a higher seat. He served with humility and had no ego over his achievements.

(l) *Adaptability.* It is displayed during his search for Sita where he changes his size from micro to macro and vice versa depending on the requirements of the situation.[9]

(m) *Aiding Intuition.* Hanuman was a senior aide to King Sugriva who had lost his kingdom to his brother Bali and was living in exile in a forest. When Lord Rama and Lakshman come to the forest during their exile, Sugriva suspects them as mercenaries of Bali and orders Hanuman to kill them. Hanuman follows his intuition and confirms the real identities of Lord Rama before execution of his task. This act of Hanuman proves to be a turning point in the epic as Rama helps Sugriva in gaining his kingdom back and, in turn, Lord Rama is helped by Sugriva and his army of monkeys in the fight against the larger army of Ravana. In addition, it was Hanuman's intuition that helped Rama to recognise Vibhishana as his friend even though he was a brother of Ravana. This was instrumental in the killing of Ravana who otherwise was proving to be invincible in war.

(n) *Strategic Thinking*. Hanuman decides not to enter Lanka by fighting with soldiers protecting the gate there. He did not want to let Ravana know of his presence before the completion of his task of finding out the whereabouts of Sita. He chose to turn small to enter the city at night to accomplish his task without giving away his intentions beforehand. Hanuman displays a wide range of qualities during the entire course of the epic *Ramayana*. The qualities shown by Hanuman represent the whole spectrum of desired qualities for any leader in any organisation.

Photo 3: Hanuman after setting Lanka alight

Mahabharata and Bhishma as a Leader

The Epic and Character of Bhishma. A terrible fight similar to the one represented in the *Mahabharata* took place in India well before 3000 BC on the Kurukshetra battlefield, not too distant from Delhi, the current capital of our nation. It was a violent battle between the cousins, the *Pandavas* and

Photo 4: Krishna confronting Bhishma

the *Kauravas*, in which the Pandavas triumphed. The magnificent old man named Bhishma, who was 116 years old during this eighteen-day fight, was the commander-in-chief of the Kauravas and was adored, admired, and cherished by the governing elite on both sides of the conflict (see photo 4). He was mortally wounded in the combat, his body punctured by hundreds of arrows, and he died there on the field of battle.

The Teachings of Bhishma. The eldest Pandava, Yudhistira, was to rule the large kingdom that he had conquered in battle, and Krishna, the Pandavas' divine mentor and advisor, asked Bhishma to teach Yudhistira the skill of leadership. A few of his teachings are given in succeeding paragraphs:[10]

(a) *Personal Conduct.* The actions of a king should be above reproach. His success depends on his self-control, humility, morality, and straightforwardness. He ought to have complete control of his emotions.

(b) *Balanced Approach.* A monarch must have compassion as part of his mental makeup, but he must be careful not to show it too much, as that will make him appear vulnerable to lesser men who may exploit him. A king requires constant attention. He should constantly research both his allies and adversaries.

(c) *Duty.* The people are a king's first responsibility. He should take care of them without thinking about how to make himself feel good, putting the needs of others before his own. He ought to watch over them just like a mother would.

(d) *Handling of Subordinates.* People ought to be able to live as freely and happily as they do at their father's home. A king's job is to safeguard the people and their happiness in a variety of ways using talent, nimbleness, and truth.

(e) *Candid and Wily.* A ruler should act covertly towards his adversary. Since simplicity or candour alone can never safeguard the kingdom, you must be both sincere and wily.

(f) *Self-Righteousness.* A king's guiding principle is dharma (righteous behaviour). There is nothing more potent.

(g) *Attention to Detail.* Pay attention to how the kingdom is doing. An environment that is old and run-down is a sign of disdain. In order to gain favour, renovate.

(h) *Use of Penalty*. Be confident in your ability to punish others and do not hold back when doing so. People are frequently motivated by punishment, therefore understand the principles of correction.

(j) *Righteousness*. Bhishma is asked if a leader should feel saddened for getting into a conflict with individuals who are close to and precious to him, or guilty for having a conflict? In response, he says that a leader must stand up for what is right, even if that means opposing, or arguing with members of his own team. A leader's main goal is to fight for the correct cause, and in the end, everyone will know what is just and right.

(k) *Team Work*. A single person cannot complete anything, not even the tiniest task. He needs help, obviously.

Bhishma as a Military Leader. Bhishma, a symbol of truth and duty, is the tallest amongst all the leaders. This peerless warrior was aware of the strength of the Pandavas and the weakness of the Kauravas. Hence, he ignored the latter's wrongdoings in the hope to reform them in time. Bhishma's magnetic personality, scholarly knowledge of statecraft, military science, religion and philosophy made him revered by other leaders. He was a true traditional leader with a traditional sense of duty to the throne of Hastinapur. Bhishma's vow of celibacy and his prolonged ascetic life made him unemotional. He was keen on bringing both the cousins close for the greater good of the country and was aware that the virtues of the Pandavas allowed them to take care of themselves without his support. He prolonged the war, hoping it would stop (see photo 5). Bhishma also taught the Pandavas about liberation, duties of a king, health,

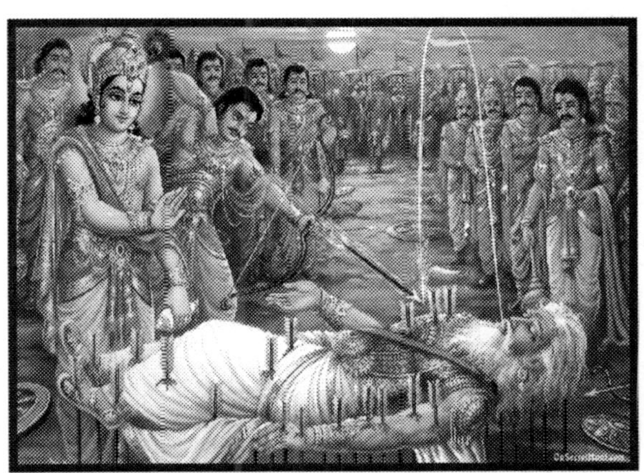

Photo 5: Bhishma on a Bed of Arrows

desire, rebirth, peace and conflict. These are captured in the chapters *Shanti Parva* and *Anushasan Parva* in the *Mahabharata.*

Spiritual Leadership Traits of Famous Indian Kings

Let us now look at some military leaders over the ages to draw out their special spiritual leadership traits.

Ashoka the Great

The grandson of the great Chandragupta of the Mauryan Age, Ashoka ruled for 27 years from 273 B.C. Acclaimed as one of most powerful kings and a military leader his name is still remembered in the world. A messenger of peace, he replaced the prevailing concept of *Dig Vijay* (conquest by force) to *Dharma Vijay* (conquest of right). His message of Ahimsa (non-violence) and Maitri (friendship) was spread all over.

Shivaji

Another crusader, a great sword bearer who kept the battle on against Muslim invaders till his last was also deeply spiritual by nature. In the words of Sant Ramdas, "Bold and liberal and earnest minded, alert and brave, you have put all kings to shame, O Prince. Immovable a heart, the protector of many, resolute to lead a holy life, rich and meditative, generous hearted – who can vie with such a one". Even his enemies praised him. He respected mosques and regarded the *Koran* with due reverence. Muslims enjoyed equality in all ways. He was tolerant towards all religions. The captured Muslim women were kept in safe custody till they could be returned to their families. He was a great motivator. *His concept of 'Hindavi Samaj' was not against Islam or for propagating Hinduism but propagated the philosophy of freedom and equal treatment to all faiths. A devotee of Shiva he never entertained the idea of establishing a command empire or a theocratic state.* He opposed feudalism and corruption.

He fought against Muslims who were well organized and overwhelming in numbers. He was brave and tactful and kept high standards of morality. Intensely religious, he respected all religions and enforced strict morality. Ever smiling, a charismatic man, he had an uncanny gift of judging character and selecting the right man for the job.

He was a great visionary leader. Despite being a foot soldier, he developed the navy. He would plan a battle to its entirety. The battle of Pratapgarh is an example of detailed planning of defensive and offensive actions. A great administrator, he constantly kept improving his fighting efficiency, besides building dams and irrigation canals. Shivaji was an effective manager. He is known to handle troops of all kinds, the bold, the timid, indifferent, thieves, etc. His man management was par excellence. Shivaji was bold and audacious and a great risk taker. His famous raid on the camp of Shaista Khan in the midst of heavy security shattered the Mughal morale, besides leaving hundreds of enemy soldiers wounded or dead.

He had a high sense of values. Noble in character, he respected women, for which even his enemies respected him. Tolerant to all religions, he had a large number of Muslims in his army. He built mosques for them to pray. A great motivator he was imbued with exceptional oratory skills which could rouse the soldiers with a few words. Hardy by nature he was wedded to his cause. His commitment was total.

Maharana Pratap

Born to a gallant leader, Udai Singh, Maharana Pratap has carved himself a niche in the annals of military history. Brought up like a warrior, he was physically and mentally robust. He displayed an exemplary character, and his strong will, sense of dedication and tremendous energy made him popular among the Rajput warriors.

He was a pioneer of the world-famous 'guerrilla warfare' against Akbar. The country recognized him for his valour, patriotism, self-sacrifice. Maharana Pratap was a virtuous leader of values. A man of his word, he led a crusade against Akbar against all odds of his clan. An ascetic, a gallant commander, he was bold and fearless.

Todd in his famous book '*Annals and Antiquities of Rajasthan*', summed up his qualities'. *"Maharana Pratap was a man of undaunted heroism, inflexible fortitude, perseverance and had the fidelity of principles. He was imbued with fervour of religious zeal, and had an unconquerable mind."*

Maharaja Ranjit Singh

He was a dashing young man who ascended to the throne at the age of 12 when his father died. By the age of 21, he had proved his military prowess and was given the title of 'Maharaja', in 1801. A self-made man, son of small chieftain, he rose to the heights of becoming a mighty ruler by dint of his strong character and great ability. He always displayed competent military leadership with deliberate and thoughtful moves. A pragmatic leader, he never crossed his limits; thus, he was never destabilised by reverses. Ranjit Singh was a rare combination of an outstanding soldier and a great ruler with soldiering as his main passion.

Guru Tegh Bahadur[11]

Guru Tegh Bahadur was the ninth guru of the Sikh religion. He is known as a warrior, poet, teacher and thinker. The Sikhs refer to him as the Srishti-di-Chadar (Protector of Humanity) on account of his supreme sacrifice for preservation of humanity. Born on 1 April 1621 in Amritsar as Tyag Mal he fought the famous battle of Kartarpur and for the bravery displayed in it, his followers started calling him Tegh Bahadur. The Guru is however more famous and more respected for the sacrifice that he made even to the extent of sacrificing his life while protecting the weak and defenceless people such as farmers and Kashmiri Pandits. In fact, many refer to his sacrifice as the first ever martyrdom in the world for human rights. On account of the above, Guru Tegh Bahadur is therefore an apt example of a spiritual military leader.

Guru Gobind Singh

Riding a blue horse with a white hawk perched on his left wrist and a 'kalgi' adorning his turban; he was a symbol of spirituality, courage and valour. He led his forces by personal example. While Guru Nanak was a peace lover, a pacifist, Guru Gobind Singh was a warrior who fought war for peace as it was the need of the hour for the survival of society. For the educated and literate, there was the image of the Guru as a patron of learning, music and poetry; he was a great poet himself. For the weak and oppressed, he had the image of a saviour. He gave them strength, courage and confidence till they were able to hold their own. He believed in attaining salvation through work. He too believed that men should strive to be like the lotus in muddy water. He believed that prayers were the answers to life's problems. He encouraged equanimity and disapproved of casteism. His concept of 'langar' (common kitchen) and 'panj pyare' (the chosen five) go to prove his point.

Military Leadership Traits

As a man, Guru Gobind Singh was a versatile genius and a man with great qualities like tolerance, simplicity, duty consciousness, confidence, bravery, obedience, sacrifice, maturity of both thought and action, love and warmth for humanity and, above all, a man of God. Some of his outstanding leadership traits were:

(a) Guru Gobind Singh had the ability to quickly assess a situation, make a quick decision and spell them out confidently, concisely, clearly.

(b) Guru Gobind Singh was imbued with humility. He attributed all his victories in the name of his Khalsa soldiers. The war cry 'Wahe guru ji ka Khalsa, wahe guru ji ki fateh', symbolises the same. He maintained that humility is an excellent trait but to be exhibited only where it is affective. Humility cannot breed gentleness in the hearts and only embolden demons and evildoers.

(c) Gifted with a sense of humour, he could laugh at situations and ease the prevailing tension in the group.

(d) His self-sacrifice and rigour were a source of great motivation. During the seige of Anandpur fort, the Khalsa army was on a starvation diet, subsisting on edible tree leaves and barks. Guru Gobind Singh's family was also on the same diet and he equally shared the adversities and hardships, which invigorated the morale of the men. When all were heartbroken on hearing about the news of his two sons being bricked alive in a wall, he consoled them and spoke.

इन पुत्रन के सीस पर वार दिए सुत चार ।
चार मुए तो क्या हुआ जीवत कई हजार ।।

"*On the martyrdom of these sons, there are thousands of sons who are living.*"

He was unquestionably honest with a high level of integrity and a strong moral character. His five golden rules which he gave to Banda Bahadur gives an indication of the same:

(a) Never approach a woman nor cast malicious looks at her.

(b) Be always faithful to the Khalsa (soldiers) and treat each other as equals.

(c) Never try to form a separate sect of your own.

(d) Never tell a lie and remain true to your word and deed.

(e) Never feel proud after a victory.

The raising of the Khalsa Panth was indeed an innovative idea. The ability to build a cohesive force of righteous fighters from a demotivated and demoralised force is an example of his charismatic and constructive genius.

He was a saviour of Hinduism but showed tolerance towards other religions. Not an enemy of Islam, he had employed Pathans to train his soldiers. He was an eternal enemy of injustice, tyranny, and oppression, regardless of its source.

A nurturant leader, his mental alertness and vision was exemplary. He had visualised that in the race for his 'gaddi' (i.e., his succession), the main purpose of raising the Khalsa Panth would be lost. To avoid this, he introduced the 'Panj Pyare' or 'panthic' rule bringing a participative or democratic way of functioning.

Guru Gobind Singh was a great motivator and warrior who led by personal example. Of the 14 main battles he fought, he was practically outnumbered in most of them by a ratio 5:1 to 20:1. Despite this he could still give the enemy a bloody nose as he believed that "*It's the men, not the weapons, the will in the heart and the mind that bring victory in the end.*"

Magnetic bearing, always well dressed and with a dignified deportment, he won his enemies by his 'genteel behaviour'. Unquestionably honest, and imbued with a good sense of humour, he would remain remarkably calm under stress. Without being arrogant he was astute. He could read the intentions of his rivals and never went wrong in his judgment. The safe passage offered by the Mughals during the Anandpur seige turned to be a bloody affair, but Gobind Singh managed to fool the Mughal Army.

S.M. Latif, a famous Muslim historian, had said that Guru Gobind Singh had within him the two important qualities of being a spiritual leader and a warrior. He felt that Sikhism as founded by Nanak and Hinduism on the whole would have vanished had he not mobilised the vanquished people towards political ascendancy and national freedom.

Guru Gobind Singh was a great scholar with a good knowledge of Persian, Hindi and Punjabi. He was fond of arts, and crafts. A lover of music, a prolific writer and a great poet, he was always inspired by nature. His '*Dasam Granth*' is revered worldwide. A developer and social reformer he never accepted low standards, be it moral or physical. He imparted tough training and continuously worked to improve the proficiency of his subordinates. He sent a number of them to master the Vedas in Banaras. He is known to have produced hawks out of sparrows and lions out of jackals. He cut down religious bigotry, eschewed casteism, abolished social evils like dowry, etc.

He considered the four Varnas of Hinduism as paan, chuna, supari and katha, which become one when well chewed.

A fearless soldier, he considered death as a mere finite subscription to the perennial proverb of life, and martyrdom for him was the most sublime act of life, and an honour to the nation. A true patriot, though he made truce with Bahadur Shah, he refused to collude with him to fight against Marathas or Rajputs.

Batra (1976) brings out the following on his temperance, humility and way of life:

(a) Not to be elated in success, or deflated in defeat. Not to be a slave to desires, but lead a simple, balanced and temperate life.

(b) Steer clear of extremes and keep the senses under check.

(c) Not to submit to injustice.

(d) Keep humility as a great virtue. Guru Gobind Singh had said that "he who so ever looks upon him as a God would be consumed in the infernal fires of hell." He considered himself as an ordinary creation of God.

He was a strong advocate of self-defence. It is righteous to unsheathe the sword when all other human devices have failed. Further, it is important to combat and defend oneself from the evil forces from within and without.

Guru Gobind Singh believed in the practicality of religion. He said that, "no nation or sect can rise unless its religion unites them for a common purpose." Simplicity, unity, patriotism, and fearless but righteous living are the arch principles of the Guru's teachings and from where spout the golden words of equality, liberty, fraternity, secularism, democracy, universal peace and progress in their true forms.

Military Leadership in Wars Fought Post Independence

The Indian military continues to be politically apolitical and cut off from society, therefore little is known about its internal issues abroad. One thing that rightfully inspires popular jubilation and gratitude for the security forces is that, with the exception of the 1962 incident, they have performed well in every foreign and internal threat since independence. Because of this, if the military's performance in wars on the ground has been determined to be great, the nation owes it to the stellar rank and file and glorious junior leadership, whose level of sacrifice is unrivalled in world history. The average Indian tends to be extremely happy and proud of the level of generalship that the Indian military has attained.[12] However, a close penetrating look would reveal that there is a definite need to sit up and introspect for better prospects.

Operations in Jammu and Kashmir 1947-48

In reality, the Jammu and Kashmir War of 1947-1948 was forced upon the nation when it was yet a young independent nation. There was little opportunity for preparation or reaction. On 20 October 1947, Pakistan began its invasion of Jammu and Kashmir State. By 24 October, it had made significant headway and Srinagar, the state capital, was in grave danger. Only on 25 October did the State of Jammu and Kashmir make a request for assistance to the Indian government. Unless the State acceded to India as required by the Partition Agreement, no military support could be provided. On 26 October, the instrument of accession was received. Any delay in the State's admission or the deployment of the military would have been an unstoppable catastrophe, costing Jammu and Kashmir heavily. High-level sagacity was required in this situation in order to comprehend the national vital Interests and political will in order to act quickly and preserve these interests. Pakistan never viewed any method of annexation of Jammu and Kashmir, including the use of force, as being unfair. On the other hand, India has consistently argued that, regardless of a state's population, the will of the people should prevail. Therefore, it was verified that the request had the backing of the populace, as represented by the biggest political party, the National Conference, chaired by Sheikh Mohammed

Abdullah, when accepting the State's accession on 26 October. Concurrently, the Service Chiefs, all of whom were British, were warned on 25 October to prepare plans and be ready to despatch essential troops for the defence of Jammu and Kashmir.[13]

The troops concerned were only nominated on 26 October and their movement commenced on the morning of 27 October. As mentioned earlier, a small number of troops were airlifted and others sent by road. It is indeed commendable that the political masters, who had little experience of dealing with such a grave situation, reacted so very soundly and promptly. Full credit must be given to Pandit Jawaharlal Nehru, the prime minister, Sardar Vallabhbhai Patel, the deputy prime minister and V.P. Menon, secretary to the Ministry of States. It may be mentioned that Gandhiji fully supported the action of the Indian Government. Subsequently, operations for evicting the aggressors were pursued relentlessly, till a ceasefire was achieved, under the aegis of the United Nations. In fact, if at the end of 1948, operations were continued, perhaps the enemy could have been evicted even from the remainder of the territory under their occupation with, of course, additional forces. However, being conscious of the need to restore peace and having complete faith and confidence in the United Nations to ensure justice, the Indian Government agreed to the ceasefire. It will also be recalled that it is the Government of India, which initially took the case to the United Nations. Thus, from the beginning of the trouble, on 20 October 1947, in Jammu and Kashmir, up to the time of the ceasefire, on 1 January 1949, great sagacity and firm political will was displayed by the political leadership of India.[14]

Maintenance of the Aim. The Armed Forces, in this case, the Army and Air Force, relentlessly pursued the objectives of the operations after receiving the required governmental directives and inspired by the rightness of the cause. The initial objective was to protect Srinagar at all costs, while the secondary goal was to drive the invaders out of Jammu and Kashmir. Both Brigadier L.P. Sen, the commander of 161 Infantry Brigade, and Lt. Col. Diwan Ranjit Rai, commander of the originally modest force, never lost sight of the goal and really pursued it with tremendous enthusiasm. The senior commanders, especially Generals Kulwant Singh, Thimayya, and Atma Singh, as well as the Army Commander, General Cariappa, then made every effort to ensure that the goal was accomplished as the forces were built up. In the early stages of the conflict, General Kulwant Singh played a crucial role in the operations to push the enemy beyond Baramulla in the Kashmir Valley and beyond Jhangar-Rajauri in Jammu Province. The operations to push the enemy out of Uri and Tithwal, as well as the connection with Leh, demonstrate General Thimayya's assertive role and unrelenting pursuit of his objective. The actions that led to the link-up with Poonch in Jammu Province similarly showed that General Atma Singh carried out his operations assiduously and never lost sight of the end goal. Overall, General Cariappa's vision and tenacity were key factors in the goal's mainly successful completion. Despite the enemy first approaching Srinagar's gates and getting quite close to Jammu, by the end of the operations, he had been driven well away from the majority of the region, and more than two-thirds of Jammu and Kashmir had been reclaimed.

Offensive Action. No war can be won solely by defensive measures, according to an aphorism. After first assuring the defence of Srinagar's airfield and city, Indian soldiers immediately went on the attack in the Jammu and Kashmir operations. Throughout the operations, this aggressive attitude persisted. With the exception of a few setbacks that occasionally occurred during the defence of Jhangar or the attack on Zoji La, which occurs in war, the Indian forces were generally imbued throughout with a high level of combative spirit. Poonch's defensive in the face of severe adversity is a prime illustration of constant defence being conducted offensively. It goes without saying that having such an attitude is essential for winning any conflict.

Surprise and Deception. It is impossible to overstate the value of surprise and deception for winning a war. The Indian Army grasped this to a large extent. These aspects received enough attention in the majority of the procedures that were performed. The use of tanks at Sheletang and Zoji La, the fortification of Leh, the Tithwal operation itself carried out in conjunction with the advance beyond Uri, the choice to link up with Poonch via Mendhar, are other significant examples of how surprise and deception contributed to Indian victory. The quickness of the operations also succeeded in surprising people on numerous occasions.

Improvisation. As brought out earlier, the Indian Army was in the process of restructuring itself following the country's division, but before it could do so, it became embroiled in significant internal security duties. It had to conduct operations in Jammu and Kashmir without any break, even after the affected population had moved and law and order had been restored. These missions were completed in harsh and challenging terrain, bad weather, with insufficient administrative and fire support. Road communications and signal communications were supported by rudimentary infrastructure. Engineers lacked suitable and contemporary tools. The equipment and attire of the troops were inadequate. Improvisation was therefore required at all levels at every stage. The troops excelled in this area and gained a lot of confidence in their abilities to continue moving forward despite all obstacles.

Cooperation and Coordination. In-depth collaboration and efficient coordination are necessary for any activity to be successful, both within and between the Services. The time to integrate troops and formations as is customary in a time of peace was limited for the reasons already mentioned earlier. However, good collaboration was achieved between the various arms and services of the Army, particularly infantry and armour, as a result of Indian forces realising the righteousness of their cause and the responsibility that lay on their shoulders. In addition to this, the Indian Air Force was crucial in providing close offensive support to the ground forces as well as transportation assistance, and it significantly aided in their success. A lack of artillery assistance was frequently partially made up for by offensive air support. The close collaboration and cohesiveness that the Army and Air Force demonstrated throughout this conflict created the groundwork for extensive inter-Service cooperation throughout all later conflicts.

Logistics. A war's ability to succeed is largely dependent on the logistical support that is given. Forethought, meticulous organisation, and execution are required for the provision of ammunition, weapons, food, fuel, and ordnance stores, as well as for medical attention and casualty evacuation, equipment repair and recovery, and prompt reinforcement of forces. Where pre-planning is practicable in times of peace, some logistical infrastructure can be created beforehand. However, as there was no way to pre-plan for this battle, everything had to be done from scratch once the fighting began. The fact that the administrative staff and the services met the demands of the fighting soldiers so successfully demonstrates the enormous contribution they made to the operations' success.

Civil Military Relations. The excellent relationship that grew between local civilians and the military that came to their assistance was a distinctive aspect of these missions. Senior politicians like Bakshi, Dhar, and Nazir kept a close relationship with the Army and even joined them on missions. The people themselves gave the Army their full cooperation and helped with logistics and information. The Army provided medical aid, conducted outreach development, and assisted in reconstruction once the areas were liberated. The State Government subsequently organised and trained the Jammu & Kashmir Militia.

1962: A Debacle

Seeds of Conflict. In a study of leadership, it is quintessential to analyse the military aspects of the 1962 War to draw important lessons. On Independence, India declared the northern boundary in Ladakh to run along the Johnson Line to include the area of Aksai Chin. Along the eastern borders it ran along McMahon Line. A Communist regime came to power in China on 1 October 1949. Their first invasion was Tibet in 1950. Pandit Nehru declined to discuss the border dispute with China on the pretext that everything had been settled between the two friendly nations. The Chinese maintained the status quo and proposed negotiations on the boundary issue. This was not accepted by the political class of India under the guidance of the bureaucracy, which at that time was reigning supreme. General Cariappa, the first Indian Commander-in-Chief, had earlier raised the concern with the Prime Minister, to which he got an angry retort from Pandit Nehru. The subject was never raised again. The irony was that the Ministry of Defence had little say in the matters of Tibet at that point of time.[15] The Khampa tribes in northeast Tibet revolted in 1956. It spread to other regions and mainly to Lhasa. His Holiness, the Dalai Lama, escaped from Tibet and sought political asylum in India. China suspecting active abetment to insurgency in Tibet deployed the PLA right up to the borders. India considered this to be provocative and adopted a forward policy. The Prime Minister ordered deployment of the Army on the borders. With the enunciated policy of forward deployment, clashes took place at Longju in the east and Kongka La in the west, in 1959. This was the flash point for the larger confrontation that ensued.[16]

The nation's political elite must formulate its policies after giving it significant thought. The country's national goal must be in line with the military's capability and its available resources. If the nation's resources and armed weapons are insufficient to achieve the national goal, diplomatic tactics must be employed.[17]

In 1962, we had inadequate machinery to take deliberate decisions. The bureaucrats and politicians took the vital decisions regarding military matters without full consultation with the military chiefs concerned. When General Thapar, the Chief of the Army Staff, asked for a written directive regarding throwing out the Chinese from Thag La Ridge area, Defence Minister Krishna Menon was away in New York. The Deputy Defence Minister got his instructions on the telephone and a mere joint secretary, sent the directions to the Chief, which read, "The Army should get ready and send the Chinese into the Kameng frontier division of NEFA as soon as he is ready, as was decided throughout prior sessions". Thus, the order which forced our troops to operations in Nam Ka Chu area was given on behalf of a defence minister half a world away. There was no cabinet meeting. What we needed in the country was a proper system for higher directions of war so that the military chiefs could play their part in defence matters instead of the bureaucrats and politicians taking ill informed decisions.[18]

We never used our Air Force which could have provided us with very useful information regarding concentrations as well as forward movements of Chinese forces. Some bureaucrats along with Director of the Intelligence Bureau, were advising the Defence Minister and the Prime Minister on the subject. The issue was never discussed in a joint forum between the Army and Air chiefs.[19]

The country and the Government must ensure that only competent and professionally sound army officers possessing excellent character are given top jobs. Open favouritism and merit were the first casualty with disastrous consequences. In 1962, the Army hierarchy spoke what Nehru wanted to hear. It proved the importance of sound military advice by Army professionals.

Lastly, the Indian Army was never defeated by the Chinese. Only six brigades took part in the 1962 operations, four in Nam Ka Chu-Bomdi La sector, one in Walong sector and one in Ladakh sector. The Indian Army then had over 38 brigades. The men and officers at lower and middle levels gave a good account of themselves. Unfortunately, absence of clear directions from the military leadership at the top level proved fatal. The ambitious bureaucrats and the intelligence chief without any military gravitas guided the uninformed politicians to jump into a conflict with China.[20]

1965 War

Introduction. The 1965 conflict began with fighting in the Rann of Kutch in April of that year and gradually intensified until a powerful force known as 'Gibraltar' was infiltrated into the Kashmir Valley by Pakistan on 1 August. The Pakistani army then started its overt armoured offensive, code-named 'Grand Slam,' on 1 September 1965, in the Akhnoor area of J&K, where it enjoyed a strategic advantage due to the topography and initiative of offensive action.[21]

Foresight in Equipment Modernisation. The leadership, even after the debacle of 1962, had failed to equip the formations on the western front up to the desired levels; a case in point is the neglect of the mechanised formations. Pakistan had superiority in tanks in terms of quality of equipment. Our Armoured Division too had not been structured as per the requirement of the day.[22] It had two brigades, one armoured brigade and a lorried infantry brigade. In contrast, Pakistan had three identical armoured brigade headquarters. India, with more than three times the size of Pakistan, and having much larger industrial and financial resources, had only one armoured division while Pakistan fielded two. The Indian Army was tactically infantry oriented and probably our military leadership had not applied their minds to make our army hard-hitting and mobile, with more emphasis on armour. In artillery also, Pakistan had a qualitative edge since it was equipped with heavier calibre, longer range guns supplied by the USA. In infantry formations, we were better but we had a larger frontage to cover since the front with the Chinese also had to be guarded. But at the section level, Pakistan had two LMGs per section as compared to one in own infantry battalions.[23]

Defensive Mindset. Since the strategy as a nation was based on being defensive, unconsciously our commanders had developed an attitude of defensive mindedness. In terms of training the formations, we had not practised deep manoeuvres, being unduly concerned with losses to tanks; the attitude was to conserve the tanks than risk them in a decisive combat.

Lack of Coordination between Army and Air Force. In case of an emergency, the Pakistan Air Force was ready to protect the area because it had been included in the operations plans.[24] Additionally, anticipating conflict, the Indian Air Force (IAF) had sent a few fighter squadrons up front. What continues to surprise is that the cabinet's prior authorisation for utilising entire military power was not acquired, despite the tactical circumstances and the anticipated Pakistani onslaught. In fact, the army chief had to wait a whole day while our ground soldiers fought it out with terrible disadvantages. However, according to General D.K. Palit, this was the general who, as acting army commander in 1961, had directed the preparation of a military attack in Goa but had instructed the operations branch not to inform the IAF and Indian Navy. Since neither the Chiefs of Staff Committee nor the Emergency Committee of the Cabinet, which had taken the role of the Defence Committee of the Cabinet, appears to have met, it is clear that the higher defence organisation has failed. Based on the army chief's proposal, the defence minister approved using the IAF. The air force gave it all it had in the late hours of the day and suffered losses.[25] However, the Pakistani march to Akhnoor was ultimately delayed. But the Indian counteroffensive into Pakistan on 6 September 1965, became the true bone of contention. Without telling the air force, the 15th division of the Indian Army made the decision to begin the onslaught at daybreak along a busy road. Lieutenant General Harbaksh Singh, Head of the Western Command,[26] has been harsh in his criticism of the divisional commander on this count and for placing the division (on the Grand Trunk Road, 'bumper to bumper,' in the General's words) in danger from enemy air raids while the IAF was essentially in the dark. Naturally, the Pakistan Air Force had a field day. However, it appears that our lack of establishing proper organisation and communications for quick close support had made matters worse. It seems we did not have a clear concept of the use of the air force during the war. The priorities it seems were not clear. The Air Force wanted to win the air battle first before giving all-out support to the army. This strategy of the Air Force was based on the allied strategy of World War II in which thousands of aircraft were available to the Allies to win the war. This concept, may be, was not applicable to us.

Superior Generalship during the Conduct Stage. Pakistan started the 1965 war with superior armour and artillery which played a decisive role in warfare in the plains. They had prepared detailed plans, yet they failed to achieve their aims. Their leadership wavered when their forces were knocking at the very gates of Akhnoor. Similarly, the breakout plan of their armoured division in Khem Karan sector was sound but its execution left much to be desired. General Chaudhuri led the army to success by first snatching the initiative from Pakistan and then retaining it till the war ended. Indian military leadership rightfully was against the acceptance of the UN resolution for peace as the Pak army had received a good beating, but the Government accepted it and in doing so repeated the same mistake it had done in 1947-48, when the Pak army was on the run throughout Jammu & Kashmir. During the war, there was a clear opportunity available to the Indian Army to have martial law declared in Jammu & Kashmir when the state government itself was recommending it and the central government only wanted a recommendation of General Choudhury to implement it. The successful aspect of the 1965 war was due to junior leaders, Lt. Cols., a few Brigadiers and two/three Major Generals.[27] At the strategic level, the aims were not met due to lack of coordination and a confused strategy. The major weaknesses were lack of air support, weak firepower and out-of-date equipment. Unfortunately, uncoordinated inter-services activity, indifferent higher command perceptions and directions of war resulted in a stalemate. By changing strategy and tactics in the middle of the war we could have brought in success.[28]

1971 War

Introduction. The 1971 war was started by Pakistan on 3 December 1971 when its air force and army attacked on our western front in Punjab as well as Jammu and Kashmir. India retaliated by attacking East Pakistan in strength while remaining generally on the defensive in the west. India won a decisive victory in East Pakistan, now Bangladesh.[29] It is an exceptional military feat. In one lightning blow, the Indian armed forces achieved Bangladesh's independence, a nation of 75 million people, after forcing the Pakistani commanders and 93,000 soldiers to submit after a 14-day conflict. The circumstances under which our forces operated, nevertheless, will not happen again.

Leadership at the National Level. In 1971, India had a capable national leader in Indira Gandhi who was both courageous and decisive. She handled political forces with a finesse that surprised everybody and wisely left military matters in the hands of military leaders.[30] To negate the influence of Pakistan, the USA and China, she outwitted them by signing an Indo-Soviet friendship treaty in August 1971. Meanwhile, she started to prepare the nation for war.

Leadership in the Army. The Indian Army was led by the outstanding General (later Field Marshal) Manekshaw. He was a competent leader possessing great vision and insight into matters military. He wielded a great influence with politicians as well as the bureaucracy. As Chairman of Chiefs of the Staff Committee, he ensured the political involvement of the government in evolving a broad strategy and laying down clear-cut directions to achieve the national aim in case of war. When brutal oppression started in East Pakistan in March 1971, one view in the hierarchy was to march into Pakistan as not much opposition was expected. But Manekshaw advised against any hasty action. He preferred to undertake deliberate and well-prepared operations rather than hasty exploitation of Pakistan's confusion and weaknesses in East Pakistan. He emphasized that the Indian Army needed time to complete regrouping and redeployment, large-scale dumping of ammunition and equipment had to take place around Bangladesh which required time and administrative arrangements. If the operations had been started in March/April, we would have been caught in the monsoon from May onwards. Manekshaw started detailed preparations for a short and intense war. The critical shortages in arms, equipment and manpower were made up. It was ensured that shortages of officers in the units were made up by pruning the static establishments, cancelling courses, and posting back the officers from training institutions. As soon as the monsoon was over, the formations and units were moved to the operational areas. There are mixed views regarding the leadership qualities of Lieutenant General J.S. Aurora; however, he was a competent officer and did very well as Army Commander in the Bangladesh war. He was physically tough and professionally knowledgeable. He had served for long under Manekshaw and was believed to acquiesce readily to his wishes. He was not regarded as a commander of any distinction but essentially a staff officer. Though he undertook a number of visits to the forward areas during the war, he was not successful in winning the trust and confidence of most field commanders.[31] Major General (later Lieutenant General) Jacob was Chief of Staff to General Aurora. He was a competent officer who was not given his due because of his professional skill and strong character; he had won the confidence of superiors. He contributed in detailed planning and during conduct of operations. Dumping of large-scale engineer stores was one case in point.

Morale. It is major battle-winning factor. To improve morale, along with the Chief of Air Staff and Chief of Naval Staff, General Manekshaw persuaded the government to give generous pensioners' benefits to the next of kin or wounded in the war. The morale of Indian troops was very high from the word go and continued to be the same throughout.[32] This was attributed to the excellent leadership of Mrs. Gandhi, Mr. Jagjivan Ram, the leadership in the Services and, of course, our dramatic victories on various fronts during the war. On the other hand, Pakistan had a poor state of morale due to weak leadership, inconsistent policies and lack of faith in the cause for war.

Jointmanship. Unlike Pakistan, which had its three service HQs located in three locations, that is, Army HQ in Rawalpindi, Air HQ in Peshawar and Naval HQ in Karachi, India had all of them in Delhi, thus achieving a greater degree of coordination. However, the Services did not have an integrated HQ under one person so plans were not actually joint.[33] At the army commanders level also, they were not integrated. Moreover the Army Commander was in Calcutta, Air Commander-in-Chief in Shillong and Fleet Officer Commanding-in-Chief in Visakhapatnam. Even though the system produced results, there were flaws which might have caused serious consequences under other circumstances.[34] The Air Force gave active support to the Army; the Indian Navy too was keen to play an active role to display its skill and prowess unlike as in previous wars. Air Chief Marshal P.C. Lal writes, "After the 1965 operations, we learned that the Air Force had not placed enough focus on the necessity to provide tactical air support for the Army in the field due to an overemphasis on the functions of the bomber and confidence in its efficacy. The order of operations was altered in 1969. Priority one continued to be the air protection of our country and air bases. Supporting the Army and Navy, with the Army taking precedence over the Navy, was the next-most critical task."[35] The IAF systematically bombed air fields, and kept them under a state of disrepair through periodic bombing. This kept the Pakistan Air Force grounded and us with unchallenged air supremacy so that maximum air support was available to the Army. The Navy ensured the sea blockade of East Pakistan so that no aid could reach Pakistani forces; also, nobody could escape by the sea route. Air support was also provided from INS *Vikrant* to the Army for operations against Chittagong, Cox's Bazar and south of Feni.

Selection and Maintenance of Aim. Any campaign's goal must be stated clearly if it is to be successful. There was a very clear political goal – something the Service Chiefs had not previously experienced. The political objectives assigned to the Chiefs of Staff were to fight a holding action in the west and the north and to liberate Bangladesh as soon as possible.[36] If attacked, to capture some ground in the west as a negotiating chip in the event that a Pakistani surprise strike was successful in seizing any territory in India.

Formulation of Strategy. Many months before the war, General Manekshaw issued a comprehensive and thoughtful directive to Eastern Command. Strategy and tactics to be followed were laid down. The task allotted to Eastern Command was to destroy the bulk of Pakistani forces and occupy major portions of East Pakistan, including the entry ports of Chittagong and Chalna/Khulna. There was no mention of Dacca. Emphasis on capture of ports was later removed on assurance of the Naval Chief that effective blockade would be carried out. The aim was to destroy the Pakistan Army in the Eastern Theatre in a short and decisive campaign, unlike earlier wars where capture of territory used to be the main aim. It was laid down that Indian forces were to advance as quickly as possible, bypassing fortified positions from the flanks and affecting deep penetrations. This was probably the first time that such a directive was issued; this was further amplified by Eastern Command in its concept of operations. Eastern Command planned a multipronged offensive from as many directions as possible. Detailed plans were then formulated for each sector giving allotment of troops to each axis of advance and a programmed progress along each axis on a D-Day basis which gave little scope to field commanders to plan operations in their sectors based on local knowledge of terrain, enemy dispositions and their own aptitudes. Wargames were then conducted and some changes made. The plans did not give any indication that the ultimate objective was Dacca. Macro planning at Army Headquarters was directed towards clearing the territory up to the rivers and was silent about the ultimate objective. There was a clear lack of emphasis on capturing Dacca initially.

Leadership during Conduct Stage in the Eastern Front. During the conduct stage, good military leadership was exhibited by higher commanders in general.[37] Three Corps operated under the Eastern Command, i.e., 2 Corps (Lieutenant General T.N. Raina), 4 Corps (Lieutenant General Sagat Singh) and 33 Corps (Lieutenant General M.L. Thapar). 101 Communication Zone was led by Major General Gurbux Singh Gill initially and thereafter by Major General Nagra. Apparently, no Corps had been given the specific task to capture Dacca. The progress of operation of 2 and 4 Corps was to be seen and thereafter made faster headway to execute the task. It is seen that Lieutenant General Sagat Singh comes in for a lot of praise for his dash and drive.[38] He carried out a blitzkrieg type of operation by bypassing the well-fortified fortresses of Myanamati, Lalmai and Lakshman; contain them initially and go straight for Daudakandi, Chandpur and Ashuganj, thus isolating all the troops on the border. Lieutenant General Sagat was a bold commander in contrast to 2 Corps Commander Lieutenant General T.N. Raina who was a bit cautious and was always worried about his flanks.

Leadership during Conduct Stage in the Western Front. In the western front, the operations were to be restricted to holding defences and limited offensives. In Chhamb, where Pakistan had attacked, the leadership of Major General Jaswant Singh, General Officer Commanding, 10 Infantry Division, has been questionable about thinking of withdrawing the brigades across Munawar Tawi to Troti Heights, but this was not allowed to be done because of the timely intervention of Lieutenant General Sartaj Singh who personally visited the forward area and gave directions to counter attack to throw back the enemy rather than moving back. The General Officer Commanding 1 Corps (Lieutenant General K.K. Singh) was found to be over-cautious in his approach when tasked to launch an offensive in the Shakargarh area. Since he did not want to lose any territory if Pakistan launched an offensive in the area, he left a fairly large number of troops in a defensive posture all along the border. He left one division out of three and one armoured regiment for the defence of Ramgarh. This could have been avoided. Since Pakistan had already launched an offensive in Poonch and Chhamb, another offensive was less likely and a justifiable risk would be part of good generalship. The offensive was spread over a frontage of 80 kilometres, thus dispersing the employment of two armoured brigades along with lesser gun densities as the total artillery availability amounted to ten field, eight medium and three light regiments.[39] Pak minefields seemed to have played an important role in making our commanders over-cautious. A mass and concentrated use of armour supported by the full weight of our artillery and infantry would have given us much better results. In the Rajasthan sector, 11 and 12 Infantry Divisions were directly under Southern Command, there being no Corps Headquarters. 12 Infantry Division was to capture Rahim Yar Khan and cut off Pak rail communications. One commando group was also to be used for the operation. 11 Infantry Division was to capture Naya Chor. An armoured squadron was made available for the operations. It would have been better if only one offensive was planned with maximum resources. Pakistan was also planning to attack in the Jaisalmer sector. It is fortunate that Pak 18 infantry division started its offensive earlier; otherwise, if we had gone in first, it would have surfaced behind us, thus causing a major embarrassment. The offensive was halted by the Air Force at Longewala.[40] This was the occasion when 12 Division could have taken advantage of the situation and delivered a decisive defeat. It had both options either to pursue the 18 Infantry Division or to go for the previously planned offensive after leaving suitable reserves behind.

Psychological Warfare. The aspect of psychological warfare was also well used to bring in early defeat. In November, operations were conducted in such a way that General Niazi was forced to move his troops forward to defend important approaches ahead of rivers, thus denuding the Dacca bowl. The troops later were incapable of falling back on the capital across the rivers. Secondly, the dropping of leaflets exhorting the troops to surrender was another technique which helped.

Surprise. Surprise as an important principle of war was not given due importance at the strategic level. There were strong indications and incidents, six to eight months preceding the war, which were bound to lead to an open confrontation. However, at the tactical level, both sides exploited this principle to gain tactical victories. A few examples which stand out are the naval missile attack on Karachi Harbour, a Pak submarine torpedoing INS *Khukri* off the Kandla Coast, para assault in Tangail, use of An-32 aircraft for carpet bombing in the western sector, air attacks in support of 23 PUNJAB against the enemy armoured thrust in Longewala.[41]

Concentration of Force. The principle of concentration of force by all the three services was commendably exploited in the east. Our leadership concentrated on liberating Bangladesh at the earliest possible opportunity and refused to attack in the west till troops could move from the east to the west.[42] Pakistan, on the contrary, flouted this principle and had to suffer reversals.

Higher Direction of War. There was an excellent understanding between the then Prime Minister, Mrs. Indira Gandhi, and the three Service Chiefs. This facilitated quick decision-making and clear-cut directions for the Services. This was a major contributory factor to our victory in 1971.[43] Apart from the excellent inter-services cooperation; coordination between the government and the war machinery was commendable. We were found wanting in this aspect during our previous engagements. At the same time, this aspect was dismal on the Pakistan side as was borne out by the statements made by some of their generals.

Unity of Command. Despite the excellent rapport among the three services during the war, there is still the requirement of a Chief of Defence Staff for strategic planning during peacetime and direction of operations.

Offensive Spirit. Some of our attacks failed due to incorrect appreciation of enemy strength and lack of deliberation in planning and mounting such attacks. Calculated risks may be taken while attacking hastily prepared defences; however deliberate planning and stage management would be essential while dealing with deliberate defences. Interrogation of some of the prisoners of war bore testimony that the Indian Army had underestimated their strength in particular areas and locations. Frontal attacks against enemy deliberate defences will always prove costly. Therefore, attempts must be made to surprise the enemy by developing an attack from an unexpected direction. Operations in Bangladesh brought out the necessity to master the techniques of clearance of built-up areas and well-coordinated employment of all arms. Bold and imaginative employment of helicopters contributed considerably in maintaining the momentum of our offensive in Bangladesh. Though our resources in terms of helicopters were limited, their employment in a terrain ridden with obstacles in terms of canals and rivers often paid handsome dividends.

Contingencies and Reserves. Instead of committing forces to decisive acts with immediate tactical consequence, there was a noticeable tendency to reserve them for some hazy distant possibilities. As an illustration, after 7 December, the 33 Corps had six infantry brigades in its operational region. But for the offensive, just one brigade was used efficiently. Thus, the formations' full combat potential was not completely employed.

Post War Negotiations. In the post-war phase, even after stupendous success, justified gains were not negotiated for settlement of all disputes.[44] The favourable conditions created by the military victory to settle our outstanding problems with Pakistan in the long-term interest of peace and normal relations were not exploited.

Op Pawan

The Indian Peace Keeping Force (IPKF) was at full war with the LTTE in Sri Lanka in 1987 in an effort to project its dominance outside of the country while achieving no national goals. It was an incredibly horrible experience and a complete breakdown of the civil and military hierarchy.[45]

No Clear-Cut Understanding of National Interests. Before the induction of the IPKF in Sri Lanka, relations between India and Sri Lanka were not very cordial as the Sri Lankan government believed that India was providing support to the Tamil rebels. There was a lack of coordination at the higher level as there was no clear indication as to what were our national interests. Initially, it was felt that we had to separate the two warring forces, that is, the Sri Lankan Army and the LTTE; later, however, this changed.[46] A great irony was that Sri Lanka, whose fight India was fighting, was supporting her own greatest enemy, the Tamil Tigers, who were demanding independence from the same Sri Lankan Government.

Ad hoc Approach. India at that time had no clear-cut infrastructure to analyse the pros and cons of different approaches to face up to a given situation and put up a suggested solution, with all its pros and cons, for a political decision. Everything was ad hoc. The Chief of Army Staff was tasked to settle the Sri Lankan imbroglio. The other two Services were given no specific responsibility, except to assist the Indian Army. The result was that the entire approach was ad hoc, even to the fact that Indian troops entering Sri Lanka were neither entitled to foreign service allowance, nor were they entitled to field service allowance.[47]

No Clear-Cut Direction to the Armed Forces. The Armed Forces were not clear as to what they were meant to do. The role of the Armed Forces is to fight and not to police, but in the ultimate analysis it was policing that was being done by the IPKF; even the name of the force suggests it. The entire expenditure of this operation was debited to the Indian defence budget, thus affecting modernisation.[48] There were no guidelines to the Force Commander, to guide the conduct of operations. There was no clear-cut grand strategy for this operation. Because the government was not clear in its decision, the organisation created was ad hoc to the highest degree; the end result was that the logistics had to be ad hoc too. The General Officer Commanding Andhra, Kerala, and Tamil Nadu Area had more than a handful of problems sorting out the logistics of the operation, in his capacity of advance base commander. There was no set-up for automatic provisioning of supplies, ordnance stores or even for induction of troops. There were many instances when troops landed at the Kanakesanturai jetty while their unit transport landed at Trincomalee.

Lack of Intelligence. At strategic and grand strategic levels, intelligence was outside the preview of the Armed Forces; this had to be provided by the Research and Analysis Wing and the Joint Intelligence Committee and was found wanting.[49] It was the Armed Forces that had to face the brunt of this. May be, higher leadership could have insisted on this. But when ordered to commence operations against the Tamil Tigers, they were caught unawares and completely unprepared. There was a complete blackout of intelligence at the tactical level.

Strategy for Conduct of Operations. A strategy of attrition was initially followed by the IPKF which probably was not suitable since the initiative always was with them. It was the strategy of isolation which worked better. When the insurgents were isolated from their base, the people, they got better results. The best example was the Town Commandant Jaffna. The IPKF could have gone strategically for the people and after the fall of Jaffna, the Vanni Jungles.[50] The Indian Forces were again saved by the ever-tenacious Indian soldier and of course the junior leaders. This is what Lieutenant General

Sardeshpande has to state about the performance of the officer cadre. "The fourth aspect was the painfully amateurish way the military professionals went about executing the nation's power projection: which became a glaring repetition of confusion and niggardliness. However, the saving grace was the stolidity of the jawan and dynamism of the junior officer, who between them brought steadiness and built the necessary ballast to maintain it."[51]

Locations of Commanders. The General Officer Commanding IPKF, Lieutenant General A.S. Kalkat, was located at Madras, in the advance base, next to the logistics centre which was rather incongruous. The General Officer Commanding 54 Infantry Division located himself at Palay, whereas he could have been at Jaffna after its fall. This would have ensured that he was acquainting himself with the problems and travails of his troops.

Poor Leadership. More was expected from the senior leadership. This affected motivation too. Lieutenant General Sardeshpande writes,[52] "Gathering information, planning, provisioning and quietly preparing for nasty contingencies and confrontation at various echelons, thus keeping their men and their attitude in an alert state for a full-blooded response, is paramount. When war did start, senior commanders could not withstand the impact and were found wanting". He adds, "Motivation was the worst casualty under the senior commanders, who, having developed initially gratifying bonhomie with the LTTE leaders and cadres, were reluctant to change stance, and later were certainly afraid to do so, when the chips actually were down. Lack of assertiveness, warmth of media coverage, and inadequate professional sheen showed up and resulted in dangerous manifestations of disintegrated and unhappy team." Instead of showing boldness of approach, the zero-error syndrome came to the fore.[53]

Equipment. Lieutenant General Sardeshpande, echoing the sentiments of all the personnel in the IPKF has this to say about the Indian equipment, "Our weapons and equipment have come in for a good deal of criticism. The 7.62 mm SLR is a weapon for soldiers in war.[54] It is not a weapon of terrorists and guerrillas, unlike the AK-47 or AK-56. What was required was a judicious mix of lighter AK weapons and the sturdy 7.62 mm SLRs. This mix never materialised, whereas even our 'friendly' militant groups, who formed the Provincial Government later, never seemed to have felt the paucity of such weapons."[55]

Organisational Voids. The standard infantry division is not an ideal organisation to face up to an insurgency. Some of the elements like artillery is not suitable for counter-insurgency operations. For liaison with the local political organisations, bureaucracy, and even diplomats, a representative from the Indian Administrative Services of the deputy secretary level or equivalent to a full colonel is required. The Divisional Signal Regiment was required to be reorganised to cater for improved signal communications as well as for counter intelligence. The intelligence set up at the brigade and divisional headquarters could have been beefed up.

Op Vijay – Kargil War

One of the highest battlegrounds in the world, Kargil is a testament to some outstanding bravery. In the lofty slopes of Ladakh, battles were waged. This area is sparsely populated and is home to numerous ethnic, linguistic, and religious communities in one of the highest mountains on Earth. 'Operation Vijay' is another name for the Kargil War.

Pakistan first sent forces into the region of Kashmir that was under Indian control and occupied key positions. This gave them the opportunity to position its artillery so that it could fire on the route that connects Drass and Kargil. This is how the Pakistani army infiltrated and took control of the Kargil heights. Al Badar was the name of Pakistan's operation.

India had to locate the infiltration and gather its forces to counter it in the subsequent stage. There were significant clashes between Indian and Pakistani forces that led to India retaking the areas held by Pakistani forces and Pakistani forces retreating across the Line of Control.

'Operation Vijay' was a small-scale military operation with two to three divisions on each side. The Pakistan Army took some actions to maintain surprise and deception in addition to keeping the strategy a secret. In contrast with other high-altitude regions of a similar altitude, the Kargil mountains swiftly lose snow cover as the summer wears on. The rough rocks below the peaks and ridgelines made ascending quite challenging. Troop movement was hard, time-consuming, and slow.

Mercenaries and professional warriors were among the intruders on the heights. They included the 3rd, 4th, 5th, 6th, and 12th battalions of the Northern Light Infantry (NLI) of the Pakistan Army. Some mujahedeen and individuals from Pakistan's Special Services Group (SSG) were among them. Initially, it was thought that there were 500 to 1,000 intruders on the heights, but later it was thought that there could have been as many as 5,000 intruders in total. The infiltrators were armed with mortars, artillery, and anti-aircraft guns in addition to small arms (rifles, machine guns, and grenade launchers). In addition, many posts were excessively mined.

Operation Safed Sagar. For the purpose of assisting the ground forces throughout the conflict, the IAF conducted an operation known as 'Operation Safed Sagar.' Despite the fact that the IAF's role was constrained by the weather, high altitude, restricted bomb loads, and scarcity of airstrips it provided a tremendous amount of additional support. The Kargil area's terrain, which is between 16,000 and 18,000 feet above sea level, was flown by several young veterans using specially trained personal aircraft. On 27 May, while assaulting a target in the Batalik sector, Flt. Lt. Nachiketa's MiG-27 experienced engine failure, forcing him to bail out. Sqn. Ldr. Ajay Ahuja was struck by a Pakistani surface-to-air missile (SAM) while searching for the downed pilot in a MiG-21. He safely exited the plane, but Pakistan later returned his body, which had gunshot wounds. Modern MiG-29s and Mirage-2000s were employed for electronic warfare, reconnaissance, and ground assault with free-fall bombs. Additionally, it launched a lethal laser-guided bomb, which significantly damaged Pakistani bunkers on the ridges at Tiger Hill and Muntho Dhalo. Nearly 180 Pakistani soldiers died in the Mirage raid on Muntho Dhalo.

The men who participated in the operation and the junior leadership in the Kargil war were absolutely superb. No Army in the world could have demonstrated the tenacity, grit, selflessness, and dedication to duty that our young soldiers did. Great acts of bravery and dedication were required to successfully drive the Pakistani invaders out of the Kargil sector, and the performance of our gunners and young 'air warriors' played a significant role in this success. Actually, they had little respect for our ability to use political judgement and assertiveness to pursue strategic goals that served the interests of the country. We should honour the gallantry and bravery of those who gave their lives so that the Kargil operation might be successful. They delivered an unmatched performance. These were the soldiers who only cared about protecting their nation and were willing to lose everything.

Insurgency

As opposed to conventional operations, these operations take place at the lower end of the 'Spectrum of Conflict' and involve the use of fighting power to strengthen 'civil control' in a target area rather than inflict 'destruction,' which is typically the goal of conventional warfare. Therefore, while the use of minimal force by the security forces is unavoidable in the early stages of a sub-conventional war fighting campaign to create a secure and favourable environment, such campaigns must inevitably hinge on addressing the root causes of the conflict, in line with our national policy and strategy. The idea of an 'Iron fist in a velvet glove,' which denotes a humanitarian approach towards the public at large in the battle zone, was born in the light of this essential premise. This also includes restricting the use of lethal force to combating foreign terrorists and other ferociously hostile individuals while giving indigenous misguided people the freedom to reject violence and blend with the mainstream. It emphasises utmost observance of human rights, upholds the law, and promotes the 'neutralisation' of terrorists by aiming for capture and surrender rather than just 'kills.' As part of the public information push, which depends on the efficient broadcast of information through the media, the concurrent conduct of perception management must be creatively handled.

Such a campaign requires that all military actions be people-centred, carried out in a way that fosters a groundswell for peace, and designed to reduce the number of terrorists in the area. As a result, the terms of interaction must be creatively crafted against a backdrop of political, legal, and moral constraints. Since the population is the operation's centre of gravity (CoG), capturing their hearts and minds is essential to all of our efforts in conflict management and resolution.

In non-conventional warfare, leadership development and training are especially important. To be effective, leaders must develop the perception of their troops and reaction skills so that they can identify threats quickly and use the least amount of force necessary to neutralise them while avoiding collateral damage. The success of such operations depends on having the right 'frames of reference,' being able to generate hard intelligence in a coordinated manner, and being able to use it in real time. By taking the initiative, making the terrorist reactive, and making him feel insecure as a result, we must put him on the defensive. To ensure the terrorist has no safe haven and that people voluntarily help neutralise him, this requires tenacity and unwavering dedication to the public. In order to effectively control public perception and public information, we must also effectively interact with the media. For the foreseeable future, sub-conventional operations will probably continue to be a significant army mission. Due to this, inter-service and inter-agency cooperation is vital for the efficient running of operations.

National Strategy. At the national level, the CoG and the desired end state are as follows:

(a) *Strategic CoG.* Since no insurrectionist movement can be perpetuated permanently without popular support, the populace always emerges as the CoG in all sub-conventional operations. Since public concerns are frequently the impetus for the start of any insurrectionist movement, corrective measures would entail their remedy. In such a dispute, the job of the armed forces is to act as a mediator to reduce the level of violence so that a political process may be started. This is why military operations focus on improving the civil administration's 'control' over the conflict area rather than employing force to inflict 'destruction.'

(b) *End State.* A national counterinsurgency campaign's ultimate goal is always 'conflict resolution.' Demilitarising the area of conflict and creating a setting conducive to peaceful resolution of any outstanding issues are required for this. By simultaneously using all aspects of national power, the necessary shaping of the environment is achieved. This entails seriously addressing the issue's underlying causes. It is a difficult journey that calls for consensus, coherence, credibility, and clarity.

Military End State. The achievement of political goals is facilitated by the creation of favourable military end states. Since the ultimate end states sought are conflict termination and their political resolution, such conditions not only make it possible for actions by the economic and informational elements of national power to consolidate, but also make it easier to start a political debate for a negotiated settlement.

Because the population is the CoG for these activities, they must be carried out with the utmost respect for human rights and in compliance with local laws. The use of military force in such operations is so well controlled that it not only gives civic authorities in the conflict zone more power but also improves their ability to control the situation. This underscores the importance of people-friendly operations that are conducted with a civil face.

Concept of Application of Military Force. The pillars governing application of force are as under:

(a) *People-Centric Operations.* In order to create a secure environment, military operations first seek to neutralise all hostile forces in the conflict zone that hinder or oppose peace initiatives, and then work to change the attitudes and will of the populace through the skilful and coordinated use of all available tools.

(b) *Manoeuvre versus Attrition Warfare.* Military force should be used primarily to target the minds of terrorists and other antagonistic participants in the environment since the goal of such a campaign is to strengthen the control of government agencies in the conflict zone. This in turn emphasises the significance of manoeuvre warfare, which makes sure to position our resources in a favourable position relative to the terrorists. Additionally, it aids in making the terrorists feel uneasy, which puts them on the defensive and forces them to respond to our proactive strategy. The requisite military circumstances cannot be achieved by such an application alone. As a result, using the attrition warfare approach during the campaign's early stages cannot be avoided.

(c) *Integrated Approach.* Since the ultimate goal of the military endeavour is to give local civil authorities more power, the campaign's management must constantly present a civic face. Therefore, counterinsurgency operations should always be coordinated at the highest levels through the establishment of an 'apex security mechanism' led by the senior state executive, despite the military's initial primacy. Such a setup makes it easier to keep track of all the campaign's facets from the right angle. The senior army officer should, however, clearly be in charge of all operational planning and execution in order to promote synergy.

(d) *Winning Hearts and Minds.* The success of sub-conventional operations depends critically on winning the public's hearts and minds, which should be accomplished by actions and by 'walking the talk.' This reaffirms the value of operations that respect people. Additionally, serious attempts must be made to meet the expectations of the people by implementing civic action programs including the revival of educational institutions, healthcare facilities, communication infrastructure, and initiatives that create opportunities for independent work.

Furthermore, certain other miscellaneous facets that assume importance are:

(a) *Public Information and Perception Building Operations.* Public communication campaigns should be carried out in accordance with artistically developed topics in order to affect the attitudes of different conflict zone participants.

(b) *Management of Stress.* Sub-conventional operations cause stress, which, if not regularly addressed, has a negative effect on the effectiveness and morale of the troops. Therefore, it is crucial that management of troops be given top priority and that methods are developed to recognise individuals who are under stress so that proper remedial actions can be implemented as soon as possible.

(c) *Ethos and Traditions.* The Indian Army's ethos, traditions, and culture, which have influenced the organization's thought over many years, are what give it its strength. A spirit of self-denial, moderation, tolerance, respect for women and senior citizens, and the capacity to live in peace and concord in a multi-ethnic and multi-religious environment is the essence of these, and they are evident among all ranks. The need for continued reiteration and consideration of these values to the troops is, therefore, sine qua non.

(d) *Constitution of 'Think Tanks'.* It is necessary to continuously examine and improve responses at many levels in the sub-conventional operations arena. The ideal way to do this is to create internal 'think tanks' of qualified officers at the Corps and Command levels who are totally committed to doing an extensive examination of various developments and events pertaining to the war zone.

Leadership. The most challenging situation for evaluating leadership skills of commanders at all levels is the sub-conventional operational arena. The environment's turbulence, uncertainty, complexity, and ambiguity have an impact on decision-making, which emphasises the significance of appropriate frames of reference and training to let commanders function well in a mostly 'grey' environment.

(a) *Challenges at Operational Level.* The challenges for leaders at the operational level are:

   (i) Ensuring that their command is properly oriented for non-conventional operations.

   (ii) Training of heterogeneous fighting resource components.

   (iii) Intelligence generation.

   (iv) Coping with subversion in various institutions during the initial stages of operations.

   (v) Ensuring effective coordination and synergy in the early stages of the campaign and eliciting accountability from different security services in the conflict zone (this is mostly due to the lack of a unified headquarters at this point).

   (vi) Preservation of own combat power and maintenance of morale.

   (vii) Coping with the time differential in creating counter-measures for overcoming the technological capabilities of the terrorist.

   (viii) Dealing with seditious media reports by subverted sections of local media.

(b) *Challenges at Tactical Level.* Challenges at the tactical level are:

   (i) Intelligence generation at grassroots level.

   (ii) Adhering to parameters laid down for engagement.

   (iii) Ensuring adherence to prescribed tactical norms during operations.

   (iv) Stress management.

   (v) Preventing attrition in own rank and file.

Leaders at all levels must have the appropriate conceptual, tactical, and technological abilities as well as an understanding of how to apply combat resources effectively if they are to meet the aforementioned challenges. Accordingly, effective leadership can be gauged from three facets, that is, 'What a leader must Be', 'What he must Know' and finally, 'What he must Do'.

Spiritual Leadership Traits of Contemporary Indian Military Leaders

India has produced a galaxy of military leaders who have been exemplary and outstanding. Of these, there have been a few who have been spiritual as well as successful. This section attempts to examine the lives of these leaders without doubting the abilities/qualifications of others. The intention of this examination is to see the ways in which spirituality has assisted these leaders to make them more effective.

Lt. Gen. Hanut Singh. From amongst contemporary Indian military leaders, Lt. Gen. Hanut Singh comes closest to the concept of an ideal spiritual military leader. Most consider him to be a thorough professional and amongst the finest tank commanders that India has seen. He was known as an officer who feared neither his enemies nor his superiors; he is supposed to be having no equal in the army. Coming from Jasol in Rajasthan, he belonged to a lineage of proud cavalry officers and thus chose to join the famous Poona Horse of which he is the most iconic officer. There are many tales about him but none better than the Battle of Basantar. During that battle, the leading tanks of Poona Horse (2/Lt. Arun Khetrapal was also one of the tank commanders and was awarded the Param Vir Chakra for the battle) reached a suspected minefield and started taking contact actions. Legend has it that on having received an urgent message, their commanding officer (CO), then, Lt. Col. Hanut Singh went into meditation and sought 'divine intervention'. Subsequently, he ordered the leading tanks to go through the minefield without fear. The tanks cleared the minefield without a casualty and got into a superior position. As a consequence, when the Pakistani 13 Lancers attacked the Indian defensive position of Jarpal, they were caught off guard by Poona Horse and were defeated in one of the fiercest tank battles ever seen in history. For this legendary leadership, the General Officer was awarded the Maha Vir Chakra. Poona Horse also earned the legendary title of 'Fakr-e-Hind' from their Pakistani counterparts for their gallant action.[56] Spiritual leadership gave General Hanut the ability to be a bold but balanced leader, who could stand up for his principles and stand by his subordinates even in the most trying times.

Lt. Col. (later Maj. Gen.) S.C. Gupta, Commanding Officer, 1/5 GR and the Battle of Sehjra.[57] One of the defining battles of the 1971 Indo-Pak War was the Battle of Sehjra. The main task of 48 Infantry Brigade was the defence of the Khem Karan sector. A secondary task was the capture of the Sehjra Bulge to deny Pakistan access to the critical Harike Barrage. The Sehjra Bulge comprised a 53-square kilometre area within which was ensconced the dominating Sehjra village on top of an escarpment. It was defended by a Pakistani battalion-plus force. The attack on Sehjra was executed on the night of 5/6 December 1971. The feasible and therefore expected direction of attack was from the north. 1/5 GR however did the impossible under their charismatic and spiritual Commanding Officer, Lt. Col. S.C. Gupta. The battalion infiltrated behind the enemy lines and attacked the Bulge from the rear or the south. Caught by surprise on account of being attacked from the most unexpected direction, the Pakistani battalion wilted and the same led to their retreat and subsequent capture of the Bulge. The success of the battalion to achieve the unthinkable in terms of a successful infiltration by the entire battalion in a heavily defended enemy area and the subsequent capture of the Sehjra salient (called by many as a copybook attack by infiltration) is largely attributable to the spiritual inclination of the commanding officer due to which he was able to lead the battalion to a decisive victory in one of the most challenging situations that one faces on the battlefield.

Lt. Gen. Sagat Singh. The visionary capabilities of Lt. Gen. Sagat Singh can be gleaned from the piece on him by Maj. Gen. Randhir Singh (retd.).[58] According to the author, the general officer came from humble origins (he was initially enrolled as a sepoy and was subsequently promoted to the rank of an officer), and was a man of determination, grit and the ability to lead his men from the front. While having an innate knowledge of the ground, he performed spectacularly on professional courses too and is one of the few to have done staff college courses at both Quetta and Haifa. He has the unique distinction being amongst the few non-parachute regiment officers to have commanded the prestigious 50 (Independent) Parachute Brigade. It was during this tenure that he gave an initial glimpse of his spiritual military leadership abilities. On being called upon to progress towards Panjim as a part of Operation Vijay (Liberation of Goa) he led an outrageous advance across the Mandovi River from three sides and reached his objective well before not only other Indian formations but even before the Portuguese expected him to do so. This resulted in the capitulation of the Portuguese resistance and the early liberation of Goa. This victory can be attributed to the ability of Gen. Sagat to enunciate a clear vision that could be followed by his formations as also the trust that he reposed in his subordinates which allowed them to function in an independent and fearless manner due to which the units undertook numerous river crossings against all odds. Spiritual leadership gave Gen. Sagat the unique ability to take hard decisions without fear of failure. An example of this is his decision as the GOC of 17 Mountain Division not to vacate the watershed in the Sikkim sector which resulted in India holding the Nathu La Pass today. But more than this, it was the bloody nose given by him to the Chinese (during the same tenure) during the Nathu La and Cho La skirmishes that changed the course of history of the Indian military. The real highlight of his style of spiritual leadership was seen during the 1971 Indo-Pak war. Without fear for his life, he used to fly in and out of the frontline in his helicopter and motivate the ground troops This and the belief he had in his subordinates resulted in his subordinate troops again undertaking taking bold and courageous crossings over the river Meghna and reaching Dacca in record time. The encirclement of Dhaka was completed within 14 days and remains one of the most decisive military operations ever. This resulted in the Pakistanis surrendering and the liberation of Bangladesh. Sagat's vision, personal courage, stamina and spiritual leadership enabled him to take bold decisions and trust his subordinates, thereby enabling them to function through a directive style of leadership. This was one of the contributors to the decisive victory that India had in the 1971 war.

The above are just three stellar examples of contemporary Indian military spiritual leadership and clearly points to the fact that spiritual military leadership has been available to some extent in Indian military leadership. This chapter has also shown in great detail that sterling military leadership and spirituality has existed in significant measure in India over the ages. Before examining how spirituality can enable Indian military leadership, let us first see what is spirituality and what benefits it can offer.

NOTES

1. World History Encyclopaedia, Bhagavad Gita, https://www.worldhistory.org/Bhagavad_Gita/
2. Satyavrata Siddhantalankar. *Heritage of Vedic Culture*, 1972.
3. Advaita Ashrama, Swami Ranganathanda. *The Message of the Upanisads*, 1980.
4. http://www.hinduwisdom.info/War_in_Ancient_India.html

5. http://www.hinduwebsite.com/hanuman.asp
6. http://www.sssbpt.info/summershowers/ss1996/ss1996-06.pdf
7. http://www.sanatansociety.org/indian_epics_and_stories/the_life_of_hanuman.html
8. http://books.google.co.in/books/hanuman+as+a+leader&source
9. http://www.joebm.com/papers/127-L00017.pdf
10. http://www.harekrsna.de/artikel/bhisma.htm
11. Shirish Shinde. *Guru Tegh Bahadur*, Kalyani Corporation, 2021.
12. Kirkland, Faris R. *Combat Leadership Styles: Empowerment versus Authoritarianism.*
13. Krishna Rao, K.V. *Prepare or Perish: A Study of National Security*, July 2021.
14. Op. cit.
15. Palit, D.K. *War in High Himalayas: The Indian Army in Crisis, 1962*, C. Hurst & Co. Publishers, 1991, p. 345.
16. Khanna, Lt. Gen. K.K. PVSM, AVSM**(retired). *Art of Generalship*, Vij Books India Pvt. Ltd., pp. 164-165.
17. Ibid., p. 167.
18. Gupta Das, Amit R. & Lorenz M. Luthi. *The Sino-Indian War of 1962 New Perspectives*, Routledge India, 2017, p. 237.
19. Nath, PVSM, Maj. Gen. Rajender. op. cit., p. 369.
20. Ibid., pp. 369-370.
21. Pradhan, R.D. *1965 War: The Inside Story*, Atlantic Publishers & Distributors (P) Ltd., 2007, p. 134.
22. Ibid., p. 156.
23. Fricker, John. Battle for Pakistan: The Air War of 1965, Ian Allan, 1979, p. 139.
24. Ibid., p. 123.
25. Palit. op. cit, p. 267.
26. Singh, Lieutenant General Harbaksh. op. Cit., p. 132.
27. Singh Amrinder, and Lt. General Tajinder Shergill, PVSM. *The Monsoon War: Young Officers Reminisce – 1965 India-Pakistan War*, Roli Books, p. 495.
28. Ibid., p. 384.
29. Singh, N/K/ *Bangladesh: Causes of Liberation War*, Anmol Publications Pvt. Ltd., 2003, p. 278.
30. Ibid., p. 234.
31. Ahmad, Maj. Iftak-uddin. *Memories of a Lacerated Heart* (1971), Trafford, 2017, p. 371.
32. Ibid., p. 329.
33. Palit, D.K. *The Lightning Campaign: The Indo-Pakistan War, 1971*, Lancer Publishers, 2012, p. 138.
34. Ibid., p. 156.
35. Air Chief Marshal P.C. Lal, *My Years with Air Force.*
36. Ibid., p. 132.
37. Ahmad. op. cit., p. 165.
38. Palit, D.K. op. cit., p. 56.
39. Lyon, Peter (2008). *Conflict between India and Pakistan: An Encyclopaedia.* ABC-CLIO. p. 166, India's decisive victory over Pakistan in the 1971 war and emergence of independent Bangladesh dramatically transformed the power balance of South Asia.
40. India-Pakistan War, 1971; Western Front, Part I. acig.com retrieved 22 December 2011.
41. Cloughley, Brian (2016). *A History of the Pakistan Army: Wars and Insurrections*, Skyhorse Publishing, Inc.
42. Three Indian blunders in the 1971 war, Rediff News, 12 December 2011.

43. Military Losses in the 1971 Indo-Pakistani War. Venik. Archived from the original on 25 February 2002. Retrieved 30 May 2005.
44. Palit, D.K. op. cit., p. 126.
45. Operation Pawan. The Battle for Jaffna. Archived 2009-03-30 at the Wayback Machine.
46. Descent Into Danger. The Jaffna University Helidrop. Archived 2011-06-09 at the Wayback Machine. Bharat-rakshak.com.
47. Ibid.
48. Ibid.
49. https://www.thequint.com/lifestyle/books/operation-pawan-sushant-singh-book-review-op-pawan-87-surgical-strike-that-went-horribly-wrong.
50. Ibid.
51. Lieutenant General Sardeshpande,'Op PAWAN, some reflections', *The Custodian,* January 1993.
52. Ibid.
53. James D. Scudieri. The Indian Peace-Keeping Force in Sri Lanka, 1987-90: A Case Study in Operations Other Than War, PN, 1994, p. 283.
54. Ibid.
55. Lieutenant General Sardeshpande. op. Cit., p. 63.
56. A.K. Singh. 'Lt. Gen. Hanut Singh – bold commander who led from front in 1971, but was never made Army chief', *The Print,* 13 April 2020, https://theprint.in/opinion/lt-gen-hanut-singh-bold-commander-who-led-from-front-in-1971-but-was-never-made-army-chief/400625/
57. Kuldip Singh, *The Tribune.* 'Battle of Sehjra that secured Harike Barrage', 4 December 2021, https://www.tribuneindia.com/news/comment/battle-of-sehjra-that-secured-harike-barrage-346053
58. Randhir Sinh, *The Tribune.* 'The visionary warrior Sagat Singh', 11 August 2021, https://www.tribuneindia.com/news/features/the-visionary-warrior-sagat-singh-294742

Chapter Three

Spirituality and its Relevance

For this section, the following questionnaire was sent to respondents. The questions were: Will spirituality have a positive effect on organisational performance? Will spirituality result in reducing the stress in today's military leaders thereby increasing their effectiveness? What really is spirituality? Who should undertake the path of spirituality? What is the relation between spirituality and religion? The responses to these questions are presented through the following pie charts.

Q 1. Spirituality in leadership will help in greater perception of trust, organisational support and commitment among all ranks; thus having positive effects on organisational performance.

822 Responses

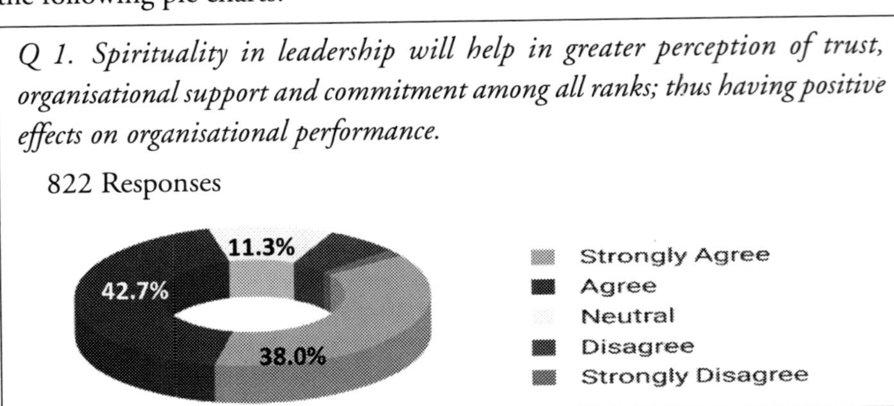

Q 2. In today's challenging environment where stress and strain are the order of the day, an understanding of spirituality and its practice would make our military leaders more effective and efficient.

822 Responses

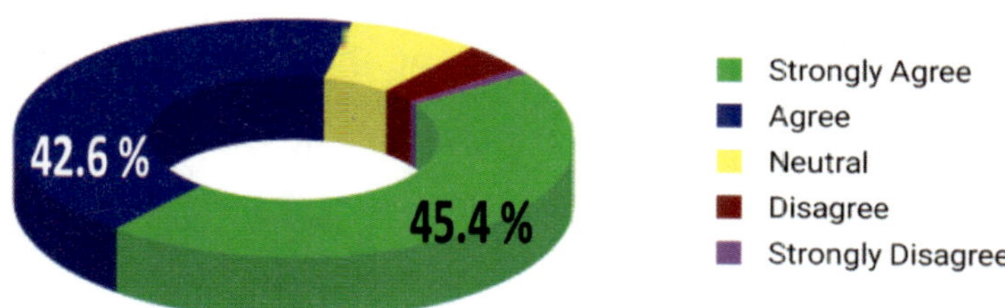

Q 3. As per you, spirituality is for those:

822 Responses

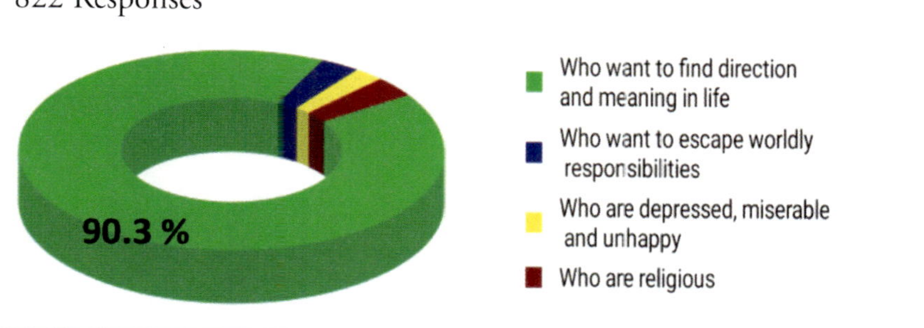

Q 4. In your perception, spirituality is:

822 Responses

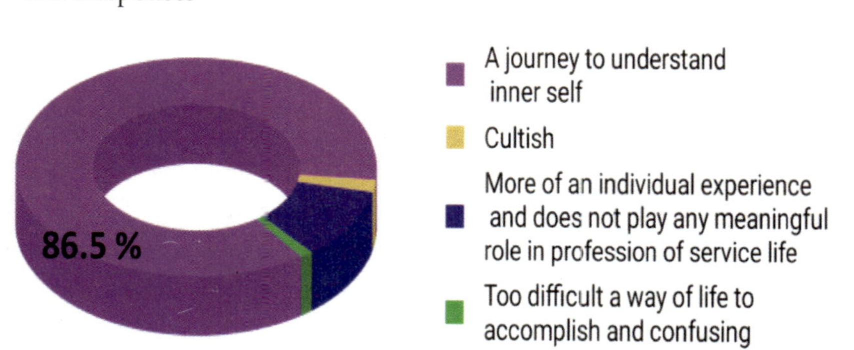

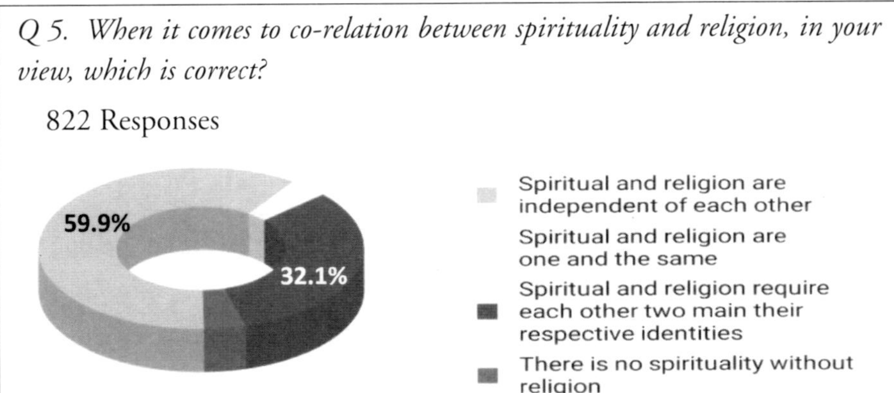

A brief analysis of the responses received in response to the questions posed in this section is as under:

(a) A majority of 81 per cent feel that spirituality will have a positive effect on organisational performance.

(b) A complete majority of 88 per cent feel that spirituality will result in reducing the stress in today's military leaders and thereby increase their effectiveness.

(c) A resounding 93 per cent majority feel that the path of spirituality should be undertaken by those who want to find direction and meaning in life.

(d) Eighty-seven per cent of respondents feel that spirituality is a journey to understand your inner self.

(e) Sixty per cent of respondents feel that spirituality and religion are independent of each other.

Having seen the analysis of the survey, let us understand spirituality and its relevance.

Quest for Intrinsic Qualities in a Leader

An analysis of various leadership models and styles leads to certain common prerequisites for a successful life like self-confidence, ability to articulate vision, empathy, persuasion, participative decision-making, self-observation, self-management, building community and shared emotional experience. It emerges that leadership is no longer an individual characteristic but is dualistic, shared and relational with intricate human dynamics. The role of values, emotions and ethics of leaders in creating meaning for followers is becoming pivotal. Intrinsically motivated leaders are driven by passion and purpose that extends beyond any tangible gains or outcomes. They are driven by a higher purpose which is not limited to achieving a mission, but a holistic growth and well-being of the complete environment. Further, they lay stress on building trust; self-confidence based on confidence in the group; a high degree of emotional intelligence that understands and regulates the emotions of the group; a belief which gives hope and meaning to one and all.

I believe "The basis of spirituality lies in living by values, ideals, and thoughts that are not only for a few but for the universal good that will lead to a responsible, secure, respectable, more inclusive, and sustainable future."[1] The quest for intrinsic qualities in a leader refers to the search for qualities that come from within the leader, rather than external factors such as position or authority. Intrinsic qualities are those that are inherent to a person's character, values, and beliefs. Qualities such as authenticity, humility, empathy, courage, vision, and resilience can help leaders inspire, motivate, and influence others. Authentic leaders are transparent and honest, and they build trust by being genuine and sincere in their interactions with others. Similarly, humble leaders are open to feedback and willing to admit their mistakes. They put the needs of the team ahead of their own and are not driven by ego or a desire for personal gain. Empathy is another facet of leadership which enables a leader to understand the feelings of others. Empathetic leaders are attuned to the needs of their team and create a supportive organizational climate where people are valued and heard. Courage is another important facet of a leader's personality where leaders are not afraid to challenge the status quo and pursue bold initiatives that can drive innovation and growth. The importance of having a vision is another essential quality of a leader, which is the ability to see the big picture and inspire others to work towards the organizational goal. Visionary leaders are well aware of the overall purpose and a compelling vision for the future that can motivate and inspire their team. They inspire great resilience, which helps them to emerge from setbacks and adversity and maintain a positive attitude and persevere against all odds, inspiring their team to do the same.

The qualities expected of a leader are not always inborn but nurtured through the journey of his career. There are numerous modes or programs of exposing leaders to transformational processes which generally are only partially successful. A need has long been felt to embark on a journey which makes leadership realise the essentials of human needs, its mode of functioning, aspirational needs, its response to internal and external influences and willing dedication to the overall cause. The leader has to rise above the confines of human limitations wherein he provides a clear vision which can be well understood and everyone enjoys being part of the journey. Spirituality can play an important role in inculcating these intrinsic qualities in a leader by providing a foundation of self-awareness, values, and purpose. It can help leaders develop a deep understanding of themselves, their strengths, and their weaknesses. Through practices such as meditation and self-reflection, leaders can become more attuned to their emotions and motivations, which can help them develop greater self-awareness and authenticity. By deeper understanding of spirituality, and when leaders lead from a higher plane, they are more likely to make decisions that align with their values, which can inspire trust and loyalty among team members. In doing so, they create a vision that inspires and motivates their team to achieve their goals. Spirituality can help leaders cultivate humility by recognising that they are part of something larger than themselves. When leaders are grounded in their spiritual beliefs, they are more likely to be open to feedback and willing to admit their mistakes, which can help them build trust and credibility with their team. If understood and practised mindfully, spirituality can help leaders cultivate empathy by recognising the interconnectedness of all beings. They get attuned to the needs of their team and create a supportive work environment.

Dissatisfied Work Environment

The present-day work environment is highly complex, fast-paced, stressful and very demanding. Leaders often find themselves lacking the fine art to emerge out of this precarious situation, keeping the group's motivation at a desirable level. A Service think tank found that "Over half of Indian Army troops appear to be suffering from extreme stress and the casualties due to stress-related incidents like fratricides, suicides and adverse occurrences are far more than that in terrorist-related actions."[2] In circumstances when leaders are under pressure, employees may feel the effects of their emotional state. As a result, workers respond with the most predictable of human emotions – dissatisfaction. This, in turn, renders the workplace unproductive as a whole and makes the leader's task far more difficult. It has been found that even where leaders are accomplished with physical and mental attributes, there exists a felt need to improve their emotional quotient in addition to them being merely professionally trained leaders.

Thus, we must move towards a 'learning organisation' from a standardised, formalised and bureaucratic organisational one. A learning organisation is love-led, intrinsically motivated, empowered, team-based, flexible and diverse. Importance is given to organising, motivating, and inspiring people to work towards the overall objective, values, goals, ethics and beliefs while maintaining high self-esteem and contentment. Learning organisations recognise that knowledge is a key resource that can help them adapt to changing environments, innovate new products and services, and improve their operations. They invest in various developmental initiatives to help employees grow all-round personally, and as a group Currently, education and training teams focus on outcomes or vocations with insufficient emphasis on how the leader provides meaning and value to the organisation. This is where the relevance of the spiritual characteristics of a leader becomes significant. Recent research has shown that a leader's ability to deal with the tensions that arise from contradictions, ambiguities, and disputes is directly correlated with his level of spirituality. Consistency between spiritual principles and proven, successful leadership has been shown through research.[3] Leaders with spirituality use skills which motivate their command to willingly work positively, foster bonds, maintain an enduring relationship based on trust, and thus help create an enabling environment.

Spirituality in Everyday Life

Spirituality is the balancing factor in everyday life. Philosophers have spoken about four domains of life – cognitive, physical, emotional and spiritual. Although it may be helpful to divide into categories to understand different facets of being, the reality is that we cannot fragment our lives into bits and pieces. Only by harmonising all parts can we become complete, which is the aim of life. Spiritual life helps lay the much-needed foundation to establish a balance in our life. Spirituality is the practice that animates our life. It focuses on meaning and inter-associations to self, others and the higher purpose. Just sitting quietly each morning for 10 minutes without outside distraction helps attain a fine balance. Many schools of thought and even religions believe one can connect to the high power (God) in household duties, the workplace, recreational activities, and anywhere. Judaism emphasises that one can take an ordinary act and make it holy, which means godliness is in every aspect of our lives.

Resistance is due to lack of Awareness. An individual's spirituality should be expressed in their everyday behaviour. John Shea argues that 'being' is the essence of spiritual life. Everything in life is perceived from a certain angle. A spiritual life is just a life, viewed from the vantage point of spirit. This encompasses waking, sleeping, dreaming, eating, drinking, working, loving, resting, recreating, walking, sitting, standing, and breathing.[4] Over the last many years, most researchers have understood this aspect and increasingly highlighted the relevance of spirituality in bringing out the much-required inner development in a leader. The language of leadership has become more spiritual than ever before. Emergent leadership models in the last two decades have worked in this direction so that the terms used in spirituality and those in relational, participative or authentic leadership become convergent. The resistance to the word 'Spirituality' is only till the time essence of spirituality and consciousness remains in the realm of vagueness.

The Essence of Spirituality

The Biggest Mystery of Life. "The goal of scientific inquiry has always been to shed light on the mysterious and uncover the previously unknown. Researchers in the scientific community are committed to unravelling the puzzles of existence. Human curiosity has pushed us to probe every corner of the universe in search of answers to fundamental questions about our origins and functioning."[5] Who we are, what we are, why we're here, how we got here, and where we go after our physical life ends, are some of humanity's most interesting questions. These questions have only been partly answered by research in the domains of biology, physics, chemistry, astronomy, geology, quantum physics, and their specialized branches.[6] They may have been able to theorise what is matter and what living beings are physically composed of but still, the mystery of the existence of the universe persists. Spirituality seeks to answer these questions. As per spirituality, some power has created the universe and everything happening therein.

The Eternal Truth – Delving into the Inner Realm. Spirituality has often been found delving into the realm of scientific discovery of complete components of existence; people, planet, animals, other living beings, matter and all other constituents of the universe. Spirituality teaches us that we all have access to a spiritual creator within. It adds meaning to everything that is happening around us. It tries to transcend beyond the physical world and delve into the metaphysical realm. Every person, at times, gets bound by the five senses and starts restricting to the cause and effect of this physical realm. What is seen and felt outwardly guides all his responses and forms the environment. The most trivial development has the potential to destabilise the complete ecosystem. Thus, the success of this ecosystem largely depends upon the response of all the entities. Spirituality helps us transcend the physical dimensions of life and look deeper into it. It achieves this through altering and trying to better the person's vision, which in turn alters and betters the person's outlook of the world. Spirituality, at its core, is turning inside to discover answers to questions only one can answer. It helps us see that everything outside of ourselves is fleeting and subject to change and that ultimately, our physical bodies will perish and be swept away like dust. In contrast, the inside world of each one of us is ageless, everlasting, and profound. When they come to terms with this timeless truth, humans may achieve a state of transcendence into a life that is boundless, complete, has a higher purpose, and is full of happiness. It helps one recognize a part of oneself that one may not have known existed before.[7] Spirituality sheds light on the reality that, despite our perceptions to the contrary, we are far more powerful than we give ourselves credit for. The human race has been discovered to be in possession of a tremendous and divine light, which gives them much more potential than they could have ever imagined. Far larger and more potent than anyone could have ever anticipated. All physical occurrences are just to be experienced during this human journey and inner calm is to be maintained in all circumstances. Every leader needs to understand this profound truth to feel more empowered, enabled, self-reliant and aware of his place in the complete ecosystem.

Defining Spirituality

It is largely understood that, "A belief in something greater than oneself is referred to as spirituality. Religious practices centred on the concept of a higher power may be included, but they may also entail a more general conviction about how each person is interconnected with others and the rest of the universe. Spirituality provides a perspective that holds that there is more to life than only what humans see and physically experience." Instead, "it implies that there is something higher that links all creatures and to the world itself". Besides arguing for the continuation of life after death, it seeks to explain such enigmas as humanity's place in the cosmos, the nature of our own individuality, and the ultimate nature of reality itself.[8]

According to Maya Spencer, "Spirituality is the recognition of a sensation, feeling, or belief that there is something greater than oneself, that being human is more than a sensory experience, and that the greater whole is part cosmic or divine in nature. Spirituality means recognising that our lives matter in ways that go beyond satisfying the base, immediate desires that fuel self-centredness and hostility. To understand this is to realize that our lives matter in the overall scheme of things."[9]

"Anything that uplifts the spirit, anything that brings more pleasure, love, joy, creativity, compassion, and zest for life is spirituality," states Art of Living.[10] The Oxford English Dictionary defines 'spiritual' as "of or relating to the human spirit or soul as distinguished from physical things."

According to Islam, the '*Rabbaniyat*' counterpart of spirituality in Quranic terminology is the process of raising one's human situation to a level where one's thoughts are directed towards the transcendental, non-material truths of divine life. It is the key to life, and unlike materialism, it has no bounds in time. Through contemplating God and his creation, believers grow cognitively, which in turn leads to a deeper spirituality.[11] As per Islam, spirituality is an all-encompassing philosophy that believes in something beyond the individual self. In Islam, spirituality is closely tied to the concept of *Tawhid*, which is oneness of God. Spirituality is defined as the inner connection of a person's soul with God, and the constant effort to maintain and strengthen this connection through various acts of worship and obedience to God's commands. Another important aspect of Islamic spirituality is the pursuit of inner peace and tranquillity. This is achieved through self-examination, deep introspection, and focusing on purifying one's thoughts, intentions, and actions. Overall, spirituality in Islam is characterised by a deep and profound connection to

God, a commitment to living a life of righteousness and virtue, and a constant effort to improve one's self and one's relationship with God.

According to Sadhguru, the essence of 'spirituality' is an experience that goes beyond the limits of physical reality. Spirituality is not a synonym for any one religion or belief system. In other words, it's a state of mind. There is a plethora of steps to do to get to your goal. Like having a garden within your own home. We need to take action if a plant's soil, sunshine, or stem conditions prevent it from flowering. We must see to it that they are cared for. Thus, spirituality is the flowering of something else inside us, if we bring our body, mind, emotions, and energy to a specific degree of maturity.[12] Sadhguru explains further that when we reach a certain level of intellectual development, all our questions are answered and we have a crystal-clear perspective on life in general.

In Hinduism, *Adhyatma* is considered to be the core of spiritual practice, and it is believed that every individual has the potential to connect with the divine through *Adhyatma. Adhyatma* means 'Spirituality' in Sanskrit. The origins of the word are the terms 'Adhi' and '*Atman*' (*Atmanaha*) meaning 'relative to the theme' and 'the soul', respectively. The soul is the divine spark at the centre of every human being, representing who we really are. The subtle body, a subset of the 'Supreme God' idea, relies on it as its primary constituent. Absolute Truth (*Sat*), Consciousness (*Chit*), and Joy (*Anand*) are their notable characteristics.[13] The central tenet of Hinduism is the idea that the soul is joyous regardless of the circumstances of its body. The path to spiritual growth and enlightenment is through the pursuit of knowledge and wisdom, through meditation, devotion, and self-realisation. *Adhyatma* is closely tied to the concept of *Atman*, which is the individual soul, and *Brahman*, which is the universal spirit that pervades all things. Hinduism teaches that the ultimate goal of spiritual practice is to achieve *moksha*, which can be understood as liberation, enlightenment, or union with the divine.

Buddhist spirituality aims to eliminate suffering by having an enlightened understanding of reality. All Buddhist spiritual practices are geared towards attaining liberation from suffering while nurturing the growth of both wisdom and compassion. Associated with this, Buddhism maintains that wisdom is viewing the world as it is – reveals the impermanency of all things and their deep inter-relatedness. The goal of Buddhist spirituality is liberation from suffering via the ego and receptivity to the truth. Buddhism is a spiritual tradition that emphasises the development of knowledge and compassion in its adherents.[14] In Buddhism, spirituality is about developing one's inner self, attaining a state of inner peace, and transcending the cycle of suffering and rebirth. Buddhist spirituality aims for attaining enlightenment as its ultimate purpose. Complete freedom from suffering and understanding the true nature of reality are both part of achieving enlightenment. The teachings of Buddhism suggest that craving and attachment lead to suffering. The Eightfold path guides one towards enlightenment by focusing on right understanding, intention, speech, livelihood, effort, mindfulness and concentration.

Spiritual practice in Buddhism involves meditation, mindfulness, and the cultivation of ethical behaviour and compassion towards all living beings. Buddhist spirituality emphasises the importance of living in the present moment, letting go of attachments and desires, and cultivating a sense of inner peace and compassion. Ultimately, the goal of Buddhist spirituality is to attain a state of complete liberation from suffering and achieve the ultimate goal of enlightenment.

Myths Regarding Spirituality

Spirituality has served as hope and inspiration to millions of people. All those who embark on journeys for varied reasons at various stages have undergone unique blissful experiences. It has become an essential facet of leadership studies worldwide. Yet, there has been some resistance in some quarters as regards embracing this life changing path. Some of these unfounded myths are:

(a) *Spirituality is something to do with Religion.* One of the myths surrounding spirituality is the belief that it is necessarily tied to religion. This popular belief scares those who do not want to be identified with any religion or give an impression of being dogmatic. But the truth is, one does not necessarily have to believe in an entity to be spiritual. While spirituality can certainly be a part of religious practice, it is not limited to any specific religion or belief system. Spirituality is more about developing a personal relationship with the divine or the sacred, and exploring one's inner self and consciousness. It can involve practices such as meditation, mindfulness, gratitude, and compassion, and can also be pursued by individuals who do not identify with any particular religion. Many people who describe themselves as spiritual may not be affiliated with any organized religion and may draw inspiration from a variety of spiritual traditions and practices. While religion can certainly provide a framework for spiritual practice, it is not a requirement for experiencing spirituality. Ultimately, spirituality is a deeply personal journey that involves exploring one's beliefs, values, and experiences, and connecting with a sense of purpose, meaning, and inner peace.

(b) *Spirituality is only for Old People.* Another myth about spirituality is the belief that it is only for old people. While it is true that many older adults may turn to spirituality as they age, it is by no means limited to this demographic variable. Spirituality is a deeply personal journey that can be pursued by people of all ages, from all walks of life. Many younger people are interested in spirituality and are exploring various practices such as meditation, yoga, and mindfulness. Research suggests that the younger generations are increasingly interested in spirituality and are seeking new ways to connect with their inner selves and explore their beliefs and values. Spirituality helps them find a sense of purpose, and inner peace that is valuable at any age and can be particularly helpful during times of stress, uncertainty, or transition. Whether one is young or old, spirituality can offer a path towards personal growth and a greater connection with oneself and others. Whether young or old, we all want happiness. There is so much happiness all around, it eludes us as we may be looking for it in the wrong places. "Our spirit is the source of all joy," says Sri Sri Ravi Shankar. Spiritual practices are a way to connect with this eternal source of joy, peace, and strength.

(c) *Spirituality is only for those who are Sad and Miserable.* This is a common myth that is not true. While it is true that some people may turn to spirituality during times of sadness or struggle, it is not exclusive to those who are unhappy or miserable. Many people who are content and fulfilled also practise spirituality as a way to deepen their understanding of themselves and the world around them and cultivate a sense of gratitude and joy. Spirituality can be practised by anyone regardless of their emotional state or life circumstances and can be a valuable tool for personal growth and fulfilment. We all have shortcomings and desires. Yet, overcoming our flaws and fulfilling our desires seems quite a challenge at times. Spirituality can help in finding our potential and strength when we are unsure of our capabilities. It can help us rise when we hit rock bottom in our life to rise again and make endeavours to reach our goals. Therefore, spirituality is for everyone.

(d) *One Needs to give up Material Pleasures to be Spiritual.* This is a common myth, which is far from true. While some spiritual traditions encourage a simple and minimalist lifestyle, it is not a requirement to give up all material pleasures to be spiritual. Spirituality is a personal journey and can manifest in different ways for different people. It is possible to maintain a balanced and fulfilling life that includes material pleasures while also engaging in spiritual practices. In fact, some traditions even view material abundance as a manifestation of spiritual growth and blessings. The key is to approach material pleasures with a sense of mindfulness and moderation and to prioritise values such as compassion, generosity, and kindness. By cultivating a sense of inner peace and balance, one can enjoy material pleasures without becoming attached to them or feeling that they are necessary for happiness. It will be a mistake to consider materialism and spirituality as facets of life which are opposed to each other. Rather, they both are complementary. Sri Sri Ravi Shankar explains through an example, "If you have a plate full of food and someone comes to you, you will not be able to eat it alone. Every spiritual person wants to give and share. But you cannot give when you have nothing to give away."[15]

(e) *Spirituality is Cultish.* While there are certainly some religious or spiritual groups that have been accused of being cult-like, this is not representative of spirituality as a whole. Spirituality encompasses a wide range of beliefs and practices, and individuals are free to explore and practise their spirituality in a way that feels authentic to them. While some spiritual communities may have strict rules or expectations, this does not necessarily make them cults. It is important to approach any spiritual community or practice with a critical and discerning eye, but this does not mean that spirituality as a whole is cultish. In fact, many spiritual practices encourage individuality and personal growth and promote values such as compassion, mindfulness, and self-awareness. Ultimately, the decision to engage in any particular spiritual practice or community is a personal choice that should be based on one's own values, beliefs, and experiences. Cults largely follow a particular belief system and do not invite questions and doubts. On the other hand, progress on the spiritual path happens with sincere questions. Unlike cults, it does not profess a single line of thought to be the ultimate truth. It is an invitation to new experiences and to re-examine our existing beliefs about ourselves and the world. Cults breed in fear. The basis of spirituality is love and a sharp intellect that can see through hoaxes.

(f) *Spirituality is only for the Weak Minded.* It is true that many individuals who are going through a rough patch look to religion or spirituality for comfort. There are various methods available in spirituality for improving the mind. When conventional psychotherapy and medical care failed, many individuals found significant relief via spiritual practices. Similar to how physically ill people visit the emergency department of a hospital when they are in a life-or-death crisis, the aforementioned stereotype of people turning to spirituality amid suffering is a frequent thing. While there will always be a need for emergency services, it does not mean that it is all that a hospital does. Prevention is the focus of care in the spiritual hospital.

(g) *To be Spiritual-Minded You should have crossed the Finish Line.* This is again a myth. While engaging in spiritual practices and cultivating a spiritual mindset can be valuable tools for personal growth and fulfilment, it does not mean that one has 'crossed the finish line' or achieved ultimate enlightenment. There is no 'there'; we may experience fleeting moments of ecstasy, which may grow as we deepen our spiritual practice. Spirituality is a journey, not a destination, and there is always room for growth and exploration. Even those who have devoted their lives to spiritual practices and teachings, recognise that there is always more to learn and understand. It is important to approach spirituality with an open mind and a willingness to learn, and be patient with oneself as one navigates the ups and downs of the journey. Ultimately, the goal is not to reach a final destination, but to cultivate a sense of inner peace, well-being, and connection with something greater than oneself. This is a lifelong journey that requires ongoing effort and dedication, and there is always room for growth and exploration.

(h) *To be Spiritual–Minded is Hard Work.* This is another myth which requires to be dispensed with. While engaging in spiritual practices and cultivating a spiritual mindset can require effort and dedication, it does not have to be hard work. Many spiritual practices can be enjoyable and fulfilling, such as meditation, prayer, yoga, or spending time amidst nature. These practices can help to cultivate a sense of inner peace, well-being, and connect with something greater than oneself. Furthermore, spirituality is not about perfection or achieving a certain standard, but rather about embracing the journey and being open to growth and learning. It is important to approach spirituality with a sense of curiosity and playfulness, rather than seeing it as a chore or obligation. Of course, there may be challenges and obstacles along the way, but these can also be opportunities for growth and learning. By approaching spirituality with an open and positive mindset, it can be a rewarding and fulfilling aspect of life. It is true that there's a trade-off between being a victim of circumstances and living a sad and uninteresting life and, making the effort to be attentive to one's thoughts and actions and the impact that they have on others. The journey to enlightenment is a joyful one.

Benefits of Spirituality: Providing the Balance

Everyone has their own reasons for spirituality it may be due to personal problems, getting over some addictions or maybe something more to our existence or due to simple love for God. However, those who put in sincere efforts to seek spirituality feel happier and more satisfied. With time and deeper involvement, they also give positivity and happiness. These spiritual traits are prerequisites which today's leader needs to establish a link with their environment.

Balanced State of Mind. One generally experiences highs and lows, when the mind is influenced by external stimuli. However as one embarks on the journey of spiritualism, the mind calms down and the effect of external stimuli starts getting reduced. As persistence sets in, the state of mind remains balanced irrespective of the situation without. Spirituality can help promote this balanced state of mind in several ways:

(a) *Mindfulness.* Many spiritual practices, such as meditation or prayer, involve focusing the mind and cultivating a sense of awareness in the present moment. This can help reduce anxiety and stress, and promote a more calm and balanced state of mind.

(b) *Self-reflection.* Spirituality often involves reflecting on one's values, beliefs, and sense of purpose. This can promote self-awareness and help individuals gain a greater sense of clarity and direction in their lives, leading to a more balanced state of mind.

(c) *Connection with something greater.* Spirituality helps in connecting oneself with something greater, someone more powerful, above the natural world. This can help individuals gain perspective and find meaning and purpose beyond their concerns, leading to a more balanced state of mind.

Ultimate Path to Self-Development. "It has been found through numerous surveys that spiritual people develop certain strong characteristics which have a very positive influence in helping the environment become more vibrant and enabling."[16] Spirituality brings a visible transformation in an individual whose positivity and vibrancy becomes infectious. They can be seen being gifted with the following:

(a) *Spiritual People are Gracious.* It has been proven through psychological studies that expressing gratitude leads to the flow of positive emotions such as optimism, generosity and overall vitality. Spiritual people may be seen as more gracious because they often have a sense of gratitude, forgiveness, and humility. These qualities which are discussed in detail below can lead them to be more appreciative, kind, forgiving, and unassuming towards others.

(i) *Gratitude.* Spiritual people often cultivate a sense of gratitude for the blessings in their lives. This can make them more appreciative of the people around them, leading them to express thanks and appreciation more readily. This attitude of gratitude can be seen as graciousness towards others.

(ii) *Compassion.* Many spiritual traditions emphasise the importance of compassion towards others. Spiritual people may be more inclined to empathise with others, show kindness, and offer help when needed. This sense of compassion can be seen as graciousness towards others. These compassionate people have been always found to be creating an environment of feeling good about even little things and looking at circumstances with empathetic eyes.

(iii) *Forgiveness.* Spirituality often involves a focus on forgiveness and letting go of negative emotions. This can make spiritual people more forgiving and less likely to hold grudges. This forgiving attitude can be seen as graciousness towards others.

(iv) *Humility.* Spiritual practices often involve a sense of humility, recognising one's limitations and accepting that there are greater forces at play in the world. This can make spiritual people humbler and less likely to seek attention or recognition for their actions. This humility can be seen as graciousness towards others.

(c) *Spiritual People Flourish.* Spiritual people experience flourishing, which refers to a state of optimal functioning and well-being across multiple domains of life. High self-esteem, compassion, and a sense of direction in life are just some of the positive outcomes associated with a spiritual outlook. Here are some ways in which spirituality can contribute to flourishing advancement:

(i) *Sense of purpose and meaning.* Spirituality helps individuals in identifying a purpose and meaning in their life, which can be a powerful motivator and source of fulfilment. By aligning with one's values and purpose, individuals become more focused and gain relevance.

(ii) *Altruism.* Many spiritual traditions emphasise the importance of compassion and altruism towards oneself and others. By cultivating these qualities, individuals can experience greater empathy and connection with others, which can contribute to a sense of well-being.

(iii) *Resilience*. Spiritual practices such as meditation or prayer can promote mindfulness and resilience, helping individuals to stay in the present and be calm in the face of stress and adversity. This can contribute to a greater sense of well-being and flourishing.

(iv) *Positive emotions*. Spirituality often involves cultivating positive emotions such as gratitude, joy, and love. By focusing on these emotions, individuals can experience greater levels of happiness and fulfilment, contributing to flourishing.

(d) *Self-Actualisation*. Spirituality can be considered as a path towards self-actualisation, wherein an individual strives towards higher personal growth and work on becoming a better individual. Self-actualisation is a concept in psychology that refers to the realization of one's full potential, including the development of one's talents and abilities, the pursuit of meaningful goals, and a sense of fulfilment and satisfaction in life. Spirituality can play a significant role in promoting self-actualisation. This is done by promoting:

(i) *Personal growth*. Spiritual practices and beliefs can promote personal growth by encouraging individuals to explore their inner selves, values, and beliefs. By engaging in self-reflection and introspection, individuals can develop a deeper understanding of themselves, which can contribute to self-actualisation.

(ii) *Association with something highly noble*. Spirituality often involves a sense of association with something higher, much greater than oneself, such as a higher power or the natural world. This enhances the sense of meaning in life, trusting something deeper and wider in its existence, an aspect which provides a much nobler purpose for living.

(iii) *Self-Transcendence*. Spiritual practices can encourage individuals to move beyond their egos and connect with others and the world around them. By experiencing self-transcendence, individuals can develop a sense of interconnectedness and empathy, which can contribute to self-actualisation.

(iv) *Authenticity*. Spirituality can encourage individuals to be true to themselves and their values, which can promote a sense of authenticity. By being true to themselves, individuals can develop a sense of purpose and fulfilment, contributing to self-actualisation.

Health Benefits of Spirituality. Studies have emphatically suggested that spirituality is beneficial to both mental health and physical health adding years to one's life. Certain proven benefits include:

(a) *Beat the Stress.* Some amount of positive stress is acceptable; however, excess stress can be quite crippling. Spirituality can be an effective tool for managing and reducing stress. Many spiritual practices, such as meditation, prayer, or yoga (all being discussed in detail, subsequently), involve relaxation and mindfulness techniques that can reduce stress and promote calmness. Spirituality can provide individuals with a perspective that transcends the stresses and challenges of everyday life, providing them with peace and making them live in the moment. This can help individuals to cope with stress by providing a broader context for their experiences. Many spiritual communities provide a sense of connection and support, which can be beneficial for managing stressful situations and a state of affairs. By connecting with others who share similar beliefs and values, individuals can feel a sense of belonging and support, which can help them to cope with stress. Spirituality often involves cultivating positive emotions, such as gratitude, joy, and love. By developing skills such as mindfulness, self-reflection, and self-compassion, individuals can build resilience and cope with stress more effectively. Thus, overall, practising spirituality is a gainful way to reduce stress levels and focus energy on positive aspects of life.

(b) *Overcoming Depression.* Depression is a widespread and significant mental health condition that has negative effects on a person's emotions, thoughts, and behaviour. Hopelessness, persistent melancholy, and a general disinterest in life are all symptoms. Spiritual practices enable such individuals to see life from a wider perspective, boosting their confidence wherein they learn to accept their feelings and experiences, which eventually helps them to overcome depression. By becoming more aware of one's thoughts and feelings, individuals can learn to identify negative thought patterns and work to replace them with more positive ones. By cultivating compassion and forgiveness, both for oneself and for others, individuals can learn to let go of negative feelings and experiences that contribute to depression. Spiritual communities provide a sense of connection and support, by connecting with others who share similar beliefs and values, individuals can feel a sense of belonging and support, which can help them to overcome feelings of isolation and hopelessness.

(c) *Lower Blood Pressure.* High blood pressure is someway intrinsically linked with stress levels. An excess of stress hormones causes the heart to beat faster and the blood vessels to constrict, leading to elevated blood pressure. In such situations, spiritual practices, such as meditation or prayer, can promote relaxation and reduce stress. By reducing stress, individuals can lower their blood pressure. While practising spirituality, one becomes more aware of one's thoughts and feelings and thus can learn to identify and manage stress triggers that can contribute to high blood pressure. Spiritual traditions emphasise healthy lifestyle habits and maintain a positive outlook towards life. These positive emotions and gratitude can help to reduce stress, control blood pressure and promote a sense of well-being, improving overall health.

(d) *Improve Social Connections.* The importance of good relationships and social adjustments are very crucial for the overall well-being of people. Faltering on this may result in anxieties, apprehensions, insecurities, and lack of confidence, which may result in cardiovascular and other dreaded ailments. Spirituality effectively helps in fixing this problem. It helps in social connections by providing a sense of interconnectedness and community, promoting empathy and compassion, and encouraging altruistic behaviour. Spirituality can help individuals recognise their connections with others and the world around them. When people feel connected to something larger than themselves, they are more likely to develop a sense of empathy and compassion for others, which can enhance their social connections. Spirituality can encourage individuals to engage in altruistic behaviour, such as volunteering or donating to charity. As spiritual practices involve mindfulness, they can help individuals be more present and attentive to their surroundings and interactions with others. When people are more mindful, they are more likely to listen and engage in conversations, which can enhance their social connections.

Positive Orientation to Life. Spirituality can provide a positive direction and purpose in life, which can lead to greater motivation and productivity. It can help individuals find a greater sense of purpose by providing a framework for understanding their place in the world and their connection to something greater than themselves. Many spiritual practices involve connecting to a higher power, whether it is God, the universe, or a divine presence. This connection can provide a positive orientation by helping individuals understand their place in the larger scheme of things. Spirituality often involves a set of values and beliefs that can guide individuals in their decision-making and actions. By aligning their actions with their values, individuals can find greater meaning and purpose in their lives. It also involves self-reflection and introspection, which can help individuals understand themselves better and their purpose. By exploring their inner world, individuals can gain clarity and insight into their strengths, passions, and unique contributions to the world. By contributing to the greater good, individuals can find a sense of purpose and fulfilment that goes beyond their own goals and desires.

Greater sense of Empathy and Compassion. Spirituality helps individuals develop greater empathy and compassion for others, leading to more positive social interactions and a greater sense of connection with the world around them. It provides individuals with a framework for understanding their connection to others and the world around them. Many spiritual traditions emphasise the importance of compassion and empathy towards others as a central aspect of their teachings. Spirituality can help foster empathy and compassion in the following ways:

(a) *Connection to a Higher Power.* Many spiritual traditions teach that we are all connected to a higher power or divine energy. This understanding can help individuals see beyond their egos and personal desires and develop a deeper understanding and empathy towards others.

(b) *Self-Reflection and Mindfulness.* Many spiritual practices encourage individuals to engage in self-reflection and mindfulness, which can help increase their awareness and understanding of their own emotions and experiences. This increased self-awareness can lead to a greater capacity for empathy towards others.

(c) *Cultivation of Love and Kindness.* Many spiritual practices emphasize the importance of cultivating love and kindness towards all beings. This can include practices such as meditation, prayer, and acts of service towards others. These practices can help individuals develop a greater sense of empathy and compassion towards others.

(d) *Acceptance and Forgiveness.* Many spiritual traditions emphasize the importance of acceptance and forgiveness towards oneself and others. By cultivating these qualities, individuals can develop a greater capacity for empathy and compassion towards those who may have wronged them.

Spirituality and Philosophy of Life

Know Thyself. Human life is one of the greatest questions posed to everyone. Human beings face the most intriguing questions: 'What am I' or 'What is the purpose of life'. 'Why have we come to this world'. The famous Greek philosopher of Athens, Socrates, who is credited as the founder of Western philosophy, famously declared that the unexamined life was not worth living. In the forecourt of the Delphic Temple of Apollo are etched two words 'Know Thyself,' which he believed encapsulated all of philosophy's commandments. It reflects the depth and importance of knowing oneself in life. Here, we want to focus on the self-knowledge that matters most in life – the inner psychological core – because that is the ultimate path to larger happiness and contentment. If we are successful in making ourselves aware of self-knowledge, we would be wiser in our life-choices.

Managing 'Self'. If we want to live a complete life, self-awareness – to know oneself both externally and internally – is very important. It will also depend on how well we manage our environment and how well we manage ourselves. Managing ourselves is not limited to our body but mind, thoughts, people we come in contact with, our emotions, our circumstances and our community. From the period of the *Vedas* and the *Upanishads*, Hindus have been informed that their faith is not exclusive to any one group of people and is instead the religion of all mankind; moreover, the greatness of Hinduism is attributed to the fact that it encompasses issues beyond the physical universe. The goal of this faith is the perfection of the person in the cosmos, and it does this not by excluding or devaluing anything from this world, but by incorporating and elevating everything in it to a higher plane.[17] Human beings often mistake things in contact as real and ultimate, not as real and valuable which can be further transcended. One needs to regulate oneself by adopting spiritual practices and teachings to cultivate self-awareness, inner peace, and a sense of purpose. By exploring one's values, passions, and interests, individuals can find themselves to be more relevant. By practising mindfulness and meditation regularly, individuals can develop greater self-awareness and learn to manage their thoughts and emotions more effectively.

Inner Journey – a Realisation. If one lives life intelligently, accurately, scientifically, and with profound understanding, then life will not become miserable. From one layer to the next, from one step to the next, from one stage to the next, it will turn into a delightful ascent toward perfection. If we lack the wisdom to adjust to the shifting conditions of our lives, we will find it a source of constant failure. Wisdom is found in the knowledge that God has given each of us a unique ability that allows us to adapt to every situation in life.[18]

Spirituality helps us understand that our precious acquisitions are not merely materialistic or restricted in the physical realm but are more profound, deeper and more permanent. There is a more transcendently impressive experience in events of our life which we often miss out on what is experienced by our body. That's why, as Socrates put it, the basic message of all philosophies, Western and Eastern alike, is to know yourself – '*Atmanamvidhi*'. Knowing oneself intimately is equivalent to knowing the entirety of creation, since we are all made of the same material – one substance manifesting in various forms – and since our bodies are nothing more than a small part of this material, it stands to reason that understanding our bodies would entail comprehending the material from which all creation is fashioned. Humanity's greatest discoveries, it has become clear, are not limited to the physical and mental realms but extend into something vaster and intangible to human sight.[19] This is the reason that leaders have to first master self-awareness, post which, all other things will fall into correct perspective.

'*Atman*' – **the Absolute.** As per Sanatana Dharma, humans are much more than physical beings. It interprets us as a multi-dimensional being which consists of metaphysically diverse elements closely interrelated and in unison to produce an effect which is our existential reality. These diverse elements, which constitute humans, work in complete harmony and integration. These include *atma* (awareness), *ahamkara* (illusory ego), *buddhi* (wisdom), *manas* (thoughts), *ahitapa* (emotions), and *deha* (body). The *Atman* stands for the genuine individual and the centre of 'I-knowing' (*Aham-pratyaya*). This is because only *Atman* is considered eternal and permanent. It is consciousness which truly lasts, the other five eventually go out of being. *Atman*, a Sanskrit term finds extensive mention even in Hinduism that refers to the individual self or soul. It is believed to be the true essence of a person, and it is often described as everlasting and unchanging. According to Hindu philosophy, *Atman* is the ultimate reality, and it is identical to the ultimate reality of the universe, known as *Brahman*. The goal of many spiritual practices in Hinduism is to realise this identity between *Atman* and *Brahman*, which is known as *moksha* or ultimate liberation. It is from this pedestal of *Atman* that a leader has to function and judge the action of others. If he can dominate the other five elements and use consciousness truly, he would be able to create a very constructive environment for the organisation to blossom. In the context of leadership, the concept of *Atman* has several implications.

(a) *Self-awareness*. The concept of *Atman* emphasises the importance of self-awareness. As a leader, understanding one's true self is essential to make effective decisions and lead with authenticity. By connecting with their *Atman*, leaders can gain a deeper understanding of their values, strengths, and weaknesses.

(b) *Empathy*. *Atman* emphasises the unity of all beings. By recognising that everyone has a unique *Atman*, leaders can cultivate empathy and compassion towards others. This can help them build strong relationships with their team and make it an effective one.

(c) *Purpose*. The concept of *Atman* emphasises the idea that every living being has a unique purpose in life. As a leader, understanding one's purpose and helping team members connect with their purpose can be a powerful motivator. This can inspire them to work towards a common goal and achieve success.

(d) *Integrity.* The concept of *Atman* emphasises the importance of living in accordance with one's true self. As a leader, leading with integrity is essential to build trust with team members and maintain ethical standards. By connecting with their *Atman*, leaders can align their actions with their values and principles.

(e) *Presence in the Moment.* The concept of *Atman* emphasises the importance of being in the present. As a leader, practising mindfulness can help reduce stress, increase focus and creativity, and improve decision-making. By connecting with their *Atman*, leaders can cultivate a sense of calm and clarity in their leadership style.

Self-Realisation: Importance of Consciousness and Bliss in Life. The importance of the eternal bliss every human strives for is very well comprised in the *'Nirvana Shatakam'* composed by the famous philosopher and spiritual guide, Adi Shankaracharya. Through Sanskrit chants, composed over a thousand years ago, he brought out the actual essence of life and unambiguously established the importance of self-realisation. Though the complete composition is aptly relevant to today's leader, the following verses will also help in understanding the meaning and purpose of life. According to it, *Nirvana* is complete tranquillity, equanimity, joy, freedom and eternal peace. *Atman* is the true self and the path to finding this true self is spirituality.

न मे द्वेष रागौ न मे लोभ मोहौ
मदो नैव मे नैव मात्सर्य भाव:।
न धर्मो न चार्थो न कामो ना मोक्ष:
चिदानन्द रूप: शिवोऽहम् शिवोऽहम्

—*Nirvana Shatakam 3*

There is no like or dislike in me, no greed or delusion,
I know not pride or jealousy,
I have no duty, no desire for wealth, lust or liberation,
I am the form of consciousness and bliss,
I am the eternal Shiva . . . . . .

Self-realisation is the understanding of the true self, beyond the limitations of the ego and the physical body. It is the realisation of our ultimate reality, which is infinite, eternal, and full of consciousness and bliss. Consciousness is the state of being aware and perceiving the world around us. It is the foundation of all experiences, thoughts, and emotions. The importance of consciousness in life is that it allows us to connect with our true being and the world around us at a deeper level. When we are fully conscious, we can live in the *'Now'*, free from any distractions of past and future. Bliss is the state of supreme happiness, which arises from the realisation of our true nature. It is the natural state of the self, unburdened by the limitations of the ego and the physical world. The importance of bliss in life is that it brings us joy, contentment, and inner peace, regardless of external circumstances. Self-realisation, consciousness, and bliss are interconnected and essential aspects of spiritual growth and well-being. Through practices such as meditation, self-inquiry, and mindfulness, individuals can cultivate these qualities and experience the fullness of our true nature. By doing so, leaders can find meaning, purpose, and fulfilment in life, and transcend the limitations of the ego and the physical world.

Yoga and Meditation: Path to Spirituality

Spirituality involves achieving a balance, creating internal alignment, healthy-mindedness, engaging our courage and living in the present moment. Maintaining a matured response mechanism and relating to challenges in a relaxed manner without getting under undue pressure by them, is the requirement of today. Leaders require to have a clear vision of emerging situations and act with strength, ease and character which not only help achieve the goal but does so by inspiring and convincing others to follow, willingly and wholeheartedly. Such actions demand a very high degree of focus, flexibility and balance. *Yoga* is one such powerful tool which is capable of providing that fine-tuning, which helps harmonise all actions into an easy flow that performs, naturally and effortlessly.

The term 'yoga' means 'union' or 'connection' in Sanskrit. As we practise yoga, we enter a state of connection and learn a set of methods that help us form meaningful bonds with any aspect of our lives. Feeling and experiencing anything is only possible via a conscious connection to that item, person, or event. Connection creates a yogic state, one that is peaceful and happy and satisfying. A state of yoga is reached when the individual's body, mind, and soul are functioning in tandem. This instrument is what helps us realize our true nature and the meaning of life. Yoga is the practice of becoming more self-aware and, in turn, more tuned with one's inner self. It helps a leader set on the path of spirituality by realising himself to be in a state of calm yet energised, 'go with flow' attitude yet focused, centred yet alert and detached yet alive to the needs of the organisation and the followers. It energises our inner state to a level where body, mind and spirit function at their maximum producing desirable outcomes. As per Sadhguru, "Once we attach the word 'Yoga' to anything, it indicates that it is a complete path by itself. Yoga, at its core, refers to an experience that grounds one in the present. The real self, or *Atman*, is what we're trying to link up with. We might also think of this as the soul. Some other terms that come to mind are disentanglement and detachment. As the ultimate aim of yoga is *moksha* or liberation, the item we are untangling ourselves from is everything that prevents us from feeling free."

There is a common notion that yoga largely refers to the physical domain limited to bodily benefits. The beautiful practice outlined in Patanjali's *Yoga Sutras*, however, provides exhaustive instruction on how to achieve this goal. Yoga, which also includes meditation focuses on a complete experience shaping it towards perfect synchronisation with nature.

Four Types of Yoga. There are only four realities, as per Sadhguru – body, mind, emotion and energy. The complete essence of mankind is around these four facets of life. Human beings use these realities as a medium to reach the ultimate.

(a) When emotions are used it is '*Bhakti Yoga*', which means the path to devotion; it teaches a person to transform emotion into unconditional love and compassion. It emphasises the importance of developing a personal relationship with a deity or higher power through various practices, such as prayer, chanting, and service. In *Bhakti Yoga*, the goal is to achieve union with the divine through selfless love and devotion. The practice is often associated with the worship of specific deities, such as Krishna, Rama, Shiva, or the goddess Devi. Similar devotion is also practised in different religions with their methods. *Bhakti Yoga* is often considered the easiest and most natural form of yoga, as it requires only sincere devotion and love towards a higher power, rather than complex rituals or strenuous physical practices. It is believed that through the practice of *Bhakti* Yoga, one can overcome the limitations of the ego and attain spiritual liberation.

(b) *Gnana* Yoga is one of the four main paths of yoga in Hinduism, and it is the path of wisdom or knowledge. As the mind is involved, that is intelligence, it is called *'Gnana Yoga'*. The leader uses his own mind to discover his true self and the universe, helping him dissolve the veil of ignorance. In *Gnana* Yoga, the goal is to achieve self-realisation or enlightenment through the pursuit of knowledge. This practice involves rigorous self-inquiry and intellectual analysis, as well as the study of spiritual texts and the guidance of a teacher or guru. This form of yoga teaches that the true nature of the self is pure consciousness and that the ultimate goal of life is to realise this truth through the purification of the mind and the elimination of all forms of ignorance and illusion. It is believed that through the practice of *Gnana* Yoga, one can attain *Moksha* and experience ultimate peace and happiness.

(c) If the body or physical action is used it is called *'Karma Yoga'*. This is the path of skilful action, where one acts selflessly mastering the art of detachment. In *Karma* Yoga, the goal is to attain self-realisation through the performance of one's duties in a spirit of selflessness and detachment. The practice involves offering all actions and their results to the Divine, without any expectation of reward or recognition. *Karma* Yoga teaches that one can attain spiritual liberation through the performance of one's duties with detachment and without selfish motives. It is believed that through the practice of *Karma* Yoga, one can develop a selfless attitude, purify the mind, and overcome the limitations of the ego. To practice *Karma* Yoga, one should cultivate the attitude of service, offer all actions to the Divine, and perform one's duties without attachment to the outcome. By doing so, one can attain spiritual growth, inner peace, and ultimately, *Moksha.*

(d) Finally, if energy is transformed to try to reach the ultimate, it is called '*Kriya Yoga*'. This is directed towards divine experience or nearing enlightenment. This helps the leader to concentrate and remain focused guided by his soul. Many thinkers consider *'Raja Yoga'* as the fourth type of yoga, which is being dealt with subsequently. *Kriya* Yoga combines techniques of breath control, meditation, and self-inquiry to awaken the spiritual energy within the body and mind. It is a systematic and scientific approach to the spiritual evolution of the individual. The origins of *Kriya* Yoga can be traced back to ancient India, but it was popularised in modern times by Yogi Paramahansa Yogananda, who introduced it to the West in his book '*Autobiography of a Yogi.*' *Kriya* Yoga is based on the concept that the human body is made up of various energy centres or *chakras*, and that the spiritual energy, or kundalini, can be awakened and directed through the practice of specific techniques, such as *pranayama* (breathing exercises) and meditation. The practice of *Kriya* Yoga aims to purify the mind and body, develop concentration, and awaken spiritual energy, leading to a state of inner peace, joy, and spiritual realization. It is believed that through the regular practice of *Kriya* Yoga, one can attain self-realisation and ultimately, union with the Divine and oneself. *Kriya* Yoga is considered an advanced practice and is traditionally taught by a qualified teacher through a process of initiation and instruction.

The four different types of yogas may hint at four separate mediums but it is impossible to separate them as independent entities. When a person is really practising yoga, their whole being, including their thoughts, feelings, and energy, are in sync with one another. A leader has to be always aware of how he feels, how he moves, and how he responds to his surroundings. Yoga is a very powerful tool which helps a person to engage mind and body to reach a state of inner calm and balance. This is going to put a leader in a position to engage compassionately, honestly and mindfully, with others. The mindful engagement with others puts him in a position to engage compassionately, honestly and mindfully with the entire environment.

'Raja Yoga'. A leader will always require compassion, effective communication, control over self, self-discipline, sharp thinking, empathy and a clear vision. *Raja* Yoga which has been well documented in *'Patanjali Yoga Sutras'*, is considered the principal form of yoga (several schools of thought consider *Raja* Yoga as the fourth type and not *Kriya* Yoga). 'Raja' means 'king' or 'royal' in Sanskrit, and the term is used to describe *Raja* yoga as the 'royal path' or primary style of yoga. *Raja* yoga has historically been used to describe both the ultimate aim of yoga and its practice used to reach that end. As this is the case, it is also thought of as the feeling of contentment and calm that comes with regular yoga and meditation.[20] *Raja* yoga guides one to strengthening personal power to improve leadership skills which are also reflective of one's

cognitive development. *Raja* yoga in leaders can significantly enhance critical thinking and automatic deductive thinking. It means a leader needs to develop the power of talking to their inner self to realise their true potential. Swami Vivekananda was one of the first thinkers to understand this aspect of *Raja* Yoga and he stated, "Talk to yourself once a day, otherwise you may miss meeting an excellent person in this world".[21]

Eight Limbs of Yoga. The eight steps to yoga or what are referred to as the eight limbs of the yoga sutras are a systematic approach to attaining inner peace, clarity, self-control and realisation.

(a) ***Yama:* Self-Control.** The yamas are five ethical qualities we carry within us, which help us to develop self-control and pure intentions that outline a code of conduct that should form the basis of our interactions with others in daily life. They are: *Ahimsa* (non-violence), which emphasises practising non-violence and compassion towards all living beings, helping oneself to be peaceful within and maintaining a positive aura; *Satya* (truthfulness), which includes being truthful in words, actions and intentions; *Asteya* (non-stealing) emphasises to refrain from stealing or taking what is not freely given; it not only refers to property but to intellectual aspects and thoughts too; *Brahmacharya* (celibacy) meaning not indulging in whims of the senses but uniting with consciousness and becoming powerful; *Aparigraha* (non-coveting), postulates practising non-attachment, non-greediness and non-possessiveness. Self-control helps us gain control over our thoughts, emotions and senses. These ethical guidelines are considered essential for living a yogic lifestyle, and they help to promote self-awareness, self-discipline, and inner peace. By following the yamas, individuals can cultivate a sense of social responsibility and contribute positively to their communities and the world around them. A leader who has achieved self-control has almost won half the battle and acquired the power to make sound decisions in the most adverse conditions. These guidelines will help leaders live in harmony with themselves, others, and the world around them.

(b) ***Niyama:* Self-Discipline.** The yamas relate to personal qualities whereas *niyamas* are inward practices or habits to improve the self. The *Niyamas* are the second limb and refer to the ethical and moral principles that govern an individual's behaviour towards oneself. They are the personal observances that one practices to maintain a positive state of mind and healthy body. They are:

(i) *Shaucha* (Cleanliness). *Shaucha* refers to cleanliness or purity of body, speech, and thought. It is an important aspect of yogic practice, as it helps to promote physical health, mental clarity, and spiritual well-being. It manifests in the form of *physical cleanliness* which involves maintaining a clean and healthy body, and keeping one's environment clean and organised; *Speech cleanliness* emphasises the use of kind, truthful, and respectful language; thus one can create a more positive and harmonious environment, both internally and externally; *Mental cleanliness* involves purifying one's thoughts and emotions, which can be achieved through practices such as meditation, mindfulness, and self-reflection; thus *Shaucha* helps in achieving physical, environmental and mental purity.

(ii) *Santosha* (Contentment). It emphasises being unconditionally happy. It refers to the practice of contentment and gratitude. It is the quality of being satisfied with what one has, rather than constantly striving for more. The practice of *Santosha* helps one to find contentment and appreciate the gifts and blessings that life has to offer. It involves developing an attitude of gratitude and focusing on the positive aspects of one's life, rather than dwelling on what is lacking. *Santosha* does not mean that one should become complacent or stop pursuing their goals and aspirations. Instead, it means finding joy and fulfilment in the process, rather than being solely focused on the end result. By cultivating *Santosha*, individuals can experience greater peace, happiness, and fulfilment in their lives, regardless of external circumstances. Practising *Santosha* can also have a positive effect on one's relationships, as it encourages individuals to appreciate and value the people in their lives, rather than taking them for granted or focusing on their flaws.

(iii) *Tapas* (Asceticism). *Tapas* means choosing to restrict oneself to keep away from bad habits through self-discipline and austerity to purify the body and mind. It involves the willingness to endure hardship and discomfort to achieve one's goals and spiritual aspirations. The practice of *Tapas* can take many forms, including physical practices such as fasting, yoga, and other forms of physical exercise. It can also involve mental and emotional practices, such as meditation, mindfulness, and self-reflection. The goal of *Tapas* is to cultivate greater self-awareness and inner strength, as well as to purify the body and mind of negative influences and habits. The practice of *Tapas* requires a strong commitment and willingness to push oneself beyond one's comfort zone. It involves a willingness to face challenges and difficulties, and embrace the discomfort that arises from the process of self-discipline and austerity. By practising *Tapas*, individuals can develop greater self-control, focus, and resilience, as well as a deeper relevance of their lives. In addition to the benefits of personal growth and spiritual development, the practice of *Tapas* can also have practical benefits in daily life. It can promote physical health and vitality, as well as mental clarity and emotional stability. It can also help individuals to overcome negative habits and patterns, such as addiction or procrastination. The practice of *Tapas* is an important aspect of leadership, as it helps a leader to develop the inner strength and discipline necessary for personal transformation in terms of selflessness and mindfulness.

(iv) *Svadhyaya* (Study). *Svadhyaya* refers to the practice of self-study and self-reflection. It involves the exploration and study of spiritual texts and teachings, as well as the examination of one's thoughts, beliefs, and actions to open one's understanding of the self and the universe. The practice of *Svadhyaya* can take many forms, including the reading of sacred texts of any religion, as well as engaging in self-reflection through meditation or other forms of introspection. The goal is to cultivate greater self-awareness and understanding, as well as to deepen one's connection to the divine as individuals can gain a deeper understanding of their nature and the nature of the universe.

They can also gain an insight into the causes of suffering and the path to liberation. By studying spiritual texts and engaging in self-reflection, individuals can develop greater clarity, wisdom, and compassion, and can move closer to their ultimate spiritual goals. In addition to the benefits of spiritual growth and personal development, the practice of *Svadhyaya* can also have practical benefits in daily life. It can help individuals to develop greater clarity of thought and purpose, as well as overcome negative habits and patterns. It promotes greater harmony and understanding in relationships, as individuals gain greater insight into their motivations and behaviours, as well as those of others.

(v) *Ishvara Pranidhana* (Dedication to God/Master). This means always remaining connected with God and thus diving into the infinite and vast consciousness of love, hope and eternalness. At times, it is also considered a complete surrender to God. It refers to the practice of surrendering one's ego and individual will to a higher power, and living by divine will, involves recognising and surrendering to a higher power, and allowing that power to guide and direct one's life. The practice of *Ishvara Pranidhana* can take many forms, including prayer, meditation, and devotion to a particular deity or spiritual tradition. It involves a willingness to let go of one's desires and attachments and to trust in the wisdom and guidance of the divine. Through its practice, individuals can develop a deeper sense of connection and reverence for the divine. They can also experience a sense of peace and contentment, as they let go of their fears and anxieties and trust in the wisdom and goodness of the universe. In addition to the benefits of spiritual growth and personal development, the practice of *Ishvara Pranidhana* does help individuals to overcome feelings of anxiety, stress, and uncertainty, as they surrender to the wisdom and guidance of a higher power. It can also promote greater harmony and understanding in relationships, as individuals learn to trust in the divine plan and accept the actions of others.

(c) ***Asana:* Physical Exercise**. *Asana* is a Sanskrit term which is generally translated as 'posture' or 'pose.' *Asana* can be referred as "a steady, comfortable seat," particularly for the purpose of meditation. The aim of practising these *asanas*, or physical postures, before beginning a meditation session is to produce the calm and ease of mind that is necessary for effective meditation. Maintaining this equilibrium is essential for good health and stability. We need to get into an equilibrium which stimulates all the glands helping the body attain physical, intellectual and spiritual balance. *Asanas* purify us and give us good health. Being a leader, a physically fit body and mind helps to achieve overall equilibrium. The practice of *asanas* involves holding various postures for some time, usually several breaths or more. The postures can range from simple, seated positions to more complex, dynamic movements. *Asanas* are typically practised in combination with *pranayama* (breathing exercises) and meditation, to create a more complete and balanced practice. Some common *asanas* include *Tadasana* (mountain pose), a standing posture that improves posture and alignment; *Adho Mukha Svanasana* (downward-facing dog pose), a full-body stretch that strengthens the arms and legs; *Virabhadrasana* (warrior pose), a series of postures that build strength and confidence; *Balasana* (child's pose), a gentle, restorative posture that promotes relaxation and stress relief; and *Padmasana* (lotus pose), a seated posture that promotes flexibility and concentration. The practice of *asanas* in yoga is incredibly important for physical, mental, and spiritual well-being. Some of the key benefits of practising *asanas* which can be highly useful for leaders are:

(i) *Physical Health*. *Asanas* help to improve overall physical health by increasing flexibility, strength, and body equilibrium. They can also help avoid injury and improve posture and alignment.

(ii) *Mental Health*. Proper practice of *asanas* can help reduce stress, anxiety, and depression. It leads to relaxation, improved focus, and enhanced mental clarity.

(iii) *Spiritual Growth*. *Asanas* are commonly employed for spiritual growth because they can help people connect with their inner selves, resulting in deeper self-awareness and consciousness.

(iv) *Improved Breathing*. *Asanas* are typically done together with *pranayama* which results in enhanced lung capacity and an increase in the flow of oxygen throughout the body.

(v) *Increased Energy.* Regular practice of *asanas* can help to boost energy levels and reduce fatigue, leading to greater productivity and vitality throughout the day.

(vi) *Improved Immune function. Asanas* help to stimulate the lymphatic system and increase circulation, which can improve immune function and promote overall health.

(vii) *Improved Digestion.* Certain *asanas*, such as twists and forward folds, can help to improve digestion and alleviate digestive issues.

(viii) *Holistic Health.* The correct implementation of laid down asanas helps in promoting complete health by taking care of all three aspects – physical, psychological and emotional. Individuals can attain a greater sense of balance and harmony in their lives by regularly practising *asanas*.

(d) ***Pranayama:* Breathing Exercise.** '*Prana*' means life force. *Pranayama* is a Sanskrit word that means 'breath control' or 'life force extension'. As defined by Patanjali, the sage, it alters the breath's pattern and duration by techniques that include breath retention and division. By focusing on various regions of the body and counting breaths to slow the breath's flow, mental clutter may be cleared away.[22] Breathing mindfully helps to improve concentration, focus, and circulation of blood. When the leader masters his breathing, he can control anxiety, restlessness, and unwanted thoughts and remain calm and unruffled in tense situations. Breathing exercises, one of the primary tools of meditation, is a fundamental aspect of yoga and helps to regulate the flow of *prana*, or life force energy, in the body. One needs to practise controlling the breath through various techniques, including deep breathing, alternate nostril breathing, and breath retention resulting in better blood circulation and enhanced lung capacity. Thus, individuals can improve their overall cardiovascular health, significantly. One of the most important benefits of *pranayama* is its ability to reduce stress and anxiety. By slowing down the breathing and focusing on the present moment, individuals can reduce the activity of the sympathetic nervous system, which is responsible for the 'fight or flight' response. This can help to reduce stress and anxiety levels and promote relaxation and calmness. *Pranayama* is also beneficial for overall physical health. It has also been shown to improve digestion and boost the immune system. In addition to its physical benefits, this highly beneficial practice is also a powerful tool for spiritual growth. By focusing on the breath and cultivating awareness of the present moment, individuals can develop a deeper sense of self-awareness and connection to their inner selves. *Pranayama* is often used in combination with meditation and other spiritual practices to promote inner peace and harmony. *Pranayama* should be learned properly, as some techniques can be quite challenging and require proper instruction and guidance. It is also important to practice it in a safe and comfortable environment and avoid pushing oneself too hard. Overall, *pranayama* is a powerful and transformative practice that offers numerous benefits for physical, mental, and spiritual well-being. By incorporating it into a regular yoga practice, leaders can experience greater peace, clarity, and vitality in all aspects of their lives.

(e) ***Pratyahara:* Regulation of Senses with External Objects**. This is a state which acts as a bridge between the internal being and the external environment. It is usually translated as 'withdrawal of the senses' and refers to the practice of consciously disengaging from external stimuli to focus the mind and cultivate inner awareness. It is attained by moving inwards towards one's own consciousness and exercising full control over the senses. *Annamaya Kosha*, the food sheath, *Pranayama Kosha,* the breath sheath, *Manomaya Kosha*, the thought sheath, *Vigyanmaya Kosha*, the intellect sheath, and *Anandamaya Kosha*, the happiness sheath, make up the five sheaths or layers of *Pancha Kosha*, that encases the inner *atman* or awareness. The goal of *pratyahara* is for the practitioner to withdraw from the external world with the use of meditation to pierce these sheaths and ultimately connect with awareness. In terms of leadership, the concept of *pratyahara* can be seen as the need for a leader to withdraw from external distractions and focus on their inner awareness and intuition. This can help them make more thoughtful and informed decisions as well as better understand the needs and perspectives of their team. A leader who practises *pratyahara* may be more able to listen deeply to their team members, recognise patterns and trends, and make decisions that are in line with their values and goals. By cultivating a sense of inner stillness and mindfulness, a leader can create a more supportive and effective work environment for their team. A good leader needs to balance their inner awareness with their ability to engage with others and respond to external challenges and opportunities. This limb helps a leader to remain unfazed due to darkness outside but take decisions based on inner consciousness.

(f) ***Dharna:* Concentration**. *Dharna*, as the word suggests, is the practice of focusing one's attention on a single object, location, or idea for an extended period of time. As one rests attention at a specific point, the mind's restlessness is controlled and it stops wavering. There is a calming effect on the body and balance is achieved. As we start concentrating, the body effortlessly enters into *dhyana*. *Dhyana* is of vital importance to oneself while one is interacting, reacting or responding to people or situations. In the context of leadership, *Dharna* can be a powerful tool for enhancing focus, clarity, and decision-making. By developing the ability to concentrate one's attention, leaders can become more effective at managing complex tasks, staying focused on long-term goals, and making informed decisions in the face of uncertainty and ambiguity. Furthermore, *dharna* can help leaders to stay calm and centred in high-pressure situations, which is essential for effective leadership. It can also improve communication skills by enabling leaders to listen more attentively and respond more thoughtfully to the needs of their team members. Overall, *dharna* can help leaders to become more mindful, empathetic, and effective in their roles. By cultivating greater concentration and focus, leaders can build stronger relationships with their team members, make more informed decisions, and ultimately achieve greater success in their organizations.

(g) ***Dhyana:* Meditation**. Meditation, which is very much a part of yoga is the state one can experience complete stillness. Deep concentration leads to *dhyana*. In this meditative state, one also achieves eternal calmness or bliss called *samadhi*. If practised properly under guidance, one can progress his meditative state to perfection – a quintessential of a good leader. A leader needs a deep focus when the mind does not get distracted by intrinsic thoughts. He needs to be conscious of the moment, and that helps him exercise full control over the situation. By improving focus and concentration and reducing stress and anxiety, *dhyana* meditation can help leaders to make better decisions. Additionally, greater self-awareness can help leaders to make decisions that are more aligned with their values and goals. There are many different techniques and approaches to *dhyana* meditation, but some common elements include:

(i) *Focus on the breath*. One of the most common techniques for *dhyana* meditation is to focus on the breath. This involves observing the breath as it moves in and out of the body and using this awareness to anchor the mind and stay present at the moment.

(ii) *Body scan*. Another technique for *dhyana* meditation involves systematically scanning the body from head to toe, observing any sensations or tension that may be present, and letting go of any physical or mental tension.

(iii) *Mantra repetition*. Some practitioners of *dhyana* meditation use a repeated word or phrase (known as a mantra) as a focal point to anchor the mind and stay present in the moment.

(iv) *Visualisations*. Another technique for meditation involves visualising a peaceful or calm scene, such as a forest or ocean, and using this image to cultivate a sense of tranquillity and relaxation.

(v) *Loving-kindness meditation*. This technique involves directing positive feelings and goodwill towards oneself and others and cultivating a sense of compassion and empathy.

(h) ***Samadhi*: Complete Realisation**. *Samadhi*, a Sanskrit term, refers to a state of complete realisation, in which the individual merges with the object of their meditation, becoming one with the universe. In this state, the individual experiences a profound sense of peace, joy, and transcendence. As one progresses from a deep meditative state and achieves *samadhi*, life becomes full of love, joy, and strength. A leader will significantly enhance his power of visualisation, analysis, thinking and retention. The power of the subconscious mind would keep him well aware of the environment and help him get over difficult situations and help him take balanced and well-considered decisions. *Samadhi* involves letting go of the ego and merging with the universe. This can help leaders to develop a greater self-awareness and understanding. By transcending their concerns and merging with a higher power or universal consciousness, leaders can develop a broader perspective of their own lives and the world around them. By quieting the mind and letting go of the ego, leaders can access a deeper level of insight and inspiration, which can lead to more creative and innovative solutions. It will help leaders tap into a deeper level of wisdom and insight, which can help them make decisions that are more aligned with their values and goals. As *samadhi* involves transcending the limitations of the physical world and experiencing a state of complete unity with the universe, it can help leaders to develop a greater sense of empathy and compassion for others, as they recognize their interconnectedness with all beings. There are many different approaches to *samadhi*, but some common elements include:

(i) *Deep concentration. Samadhi* requires deep concentration, in which the individual focuses their attention on a single object or idea. This concentration must be sustained for an extended period, to achieve the state of complete realisation.

(ii) *Letting go of the self.* In *samadhi*, the individual lets go of their sense of self and merges with the object of their meditation. This is a challenging process, as it involves letting go of the ego and surrendering to a higher power or universal consciousness.

(iii) *Complete stillness. Samadhi* requires complete stillness, both physically and mentally. The individual must be completely present in the moment, without any distracting thoughts or movements.

(iv) *Transcendence. Samadhi* involves transcending the limitations of the physical world and experiencing a state of complete unity with the universe. In this state, the individual experiences a profound sense of peace, joy, and freedom from suffering.

Yoga and Meditation for Military Leadership. Yoga and meditation can be powerful tools for military leaders, helping them to develop the physical, mental, and emotional resources they need to lead with confidence, resilience, and compassion. By regularly practising yoga and meditation, military leaders can cultivate the inner strength and develop the clarity that they need to succeed in even the most challenging situations. If the leader develops his inner voice, he can connect with the troops in a meaningful manner. The act of breathing helps to understand the importance of focus in life and thus remain concentrated on the target. The mental discipline developed helps managing own and others' emotions. An individual's self-awareness is linked to their degree of achievement. Yoga and meditation can help the leaders to develop the inner resources they need to lead with clarity, purpose, and integrity. The major benefits of yoga and meditation for military leaders can be summarized in the following ways:

(a) *Improved resilience and stress management.* Combat situations are often high-stress and demanding, and yoga and meditation can be effective tools for managing stress and improving resilience. By cultivating mindfulness and relaxation, military leaders can better cope with the challenges they face and make better decisions under pressure.

(b) *Enhanced physical and mental performance.* Yoga involves physical postures, breathing techniques, and meditation, all of which can help military leaders to enhance their physical and mental performance. By improving flexibility, strength, and focus, yoga can help leaders to perform at their best, both physically and mentally.

(c) *Increased self-awareness.* Yoga and meditation involve introspection and self-reflection, which can help military leaders to develop greater self-awareness and emotional intelligence. By understanding their strengths, weaknesses and triggers, leaders can better manage their emotions and communicate more effectively with their team members.

(d) *Improved decision-making.* By improving focus, clarity and resilience, yoga and meditation can help military leaders make better decisions. Additionally, greater self-awareness and emotional intelligence can help leaders to make decisions that are more aligned with their values and goals.

(e) *Enhanced teamwork and collaboration.* Yoga and meditation can also help military leaders to develop greater empathy, compassion and collaboration skills. By cultivating a sense of unity and interconnectedness with others, leaders can better understand and relate to their team members, fostering a more positive and productive work environment.

Spirituality and Leadership

The apparent resemblance among the spiritual leanings of great leaders has fuelled a recent uptick in academic pursuits of the connection between leadership and spirituality. The importance of ethics and values has risen to the forefront of every business. In today's world, there are numerous examples where the positive impact of spirituality is experienced with minor variations, be it a challenging environment of the Armed Forces, competitiveness in corporate sectors or other government sectors. "Encompassing ideals that create feelings of transcendent connection between individuals, 'workplace spirituality' is a popularly growing term. The followers/workers find personal fulfilment in their job. A sense of calling that embodies the feeling of transcendence via one's job forms the cornerstone upon which workplace or organisational spirituality rests. There is a craving for participation, togetherness, and human interaction."[23]

Business in yesteryears was always established on spiritual principles but as the Industrial era set in, people became more obsessed with unethical profit-making, reasoning, deceptive marketing and maximising profits. However, now again, the world over, businesses are on the verge of major transformation as today's working environment appears under severe materialistic threat. Once again, there is a felt need to explore the intrinsic facets of human values and achieve the desired congruence and meaning at the workplace. In the existing environment, spirituality is one such golden discovery, which will help an individual to connect to their inner self to others and with the ultimate reality, thus, helping him to live harmoniously in the shared community. Research has shown that leaders who are real and have integrity reflect on their life to find their purposes.[24] It has been theorised that visionary and behavioural pattern of a leader may all be directly influenced by the inner direction they get via contemplation, prayer, and meditation, leading to an increase in the organization's bottom line.[25] Further, meditation, one of the limbs of *raja* yoga, can significantly, enhance an individual's effectiveness, his outlook, provide calmness, develop empathy and reduce anxiety – all contributing towards helping the leader in making proper judgements, formulating good plans and making sound decisions.

Spiritual Leadership Theory. L.W. Fry's research of the spiritual leadership theory is one of the first attempts to conceptualise the interplay between spirituality and leadership. The theory is based on the intrinsic motivational model founded on goal identification and the tasks involved. As per the proponents of the theory, a leader with spirituality should adopt in his functioning, faith and culture of altruistic love. Faith is an integral aspect of vision, providing a spiritual foundation for the whole process. The results of selfless love and the development of spiritual meaning are an environment where work is enjoyable and people are at peace and contentment.[26] Another researcher, Laura Reave, brings out the consistencies between spiritual values and successful leadership. That is, "leaders that apply spiritual principles use comparable skill sets that build an atmosphere that meets goals, motivates workers, creates a great work environment, and displays trust and ethical behaviours that promote positive connections," she argues. As a result, the leader is capable of increasing production, lower resistance, and ensuring the organization's long-term viability. Subordinates are looking for a leader who value their relationships with others; therefore, a spiritual approach to leadership is also universal. With the advent of globalization, this has been the most preferable choice.[27]

The spiritual leadership theory emphasizes the significance of spirituality and ethical values in leadership when analyzed. According to this theory, inspiring and motivating followers towards achieving higher performance levels is what makes a leader effective. A feeling of significance and direction is also upheld by them in their work. The idea behind the spiritual leadership theory is that leaders should be directed by a group of core ethical and spiritual values. These include compassion, integrity, and social responsibility. These values should be reflected in the leader's behaviour, decision-making, and interactions with others, and should be used to inspire and motivate followers to achieve their goals. The spiritual leadership theory also emphasises the importance of creating a sense of community and belonging among followers.

Leaders must foster a culture of shared values, purpose, and vision, and must create opportunities for followers to collaborate, communicate, and support one another. Another key aspect of the spiritual leadership theory is the idea of servant leadership. This approach emphasises the importance of leaders serving the needs of their followers, rather than using their power and authority to control or manipulate them. Leaders who follow this are often seen as humble, caring, and compassionate, and are focused on creating positive change in the world. The spiritual leadership theory offers a unique perspective on leadership, emphasising the importance of ethical and spiritual values, community building, and servant leadership. By adopting this approach, leaders can inspire and motivate their followers to achieve their goals, while also creating a more compassionate, purpose-driven, and meaningful work environment.

Spirituality, Leadership and Value System. A leader's strong value system has been clearly shown by previous research on leadership theories and spirituality. As per Russell's argument (2001), our values constitute the underlying belief system inside us that reflects in thinking patterns and, consequently, manifests as behaviour. A leader's values and worldview are reflected in their personal acts of leadership, which can have significant impacts on their followers.[28] Russell has further explained that the value system in any leader forms his base for conduct. A value system like honesty, integrity and fairness is adopted for everyday conduct along with qualities like compassion, concern for others and altruistic love. All these value systems which are traits of good leadership have been intrinsically found in spiritual individuals. Bertrand Russell, a philosopher and mathematician, believed that the value system of a leader is the foundation of their conduct. According to him, a leader's values are reflected in their actions and decisions and are essential for guiding them through difficult situations.

Russell argued that principles of justice, compassion, and integrity should be the cornerstone on which a leader should base his value system. These values should be grounded in a commitment to fairness, equality, and respect for human dignity, and should be reflected in the leader's behaviour, decision-making, and interactions with others. In practice, this means that a leader's value system should guide their actions and decisions, even in challenging or uncertain circumstances. For example, if a leader values honesty and transparency, they should be willing to communicate openly with their team members, even if the news is difficult or unpopular. Similarly, if a leader values fairness and equality, they should ensure that all team members have equal access to resources, opportunities, and rewards. Russell also believed that a leader's values should be rooted in a commitment to social justice and the common good. This means that leaders should be mindful of the impact of their decisions and actions on society as a whole, and should work to promote the well-being of all people, not just their interests or those of their organization. Thus, Russell's perspective highlights the importance of a leader's value system in shaping their conduct and guiding them through complex and challenging situations. By adopting a values-based approach to leadership, leaders can inspire and motivate their team members, while also creating a more just, compassionate, and ethical work environment.

A key finding comes from the work of J. Cranston Barsh and R.A. Craske, who conducted interviews with leaders (in this case, women leaders) from all around the world. Those that make spirituality a component of their daily lives exhibit these values. They found that leaders could be classified along five distinct personality traits meaning, selfless love, introspection, foresight, and authenticity are amongst them.[29] These traits developed through spirituality do lay a strong foundation for a leader, which helps in achieving organizational success and are being discussed in detail.

(a) *Finding Meaning.* The 'meaning' is, what and why we do what we do. The force behind our actions. Finding out what pushes them, and what pushes them farther, is something that fascinates people. The topic reignites their interest and stirs their enthusiasm. Work with a purpose becomes a 'calling' when compared to a job without one. In what ways is meaning crucial for leaders? Professionals that feel this way are demonstrated to have better levels of work satisfaction, more productivity, lower turnover rates, and greater loyalty in studies. Feelings of transcendence are another perk, when you give to a cause larger than yourself, you get a better understanding of its significance and a sense of fulfilment that feeds on itself. Several of the women leaders were able to go forward on uncharted courses and take the necessary risks due to having found a deeper purpose in their work.[30] A leader's sense of purpose is crucial to their own health and the success of their organisation. When leaders are fulfilled in their work, they exude an enthusiasm for their mission that belies their seriousness about achieving it. The preceding studies discovered that a leader's sense of significance in their job was the most essential value, working as a powerful motivator to help them get through difficult times, discomfort, and fear of the unknown. Finding meaning and relevance for military leaders is a crucial aspect of leadership development, as it can help leaders navigate the complexities of their roles, and inspire and motivate their teams to achieve their goals. Cranston Barsh and R.A. Craske, in their book '*Managing Strategic Innovation and Change*,' provide several insights into how military leaders can find meaning and relevance in their work. Aligning personal values with those of the organization is crucial for success. By aligning personal values with organisational ones, leaders can establish a profound sense of purpose and significance in what they do. The same could be inspired among their team members. Another observation is that building a sense of community and belonging among teammates is significant. Promoting a culture of trust, respect, and shared purpose can help leaders create a supportive and collaborative work environment. This leads to improved team performance and satisfaction. Barsh and Craske stress that it is crucial to maintain a focus on the broader mission and purpose of the military organisation. Even when facing challenges or uncertainty, leaders who prioritize their mission can remain motivated and inspired.

(b) *Altruistic Love*. Altruistic love's impact on workplaces is explored extensively through research carried out by Laura Reave who is an expert and scholar of organisational behaviour. She has divided altruistic love into five sub-values in her work, which enables a more complete comprehension of the concept. The concept of altruistic love revolves around displaying disinterested, dedicated, all-encompassing, and gracious care, concern, and esteem for oneself along with others. Caring for others without expecting anything in return is emphasized as important. Reave discusses how benevolent love impacts companies while breaking down its components into five sub-values that enhance understanding and involve deeper investigation.[31] Reave's research suggests that when these sub-values of altruistic love are present in the workplace; they can have a range of positive consequences, including increased employee engagement, satisfaction, and well-being, as well as enhanced team cohesion, trust, and collaboration. Furthermore, Reave argues that altruistic love can build a very effective work atmosphere, where everyone feels relevant, valued, and supported. This would help in increased productivity, creativity, and innovation, as well as a more positive organizational culture. Reave's research on the sub-values of altruistic love in the workplace highlights the potential benefits of fostering a more caring and compassionate work environment and provides guidance for leaders and organizations seeking to enhance the well-being and performance of their employees. The following five sub-values form the foundational values for any leader – military or others.

(i) *Humility*. Most religious or spiritual philosophies stress the need for humility in one's spiritual journey. As Reave's study shows, followers have a preference for leaders who are self-effacing. Humility is an essential trait for military leaders to possess because it allows them to lead with a sense of openness, self-awareness, and accountability. It allows leaders to acknowledge their weaknesses, learn from their mistakes, and seek feedback from others. This helps to promote continuous learning and growth, which is critical for military leaders who need to stay adaptable and innovative in the face of changing situations. Humble leaders recognise that they are not infallible and rely on the expertise and perspectives of others to make informed decisions. This creates a sense of teamwork and collaboration among team members, which can lead to more effective problem-solving and decision-making. Humble leaders are more likely to prioritise ethical and moral behaviour over their self-interest. This promotes a culture of ethical behaviour and can help to prevent abuse of power or corruption. Leaders with humility are generally found to be more open and approachable, making it easier for team members to communicate with them. This fosters a sense of trust and openness, which is essential for effective communication in the military. Thus, they are likely to earn the trust and respect of their subordinates because they are seen as approachable, accountable, and authentic. This enhances their credibility as leaders and can help to promote a culture of respect and trust in the military.

(ii) *Respect for Others*. Leadership that takes into account the workers' values results in independence rather than dependency, as well as long-term success rather than fleeting glory. Researchers have tracked the productivity of workers whose managers showed care and sympathy. Over the years it has been found that respecting others was a crucial aspect of effective leadership, as it fosters a culture of trust, collaboration, and mutual respect among team members. When leaders show respect to their subordinates, it fosters a sense of team cohesion and unity. This is particularly important in the military, where teamwork and collaboration are essential for effective mission accomplishment. Respecting others promotes trust among team members, which is essential for clear communication, sound decisions, and building of trust. Leaders who respect their subordinates are more likely to prioritise ethical behaviour, fairness, and justice in their decision-making. This in turn results in subordinates trusting their leaders and are more likely to follow their directions, even in challenging situations. Respecting others, regardless of their background, promotes diversity and inclusion in the military. This creates a more inclusive work environment, where everyone feels valued and respected. When leaders show respect to their subordinates, it enhances their job satisfaction and commitment to the organisation's goals. This can lead to higher retention rates, which is particularly important in the military, where turnover can be costly and disruptive.

(iii) *Treating Others Fairly*. When we value other people, we naturally treat them with fairness. When workers feel their leaders have their best interests in mind, they are more engaged in their job, and their output rises as a result. Treating others fairly is an essential aspect of effective leadership in any setting, including the military. In the military, leaders are responsible for creating a culture of respect, trust, and fairness, which can help to enhance team performance, morale, and well-being. There are several reasons why treating others fairly is particularly important for military leaders. Firstly, in the military, trust and respect are essential for effective mission accomplishment. When leaders treat their subordinates fairly, they are more likely to earn their respect and trust, which can enhance the overall effectiveness of the team. Secondly, fairness is critical in promoting organisational justice, which refers to the perception of fairness and equity in the workplace. When employees perceive that they are being treated fairly, they are more likely to be satisfied with their job and commitment to the organisation's goals. Conversely, when employees perceive that they are being treated unfairly, it can lead to resentment, conflict, and disengagement. Thirdly, fairness is essential for promoting diversity, equity, and inclusion in the military. When leaders treat all team members fairly and equitably, regardless of their background, they can create a more inclusive and diverse work environment, where everyone feels valued and respected. Finally, treating others fairly is a critical component of ethical leadership. Ethical leaders are those who prioritise doing what is right, even in the face of adversity or personal gain. By treating others fairly, leaders can demonstrate their commitment to ethical behaviour and serve as role models for their subordinates.

(iv) *Caring and Concern*. In addition to being fundamental to effective leadership, the qualities of care and concern are emphasised by the vast majority of faith traditions. Rego's 2008 study found that "subordinates' mental health was improved when their superior showed empathy and compassion." Leaders who cared about their followers' well-being tended to see gains in productivity for the team as a whole. Military leaders who demonstrate care and concern for their subordinates can create a culture of trust, respect, and support that enhances team cohesion and mission success. When military leaders show genuine care and concern for their subordinates, it enhances their morale and raises their spirits enhancing their commitment to the mission.

This important aspect builds trust and loyalty which are essential for mission success. It improves communication and subordinates are more likely to share their thoughts, concerns, and ideas with leaders whom they perceive as caring and approachable. Eventually, it helps in team cohesion creating a sense of camaraderie and support that enhances teamwork and collaboration. This can lead to improved mission accomplishment and overall performance.

(v) *Appreciating the Contributions of Others.* The value of others is a concept preached by many religions. More dedication, productivity, and contentment in the workplace might result from a spiritual leader's real appreciation. In military life, recognising and appreciating the contributions of others can boost morale among the troops. When soldiers find their efforts being recognised, they are more motivated and work harder. The military is all about teamwork, and recognising the contributions of others is a way to promote a sense of teamwork and unity. They get inspired to be fully loyal to their leaders and their country. They are also more likely to stick with their unit and complete their mission. Their effectiveness and efficiency increase substantially, and they are able to make significant contributions to the achievement of the unit's goals.

Self-Awareness. The ability to "sensing that permits people to have a more exact and accurate understanding of the leader's moods and feelings" is one definition of self-awareness. It largely involves understanding one's thoughts, emotions, and behaviours, and how they impact oneself and others. Engaging in reflective techniques that elicit one's inner sentiments, emotions, and state of being is essential to develop self-awareness. This reflective process is one of the essential aspects of spirituality. The process can take the form of meditation, deep thinking, prayers or preaching. Yoga and meditation augmented with discourses on spirituality can help an individual become self-aware and understand issues from the correct perspective. It makes him aware of his strengths and weaknesses and so too of his team. Spirituality can provide a framework for individuals to explore and understand their inner world, as well as their connection to the world around them. Practices such as meditation and mindfulness can help individuals develop a greater awareness of their thoughts, emotions, and physical sensations. By learning to observe these experiences without judgement, individuals can gain a deeper understanding of their inner core. This process can help individuals gain a clearer understanding of what is important to them and what motivates their actions. Useful spiritual practices such as journaling and contemplation can help individuals reflect on their experiences and gain insights into their patterns of thinking and behaviour. The importance of compassion which can be developed through spiritual means has been adequately covered before. Spirituality can encourage individuals to cultivate compassion and empathy towards themselves and others. This can help individuals become more aware of how their actions impact others and can inspire them to make positive changes in their lives. Thus, by exploring their inner world and developing a deeper understanding of themselves, leaders can become more self-aware and better equipped to navigate the challenges of life.

Visioning. Visioning involves understanding the relationship between controlling thoughts, having faith, and visioning. As per all spiritual teachings, control over one's mind is the most important prerequisite for a leader. As per the *Vedas*, this aspect has been symbolically shown by a chariot with a rider. The rider who symbolises the intellect of an individual is riding the chariot (physical body) and through the reins (mind) controlling the horses (senses). Visioning relies heavily on one's ability to keep their thoughts under check. 'The best of friends when controlled but worst enemies when uncontrolled' – this is how Krishna describes our minds to Arjuna according to the *Bhagavad Gita*.[32] Mental mastery contributes to better focus abilities. The entire team will be compelled to act similarly if their leader shows total dedication towards achieving organizational objectives. Any resistance at any level gradually diminishes, if present. For military leaders, visioning is an essential skill as it provides a clear direction and purpose to their organisation. A vision is a compelling image of the future that inspires people to work towards a common goal. By creating and communicating a vision, military leaders can motivate their teams to achieve their goals and objectives. This important facet of spirituality can enable leaders in many ways:

(a) *Creates a sense of purpose.* A clear vision helps military leaders communicate the purpose of their organization and how it contributes to the larger mission. This helps to motivate and inspire team members to work towards a common goal.

(b) *Provides direction.* A well-defined vision provides a clear direction for the organization, which helps military leaders make strategic decisions and allocate resources effectively. It also ensures that everyone is working towards the same goals and objectives.

(c) *Fosters innovation.* A compelling vision encourages military leaders to think outside the box and explore new ways of achieving their goals. It encourages creativity and innovation, which leads to new approaches and solutions.

(d) *Increases engagement.* A clear and inspiring vision can increase engagement among team members, which can improve morale and performance. When people are motivated by a common overall aim, they work together and support each other wholeheartedly.

(e) *Enhances Accountability.* A well-communicated vision provides a framework for measuring progress and holding team members accountable for their actions. It helps to ensure that everyone is working towards the same goals and objectives and helps to identify areas for improvement.

Authenticity. "In other words, authenticity is when a person takes responsibility for their own feelings, values, and opinions and acts accordingly."[33] Authenticity, when reflected in the leader has an infectious effect on subordinates, who start believing in the purpose of the action. Integrity and loyalty are reflected in the complete team's effort, all emanating from the authenticity and ethical behaviour displayed by the leader. A complete environment of trust, camaraderie and loyalty to the organisation sets in. Authenticity is a critical requirement for military leaders as it establishes trust and credibility with their teams, and enables them to lead with integrity. Authentic leaders are transparent, honest, and genuine in their communication, actions, and interactions with their teams. By being true to themselves and their values, military leaders can build strong, cohesive teams that are capable of achieving their goals even in challenging circumstances. They are true to themselves and their values, and their behaviour is consistent with their words. The importance of authenticity for military leaders holds special significance as it helps in:

(a) *Establishing trust.* Authenticity builds trust and credibility with team members. When military leaders are authentic, they are perceived as genuine, reliable, and dependable, which can increase the confidence of team members in their leadership.

(b) *Enhancing Communication.* Authentic leaders communicate openly and honestly with their teams, which can increase the effectiveness of communication. When team members feel that their leaders are sincere, they are more likely to be receptive to their message.

(c) *Inspiring loyalty.* Authentic leaders inspire loyalty and commitment in their teams. When leaders demonstrate a strong commitment to their values and their team's goals, team members are more likely to follow their example and work towards achieving those goals.

(d) *Building resilience.* Authentic leaders can help build resilience in their teams by creating a culture of trust and transparency. When team members feel that they can be themselves and express their opinions openly, they are able to handle adversity with a higher degree of success.

(e) *Promoting ethical behaviour.* Authentic leaders exhibit ethical behaviour and hold themselves and their teams accountable to high standards of integrity. This can help prevent unethical behaviour and promote a culture of honesty and fairness.

Having seen the relevance and benefits of spirituality in general and as it pertains to leadership in particular, in the next chapter an in-depth analysis of spirituality and its impact on military leadership will be carried out to see how spirituality will enable Indian military leadership, as also, understand ways in which it could prepare military leaders to be more effective in combat and non-combat situations.

NOTES

1. Houston George Gregory, "Spirituality and Leadership: Integrating Spirituality as a Developmental Approach of Improving Overall Leader Effectiveness" (2014). *Dissertations & Theses.* 87. Accessed on 10 June 2021 at https://aura.antioch.edu/etds/87/http://aura.antioch.edu/etds/8
2. Peri Dinakar. 'Over half of Army personnel under severe stress: Study', *The Hindu*, 8 January2021. Accessed on 19 June 2021 at https://www.thehindu.com/news/national/over-half-of-army-personnel-under-severe-stress-study/article33528310.ece
3. Reave Laura. 'Spiritual values and practices related to leadership effectiveness,' *The Leadership Quarterly*, vol. 16, issue 5, 2005, pp 655-687.

4. Frederic and Mary Ann Brussat. '*What is Everyday spirituality?*' Accessed on 21 June 2021 at https://www.spiritualityandpractice.com/about/what-is-everyday-spirituality
5. Sant Rajinder Singh Ji Maharaj. '*Science of Spirituality*', Accessed on 15 June 2021 at https://www.sos.org/science-of-spirituality/
6. Ibid.
7. Sharon Jennis. '*Spirituality for Dummies*', Accessed on 7 May 2021 at https://www.spiritual-happiness.com/sfdch1.html
8. Elizabeth Scott. '*What is Spirituality? Spirituality Can Benefit Your Health and Well-Being*', Accessed on 7 May 2021 at https://www.verywellmind.com/how-spirituality-can-benefit-mental-and-physical-health-3144807.
9. Spencer Maya. '*What is spirituality? A personal exploration*', Accessed on 13 February 2023 at https://www.rcpsych.ac.uk/docs/default-source/members/sigs/spirituality-spsig/what-is-spirituality-maya-spencer-x.pdf?sfvrsn=f28df052_2#:~:text=Dr%20Maya%20 Spencer,cosmic%20or%20divine%20in%20nature.
10. Sri Sri Ravi. '*What Spirituality Can Do For You - What Sri Sri Said*', Japan, 2 April 2017. Accessed on 21 June 2021 at https://www.artofliving.org/wisdom/wssst/transcript-of-osaka-2-april-2017.
11. Spirit of Islam. '*Spirituality in Islam: Towards Global Peace and Spiritual Living*', February 2015. Accessed on 21 June 2021 at https://spiritofislam.co.in/spiritnew/index.php/ari4.
12. Sadhguru. '*Spirituality is a Certain Way of Being*', Accessed on 10 June 2021 at https://isha.sadhguru.org/yoga/yoga-articles-spirituality/what-is-spirituality/
13. *Hindu Janjagruti Samiti*. 'Why is man interested in Spirituality?', Accessed on 10 June 2021 at https://www.hindujagruti.org/hinduism/knowledge/article/why-is-man-interested-in-spirituality.html#:~:text=The%20word%20'adhyatma%20(%E0%A4%85%E0%A4%A7%E0%A5%8D %E2%80%8D%E0%A4%AF%E0%A4%BE%E0%A4%A4%E0%A5%8D%E2%80%8D%E0%A4%AE), to%20the%20soul%20(Atma).
14. Mark W. Muesse. 'Buddhist Spirituality', *Centre for Spiritual Growth in Memphis*, Tennessee, 2002. Accessed on 13 August 2021 at http://www.explorefaith.org/livingspiritually/following_a_sacred_path/buddhist_spirituality.php
15. The Art of Living. '*7 myths about spirituality debunked*', Accessed on 23 February 2023 at https://www.artofliving.org/in-en/wisdom/spirituality/myths-about-spirituality
16. Howell Ryan T. '*Why Be Spiritual? Five Benefits of Spirituality*', February, 2013. Accessed on 16 July 2021 at https://www.psychologytoday.com/us/blog/cant-buy-happiness/201302/why-be-spiritual-five-benefits-spirituality
17. Swami Krishnananda. '*The Philosophy of Life*'. Accessed on 21 July 2021 at https://www.swami-krishnananda.org/disc/disc_365.html.
18. Ibid.
19. Ibid.
20. Yogapedia. '*Raja yoga*', 10 September 2020. Accessed on 10 July 2021 at https://www.yoga pedia.com/definition/5338/raja-yoga
21. *Good Reads*, 'Quotes of Swami Vivekananda'. Accessed on 13 July 2022 at https://www.goodreads.com/quotes/7174617-talk-to-yourself-at-least-once-in-a-day-otherwise
22. The Art of Living. 'The essential guide: 8 limbs of yoga by Maharishi Patanjali', Accessed on 17 July 2021 at https://www.artofliving.org/in-en/yoga/yoga-beginners/types-of-yoga
23. Giacalone, R. A.; Jurkiewicz, C. L. & Fry, L. W. (2005). 'From advocacy to science: The next steps in workplace spirituality', A research. In R. F. Paloutzian & C. L. Park (eds.), *Handbook of Psychology and Religion,* pp. 515-528). Thousand Oaks, CA: Sage. Accessed at http://

psychology.iresearchnet.com/industrial-organizational-psychology/leadership-and-management/spirituality-and-leadership-at-work/

24. Korac Kakabadse, N., Kouzmin, A. and Kakabadse, A. (2002). "Spirituality and leadership praxis", *Journal of Managerial Psychology,* vol. 17, no. 3, pp. 165-182. Can be accessed at https://doi.org/10.1108/02683940210423079
25. Riger, M. & Seng, Y. (2005), Leadership with inner meaning: A contingency theory of leadership based on the worldviews of five religions, *Leadership Quarterly*, 16, 771-806. Accessed at https://cpb-ap-se2.wpmucdn.com/thinkspace.csu.edu.au/dist/b/3332/files/2017/06/leadership-with-spiritual-meaning-2dyqf07.pdf
26. Server, Prem. 'Spiritual values in leadership and the effects on organizational performance: A literature review', University of Northern British Columbia, April 2013. Pp. 10-12.
27. Reave, Laura. 'Spiritual values and practices related to leadership effectiveness,' *The Leadership Quality Journal,* vol. 16, issue 5, October 2005, pp. 655-687. https://psycnet.apa.org/doi/10.1016/j.leaqua.2005.07.003
28. Russell, R. F. 'The role of values in servant leadership'. *Leadership & Organization Development Journal,* vol. 22, no. 2, 2001, pp. 76-84. https://doi.org/10.1108/01437730110382631
29. Joanna Barsh, Susie Cranston, and Rebecca A. Craske. 'Cantered leadership: How talented women thrive', *Mckinsey Quarterly,* 1 September 1, 2008. Accessed at https://www.mckinsey.com/featured-insights/leadership/centered-leadership-how-talented-women-thrive
30. Ibid.
31. Reave. op. cit.
32. Swami Mukundananda. '*Commentary on Bhagavad Gita: Chapter 6, Verse 6*'. Accessed on 16 July 2021 at https://www.holy-bhagavad-gita.org/chapter/6/verse/6
33. Gardner, W. L. & Schermerhorn, J. R., 'Performance gains through positive Organizational Behaviour and Authentic Leadership'. *Organizational Dynamics,* 33(3), 2004, pp. 270-281. http://dx.doi.org/10.1016/j.orgdyn.2004.06.004

Chapter Four

Spirituality and Indian Military Leadership

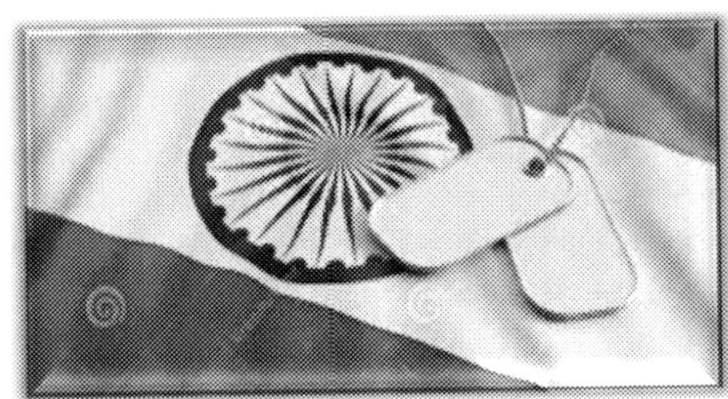

अमृतं चौव मृत्युश्च द्वयं देहे प्रतिष्ठितम् ।
मोहादापद्यते मृत्युः सत्येनापद्यतेऽमृतम् ।।

Immortality and death, both reside in the body only.
Death comes out of delusion, and immorality comes out of the truth.

– ***Adi Shankaracharya***

For the section, a questionnaire was sent to the respondents. The questions were: Is there a need to create an intrinsically motivated Indian Armed Forces that has a high level of spiritual fitness? Will spirituality enable Indian military leadership by making it more humane and empathetic? Will spirituality help in developing attributes such as empathy, sacrifice, and compassion? Which amongst these is most important: Physical fitness, emotional fitness, spiritual fitness, or intellectual fitness? What is the level of spiritual quotient in members of Armed Forces presently? The responses to these questions are presented through the following pie charts.

Q 1. There is a need to create an intrinsically motivated, learning Indian Armed Forces having high level of spiritual fitness.

822 Responses

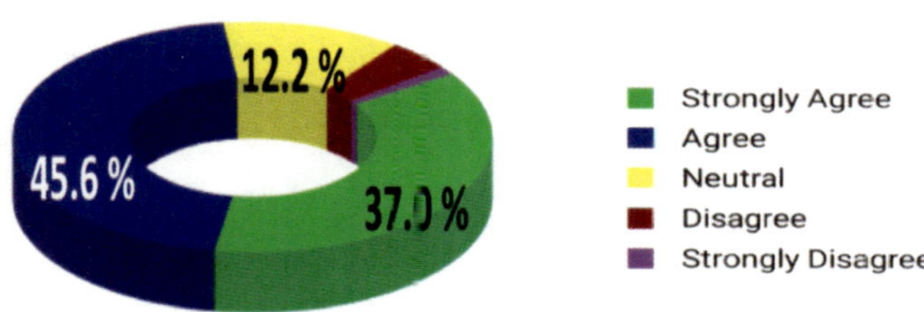

Q 2. Spirituality can enable military leadership by making it more humane and empathetic.

822 Responses

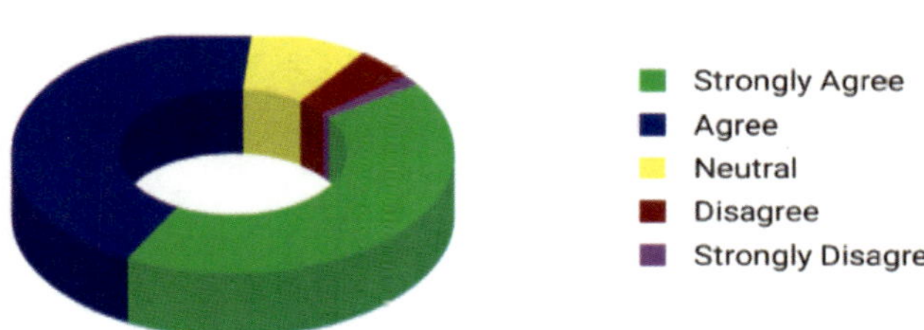

Q 3. Qualitative aspects of leadership like integrity, motivation, sacrifice, empathy, compassion, etc., can be developed by focusing on spiritualism.

822 Responses

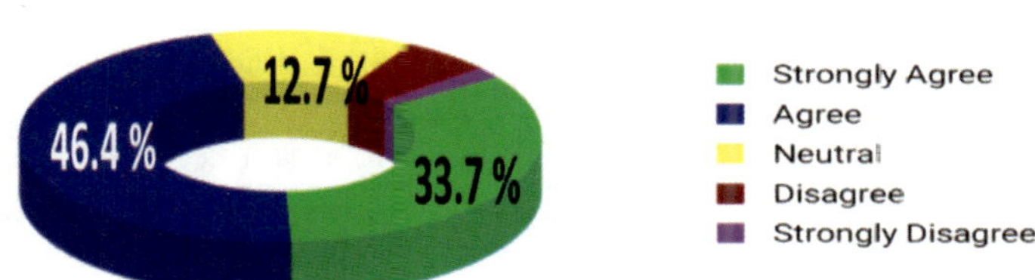

Q 4. Aspects of physical fitness, emotional fitness and intellectual fitness are well known. Spiritual fitness can be defined as the ability to adhere to beliefs, principles and values needed to persevere and prevail by a deeper understanding of the self. Based on this understanding, as concerns Indian military leadership, rank as per order of importance from 1 to 4 (with '1' being most important and '4' the least) (Pan to the left for viewing all options).

822 Responses

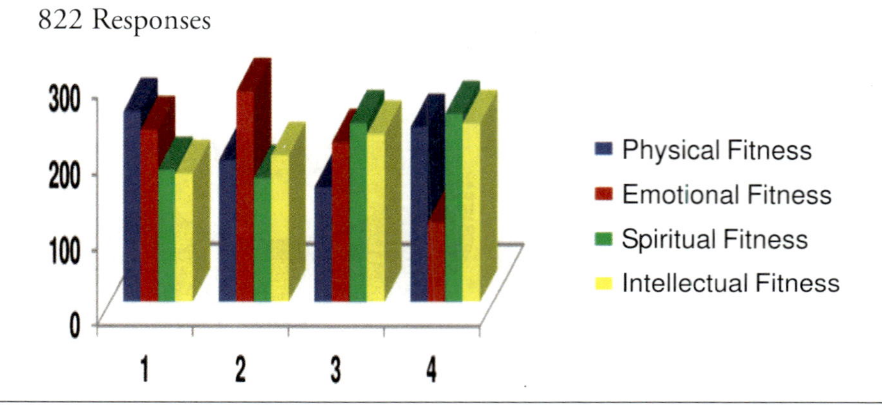

Q 5. In your opinion, what level of Spiritual Quotient do members of Indian Armed Forces possess?

822 Responses

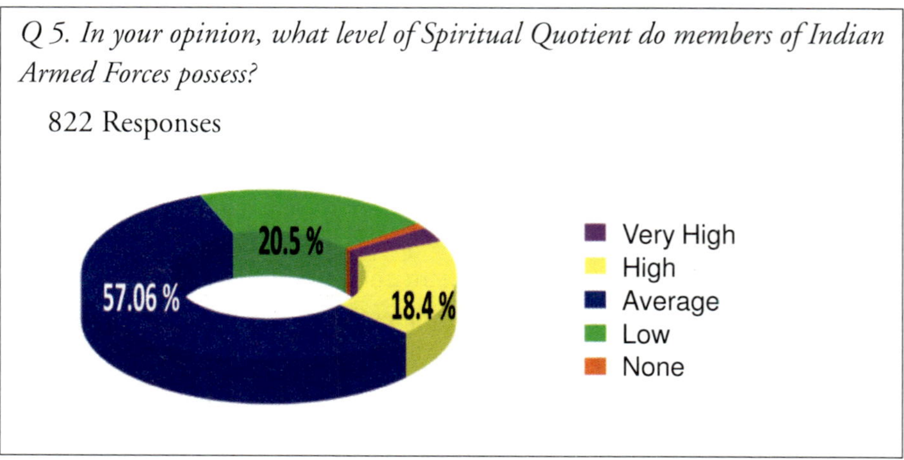

A brief analysis of the responses received is as under:

(a) A majority of 83 per cent feels that there is a need to create an intrinsically motivated Indian Armed Force that has a high level of spiritual fitness.

(b) A sizeable majority of 86 per cent feels that spirituality will enable the military leadership to make itself more humane and empathetic.

(c) A majority of 81 per cent feels that spirituality will help in developing attributes such as empathy, sacrifice, and compassion.

(d) As regards fitness levels, the order of importance is: emotional fitness, spiritual fitness, intellectual fitness, and physical fitness.

(e) About half the respondents believe that the level of spiritual quotient amongst the members of the Armed Forces is 'Average'.

Having seen leadership, particularly, Indian military leadership and spirituality in the previous chapters, this chapter examines the suitability/compatibility of spirituality in the domain of Indian military leadership. Chapter 2A has elucidated at length upon the stresses and challenges that are faced by today's Indian military leadership. Chapter 3 has brought out the numerous benefits that spirituality has to offer. This chapter looks at the feasibility of spirituality and Indian military leadership co-existing and that too in a beneficial manner.

Spirituality: An Enabler of Indian Military Leadership

कर्मण्येवाधिकारस्ते मा फलेषु कदाचन ।
मा कर्मफलहेतुर्भूर्मा ते सङ्गोऽस्त्वकर्मणि ॥

—*Bhagavad Gita, Chapter 2, Verse 47*

"*Thy business is with action only, never with its fruits,*
So let not the fruit of action be thy motive, nor be thou to inaction attached."

General. In consonance with our democratic traditions and ethos, the Indian Army prides itself on its apolitical nature and a strong secular base. Soldiers, generally from the rural areas, come from different social, regional and religious backgrounds and are mostly deeply influenced by spirituality and age-old cultural values. Spirituality per se may not be able to provide solutions to strategic, operational or tactical problems associated with soldiering but it will no doubt assist in building the character of soldiers, enabling them to imbibe a better human value system and this in turn will improve their judgment, decision making, exploitation of opportunities presented, crisis management, etc. The following paragraphs bring out the benefits that spirituality will offer to military leadership.

Enhances Work Effectiveness

Spirituality and Work. It is largely believed that spirituality and work effectiveness are non-related. While spirituality is a religious experience felt individually or collectively, work effectiveness is related to intellectual activity that results in tangible results. Such an understanding may be misplaced.

We understand that the essence of any effectiveness (could be related to work) is defined through results. Thus, any factor that assists in improvement of effectiveness should be seen to be contributing towards it. We have already seen earlier in the research that in today's work environment (Indian defence forces included), effectiveness at work is affected by numerous factors such as societal pressures, materialism, etc. This is where spirituality can be the game changer. Through an enhanced understanding of human behaviour and development of EQ, the individual would be better equipped to handle work pressures and thus his work effectiveness would be exponentially enhanced.

In earlier chapters we have seen that a soldier is exposed to a variety of negative socio-economic and professional pressures, resulting in undesirable effects on him as well as on the organisation. These pressures and their ill effects can be countered with a spiritual or divine awareness which will achieve the following:

(a) Manage tension, negative beliefs, anxiety, nervousness and fear.
(b) Cope with and avoid anger.
(c) Manage time and health in a better manner by incorporating life changes.
(d) Practice interactive decision making.
(e) Achieve happiness and satisfaction.

Having achieved the above, the following would be developed leading to resultant enhanced work efficiency:

(a) Improved unit cohesion.
(b) Sense of uniqueness and eliteness.
(c) Orientation towards mission achievement.
(d) Increased alertness and vigilance.
(e) Strength and endurance.
(f) Improved tolerance to hardship, discomfort, pain and injury.
(g) Sense of purpose.
(h) Heroic acts of courage and self-sacrifice.

(j) Increased human touch.

(k) Robust mental health.

Develops Calmness of Mind

The key to happiness and peace with associated benefits is the control of the mind. While it can be easily achieved in good times, doing so in adverse situations is the challenge. One of the key components to achieving it is contemplation and introspection. In the fast life of today, this remains a major challenge.

For every soldier and more so a military leader it is therefore essential to connect with oneself through contemplation and introspection. Doing so would enable calming of mind and lead to a better understanding of the self. This is an important pre-requisite for a soldier who is being regularly called on to handle life and death situations in difficult terrain and adverse climatic conditions.

Improves Concentration

Achievement of any aim or goal is facilitated by concentration. It is the ability to not get distracted from the task at hand and work towards the achievement of the desired end state without being distracted. In the *Mahabharata* it is said that when Arjun was to shoot an arrow at a fish placed on the top of a revolving pole by looking only at its reflection in the water, he concentrated solely on the eye of the fish and thus hit the target. In essence, mindfulness, right effort and concentration will lead to task/goal accomplishment.

Thus, soldiers must know the art of improving their concentration, propagated by various yoga proponents. One such scientific method of developing the power of concentration, the 'Hong-Sau' technique, was propagated by Sri Paramhansa Yogananda (the author of '*Autobiography of a Yogi*') and has been found to be very effective by all those practising it.

Enhances Will Power

A strong will power is a hallmark of a man in uniform; in fact, it is more or less a prerequisite for a soldier. It is even more essential for a leader in the Armed Forces. Yoga techniques combine physical well-being with the discoveries of modern physiological science. One such form of yoga known as

'Hatha yoga' facilitates a number of *asanas* and postures that strengthen and develop will power. In this, development, will and body are inter-linked and interdependent and one leads to another.

Countering Stress with Yoga/Relaxation

It has been seen in the earlier parts as to what negative impact could be caused on human beings, including soldiers, due to excessive stress, accruing due to a variety of reasons. Therefore, there is a need to manage this stress. Though a number of steps are being taken in the Armed Forces to counter the effect of this menace, medical research has proved that spiritual approach is possibly the best one!

Countering Stress. Most practitioners feel that the practice of yoga, meditation and *pranayama* helps in combating and countering stress. This is so as they not only affect the body but actually touch the source of our being. In doing so, they allow us to turn inwards. This in turn reduces stress significantly as the source of all stress that we feel and perceive is on account of our interaction and subsequent reaction to stimuli coming from external sources.

Assists in Controlling Anger and Overcoming Fear

Controlling Anger. Anger is one alphabet short of DANGER. Anger is the root cause of misery and stress. It gives birth to brain paralysis, revengefulness, destructive instinct, spite, jealousy, hatred and temporary insanity which leads to loss of control and an unstable mind.

Anger can be controlled through keeping one's mind calm. At junctures like these it is essential to take a pause or a step back and slow down the process thereby allowing for oneself the time to recollect and calm the mind.

Overcoming Fear. Fear results in anxiety, tension and lowering of confidence and these in turn lead to failure or non-achievement of the aim. An inculcation of spirituality that leads to self-actualisation helps us to develop a better understanding of our fears and thus helps in combating them better.

Creates Individuals of Strong Character

Character is the priceless attribute of an individual and is the net total of a person's values, beliefs and personality. Our behaviour and our actions are a reflection of our character. To succeed, a strong character is essential and thus character has to be developed and preserved at all costs.

Mostly, individuals of strong character have a good understanding of themselves and thus are good judges of the reasons for their failure or success. In trying times, they can stand up and take responsibility for their actions and do not look to apportion blame to others. They are also not affected or distracted by negative and adverse conditions/circumstances and can withstand the strongest of storms. Thus, they are ideal leaders for all situations. Character can be developed and enhanced through spirituality.

Teaches us that 'To forgive is Divine'

> "*Anger dissolves affection therefore; man should subvert anger by forgiveness.*"
>
> —*Samana Suttam*

Most organisations suffer from the 'zero error syndrome' wherein mistakes/errors are reacted to in a violent/disagreeable manner and thus subordinates rather than owning and reporting their mistakes, end up hiding them. There could also be occasions where individuals who are of a weak personality look to let others down on account of them falling prey to their own fears or weaknesses. In situations where someone is looking to hurt you or when mistakes are made, the ability to forgive plays an important role. Such ability is feasible when a person has inherent strength and calm assuredness to be secure in his skin. Invariably, individuals who are able to forgive and look beyond small things are spiritually evolved.

Facilitates Decision Making

On the face of it, success stories appear to be smooth sailing and easy going wherein the downs and risk are non-existent. This though is far from the truth. Succeeding mostly involves strong and timely decision making and at times this involves taking calculated risks. Calculated risk taking is completely different from rash behaviour and is in no way connected with bad luck.

While the ability to take risks is relative, it is generally seen that individuals who are spiritually inclined are not risk averse and can take greater calculated risks. Why is this so? This is on account of the fact that a spiritual person being aware of oneself is more confident in his abilities and also ready to face the consequences of decisions going wrong. Thus, while sky diving seems to be a dangerous sport fraught with huge risk, for trained sky divers the same may not be so as it is a skill set developed through knowledge, training and the courage to act while facing fear. These attributes are built through an awakening of spirituality. A person who takes calculated risks does so because he realizes that taking timely decisions on incomplete information is better than delayed decisions based on detailed information. There is no doubt that spirituality improves decision making by enhancing the ability to make decisions in situations involving risk.

Teaches how to Treat a Subordinate

Rebuking a subordinate or colleague in public (not acceptable at all) or in private tends to demoralize the individual and leads to a loss of confidence and self-esteem. By destructive criticism one pushes an individual deeper into the mire of despondency. Such individuals will underperform and never be able to contribute their full potential. Thus, not only the individual but his team and the organization will always be at a disadvantage.

The job of a leader is to prop up a subordinate with loving and encouraging words leading to constructive criticism. This ability comes in a spiritually awakened leader as he can empathize with a subordinate and be benevolent to him even when he errs.

Spirituality and Economy of Effort

Vedic philosophy and scriptures always speak of accomplishing more with less. Thus, the aim is to ensure that by performing to your optimum potential the least amount of effort is expended to achieve any given aim/task. Such ability arises when the team functions with a sense of belief awakened by a leader who always puts the team's requirements above his own. Having the ability to do so arises in a leader who can stay out of the spotlight and be secure even without being given credit. Leaders who are inclined towards spirituality will be able to do the above with ease.

Develops *Vaak Shakti*

Shardha Batra in her piece in *The Times of India*[1] has spoken about the power that a spiritually awakened person wields as regards the ability to speak while keeping the other person's views in mind. She says that the *Shabd Brahm* is the essence of all that exists. According to her a spiritually awakened individual has the ability to listen and hold diametrically opposite/contrary views of the other with all due respect. This ability comes with the belief that the knower's consciousness is one with the consciousness of the known and thus there is only one truth with the balance perceptions being false. Thus, a spiritually awakened individual is also known as a '*vachaspati*' or an individual who transcends fixed opinions created by the self-serving and manipulating ego.

Pay-offs of Spirituality

Having seen the ways in which spirituality will enable military leadership, let us summarize the major spin offs of this enabler. They are as under:

(a) Meaningfulness.
(b) Nurturing leader.
(c) Overall happiness.
(d) Work that makes sense.
(e) Felt connection with subordinates and superiors.
(f) Integration of head and heart.
(g) Common goal.
(h) Avoiding burn out and maintaining sound health.
(j) Effective stress management.
(k) Control over negative emotions, for example, fear, anger, etc.
(l) Morals and ethics.
(m) Self-actualization.
(n) Open and honest dealings.
(o) Treating subordinates humanely and with respect.
(p) Getting the job done with dignity.
(q) Strong character and will power.
(r) Enhanced risk taking and intuitive abilities.
(s) More effective decision making.
(t) Transcend BMI.
(u) Team spirit.
(v) Economy of effort.

(w) Mutually supportive and co-operative attitude.

(x) Equanimity.

(y) Non-judgmental.

To summarise, a spiritually enabled military leader will be able to do the following:

(a) Open lines of communication, leading to more informed, wise decisions.

(b) Keep his word, thus building trustworthiness.

(c) Foster proactive responses and focus on resolving issues, rather than reacting.

(d) Generate a sense of sincere caring for his subordinates.

(e) Have an uplifting spirit of collaboration and respect for people resources, and the environment.

On the basis of the deliberations undertaken in the research till now, the following emerges:

(a) Due to domination of the world by the Western powers for a prolonged period, leadership styles have been influenced by Western values. These may not be best suited for leadership, especially military leadership to be undertaken in an Indian context. Thus, there is a felt need to review the leadership principles/practices in vogue. It would be therefore prudent to arrive at a leadership theory that amalgamates the best from the West with the strengths of Indian philosophy.

(b) There is ample evidence that spirituality is the need of the hour It improves the quality of leadership to include military leadership and people the world over are falling back to it.

(c) Inclusion of relevant extracts from scriptures, life histories/biographies of brilliant and successful leaders of yesteryears, yoga, *pranayama* and meditation in leadership training will help in developing better military leadership.

Spiritual Military Leadership

Having seen how spirituality will enable and benefit military leadership, let us now build upon the concept of spiritual military leadership.

Why is Spiritual Military Leadership Required? Before moving any further let us quickly summarise as why spiritual military leadership is required in today's contemporary environment. From chapter 2 we are aware of the fact that the demands on military leadership have changed significantly. Until the last decade, having professional soundness, vision, and man management skills were considered to be adequate to become a successful leader. Contemporary leadership though demands the following:

(a) Bring out the best in subordinates.

(b) Foster psychological and physical well-being.

(c) Help soldiers to find meaning, connection and balance.

(d) Encourage organization/team commitment, responsibility, strong sense of trust, open communication and awareness.

(e) Always be fair and transparent in all decisions and dealings.

(f) Embrace change and explore chances for growth.

(g) Have genuine care about your team, community and society.

The above requires more than just skills and competencies; it requires leaders to be truly developed as human beings and committed to their own wellbeing and that of their subordinates and organization. A leadership developed with spirituality as the spinal cord, can possibly exhibit a higher form of military leadership.

Ankur Rommel in his piece '*Science, Art and Philosophy of War*'[2] stated that while many have written about the art and science of war, there is very little material on the philosophy of war. This has resulted in an incorrect understanding about the connect between spirituality and military leadership. According to him, the philosophy of war, besides other aspects, deals with the moral and ethical dimensions of war. He therefore feels that the philosophical aspect of war is far more important and critical than the art and science of war. Thus, he believes that while the tactical and operational military leaders can handle the art and science of war, the strategic military leaders should look at the philosophy of war.

Who is a Spiritual Soldier? At the outset, it is essential to understand who is a spiritual soldier. This is necessary as it is felt in certain quarters that a spiritual soldier would be someone who renounces worldly pleasures and goes to the mountains to live like an ascetic!! Such a thought therefore further expands into believing that spiritual leadership would be too weak to take strong decisions and would essentially comprise religious-minded bigots who would radicalize the army and thus destroy its secular fabric. From all that has been elucidated in this research earlier, it would be evident that nothing can be farther from the truth. Spiritual leaders are self-aware individuals who have the capacity to provide a vision for others to emulate, while being non-judgmental, kind and compassionate.

Are Soldiers inherently Spiritual? Essentially, all military leaders are soldiers. Before looking at the benefits of spirituality for soldiers, let us take a look at the question whether soldiers are spiritual?

Spirituality is being responsible for one's life and to value life. Similarly, a soldier values life and is committed to protect life, and is committed to his role. A soldier is aware that he is there because of all that his country stands for and his country thrives because of what he does. Thus, a soldier works for a higher ideal with selflessness. Selfishness is human; selflessness is divine and spiritual.

A soldier is the only person who is perpetually confronting death in trying to protect life, society and his nation. He therefore remains committed and shoulders a responsibility of the highest order. That is why he is spiritual. Other virtues are easy to understand and co-relate.

If this be the case, all that is needed is to make soldiers aware of their inherent 'spirituality' so that they are able to use it to optimize their individual output as well as contribute to the overall enhancement of his organization and the nation.

Tenets of Spiritual Military Leadership

A spiritual military leader is one of a 'pure mind'. To have a pure mind, five tenets are essential to understand and imbibe. Thus, there are five tenets of spiritual military leadership. These are as under:

(a) Lower Self vs. the Higher Self.

(b) Guna Dynamics (The Theory of Psychological Forces).

(c) Karma Theory (Laws of Cause and Effect).

(d) Karma Yog (The Art and Science of Work).

(e) Panch Wrin (Giving Model of Motivation or Five-fold Indebtedness).

Lower Self vs. Higher Self. The human personality has two layers as it were; the empirical lower self (*Vyavaharik Vyaktitva*) and the trans-empirical higher, deeper self (*Parmarthic Vyaktiva*). The empirical self or the lower self is deficit driven, conditional, dependent, apprehensive, insecure and hence prone to pettiness. The higher self is constitutionally *poorna* (complete), unconditioned, independent and fearless. The higher self is ever secure and hence prone to dignity. As long as we are tied up exclusively with the lower-self base, we have little hope of moving away from petty behaviour. For higher order behaviour, we need to awaken the dormant higher self, which is present in each one of us. The characteristics of the higher self are eternally perfect, constantly blissful, entirely self-sufficient and in fact truth and light in itself.

Thus, the important question is: How do we transform our lower self into the higher self? Reflection, meditation and concentration are the means to build the alternative platform of SELF in our consciousness. In short, for realizing the higher SELF we need to de-link with the lower SELF and completely link with the higher SELF.

Guna Dynamics (Theory of Psychological Forces). The focus of the Guna theory is on the basic attributes of the human being. The three *gunas* are '*Sattwa*', '*Rajas*' and '*Tamas*'. They are inter-related in a hierarchical order, where *Sattwa* is relatively the highest or best, *Rajas* the middle and Tamas the lowest or worst. Aurobindo says that *Sattwaguna* is the first mediator between man's lower and higher natures. *Sattwa* represents the ascending thrust, *Rajas* the lateral expanding pressure and *Tamas* the descending pull in man's character.

An analogy can be drawn between these psychological forces and a candle. The light of the flame or the illumination provided by the candle is '*Sattwa*', the wax is the '*Rajas*' and the wick is the '*Tamas*'.

Karma Theory (Laws of Cause and Effect). The essence of the Karma theory (or laws of cause and effect) can be summarized in the following five rules:

(a) Every cause will lead to an effect some time in the future.

(b) Effects in the present, would have causes from the past.

(c) Every effect can be traced to its cause.

(d) The effect is in direct correlation to its cause.

(e) All causes will have their effect without exception.

In effect, the law of Karma, explains the driving force in man, which impels him to act. Essentially, every individual makes or breaks his own destiny. Through repeated actions, habits are formed, these in turn form an individual's character and this defines his destiny. Thus, only through self-awareness and self-discipline can an individual achieve mastery of self and this would lead to the cycle of good karma.

***Karma Yog* (The Art and Science of Work).** The study of scriptures exemplifies '*Nishkam Karma*' as one of the most important facets of one's own ancient wisdom. This theory states that the entire cosmos is working without any desire and thus all actions have to be taken without the desire of the fruits of one's actions. This theory is said to have the following components:

(a) Every individual (leader or soldier) is only concerned with work.

(b) An individual should not have any desire for rewards; however rewards would be given as destined.

(c) Work is not defined by its nature but by the attitude with which it is done.

(d) Work which is done with complete sincerity and consciousness is one which is considered to be of the highest order.

Following this theory would lead to the establishment of an ideal work environment in any organization. This is however easier said than done, as the essence of human nature is to seek rewards for actions. This is more the case in today's world where there are no actions without an end result in mind. Thus, to ensure the successful accomplishment of this theory, a spiritual leader should show the way with his transparent and sincere methods and selfless actions.

***Pancha Wrin* (Giving Model of Motivation).** While the Western view has largely linked actions with rewards and a favourable end state, the same is not the case with ancient Indian wisdom and philosophy. In our philosophy, it is always about 'giving' and never about 'taking'. An understanding of what is meant by this can be gleaned from the nature around us wherein, forests and trees are always giving us without taking anything or expecting anything in return. This 'Indian giving model' is not only restricted to the action of parting with something but also doing so with all humility and gratitude on account of being indebted for all that one has already received in life. Hindu philosophy speaks of five types of indebtedness:

(a) *Deva Wrin.* Indebtedness for air, light, water and land to powers greater than us.

(b) *Rishi Wrin.* Indebtedness for the higher truths and heritage given to us by our sages and seers.

(c) *Priti Wrin.* Indebtedness for our present life and state to our parents and ancestors

(d) *Nri Wrin.* Indebtedness for all the things that one is getting but has not worked for on account of the contributions of others who one may know or nor know, remember or forgotten.

(e) *Bhuta Wrin.* Indebtedness for all the experiences provided by species that are sub-human like flora and fauna.

Having seen the five tenets of spiritual military leadership, let us now turn towards practising spiritual military leadership.

Developing and Practising Spiritual Military Leadership

A study of successful leaders will show that they are men of high values who have the right attitude and always display positive behaviour. This coupled with the deliberations undertaken in this research on spirituality, military leadership and the interconnect between them, has helped me to arrive at a methodology for developing and practising spiritual military leadership. Based on the understanding reached through this research, it can be deduced that the development and practice of spiritual military leadership can be devolved into three words Imbibe – Build – Exhibit or IBE, wherein development of spiritual military leadership is undertaken through two simultaneous processes, namely, 'Imbibe High Values' and 'Build Right Attitudes'. Post this, spiritual military leadership can be practised through the process of 'Exhibit Positive Behaviour'. Thus, developing and practising spiritual military leadership can be achieved by the following processes:

Imbibe High Values + Build Right Attitudes = Exhibit Positive Behaviour

Imbibe High Values. 'Value' is defined as 'something (such as principle or quality) intrinsically desirable'. A spiritual military leader should aspire to develop and imbibe virtues such as loyalty, integrity, honesty, high morals and courage. While each of these values is important, what defines an individual is his character. Character is the resulting individuality of a person, which is achieved post the imbibing of these good qualities; it is reflected in his conduct. An understanding of character can be gleaned from the following description given by the veteran of World War II, General Mathew B. Ridgeway of the US Army:

> "*Character stands for self-discipline, loyalty,* ***readiness to accept responsibility*** *and* ***willingness to admit mistakes****. It stands for selflessness, modesty, humility and* ***willingness to sacrifice*** *when necessary and, in my opinion,* ***Faith in God****."*

Imbibing Right Values to Develop Unimpeachable Character

Build Right Attitude. 'Attitude' is defined as the state of readiness to respond to a stimulus. A spiritual military leader has to develop the right attitude wherein he is non-judgmental so as to be able to be kind and forgiving. He trusts his subordinates so as to allow them to function independently and is mature in the way he functions. He has the compassion to allow for the weaknesses of his subordinates and most importantly shows gratitude for all that he has got in life. A spiritual military leader with the right attitude will lead by example and show the way for his subordinates to learn and emulate.

Building the Right Attitude

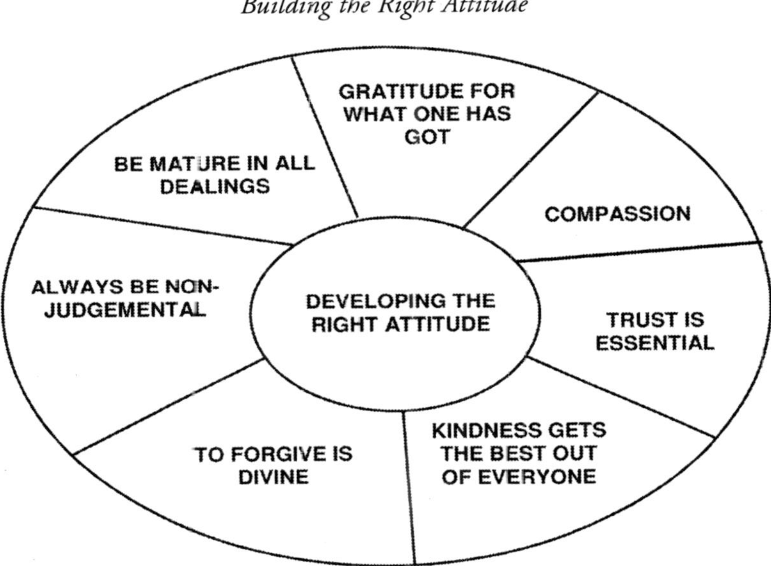

Exhibit Positive Behaviour. 'Behaviour' is defined as 'the response of an individual to his/her environment'. It has already been explained above that development of high values and right attitude will always and without fail result in the exhibition of positive and encouraging behaviour. The journey of developing a positive behaviour that would result in effective spiritual military leadership should commence with an attempt at understanding yourself or developing 'self-awareness'. This is an experiential learning where the learner attempts to gravitate from an external or outward-oriented understanding of oneself to that of looking inwards. An awareness of oneself is not sufficient though, it is also important that the spiritual military leader develops a clear and comprehensive understanding of his job and his environment. Thus, professional competence is a must. Having done this, it is essential to think about others before yourself, that is developing 'selflessness'. What separates a military leader from a spiritual military leader are two essential behavioural attributes: 'nurturing and equanimity'. Thus, a spiritual military leader will pass on his knowledge and provide such an environment wherein his subordinates can grow, by encouraging and nurturing them. More importantly, as life throws up all kinds of situations at a leader, he should display equanimity during the highs and lows of life so as not to be affected by either of them. By doing so, over a period of time such a spiritual military leader will become self-actualised. At that juncture, it is of paramount importance that such a leader should utilise this for the good of the organization and its people. If a spiritual military leader is able to exhibit such positive behaviour, he would be said to have transcended the Body Mind Intellect (BMI).

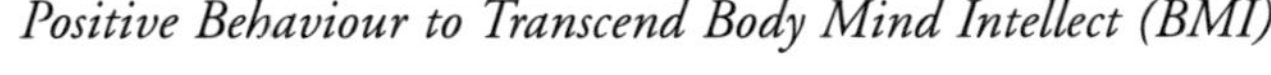
Positive Behaviour to Transcend Body Mind Intellect (BMI)

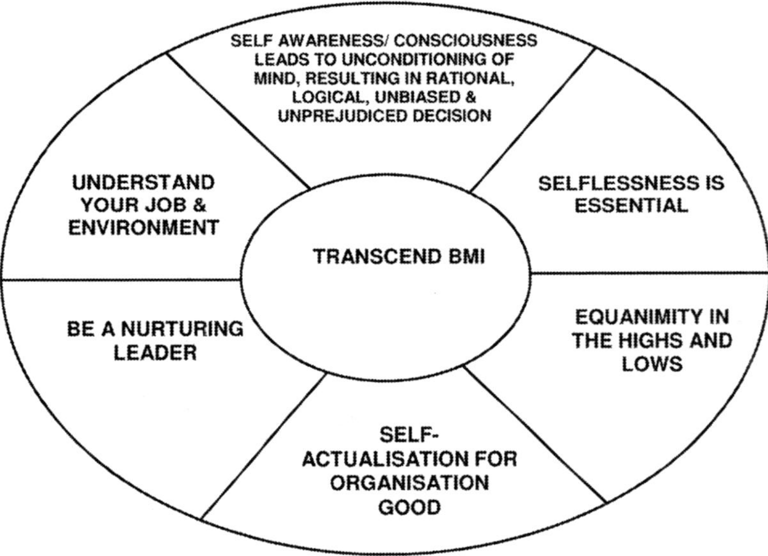

Essentials of a Spiritual Military Leader. Thus, for any leader to develop and practice spiritual military leadership, he should develop and display certain essential values, attitudes and behaviour. These are summarized as under:

Values	*Attitudes*	*Behaviour*
Loyalty	Non-Judgemental	Understand Self/Self Awareness
Integrity	Maturity	Understand job & environment
Honesty	Forgiveness	Nurturing Leader
Courage	Kindness	Selflessness
Morals	Trust	Equanimity
Character	Compassion	Self-Actualisation
Will Power	Gratitude	Transcend BMI

Spiritual Leadership Theory

Having seen what a spiritual military leader should be and how should he lead, let us turn to another important aspect, namely, the development of a spiritual leadership theory that would enable the creation, sustenance and propagation of such spiritual military leaders. While a number of leadership models do exist and these have been discussed at length in Chapter 2A, the model that comes closest to a spiritual leadership model is the transformational model wherein the leader aims at transforming his subordinates for their own good and the larger good of the organisation. One of the transformational leadership models that looks at development of spirituality for the betterment of leadership is the one propagated through the article 'Towards a theory of spiritual leadership' by Louis W. Fry.[3]

In it the author has argued that transformational leadership that incorporates spirituality for the betterment of the leader and the subordinate in the long-term benefits both of them and enhances organizational efficiency and effectiveness. This, according to him is achieved by shifting from an 'External Motivation' to an 'Internal Motivation' model and can be depicted as under:

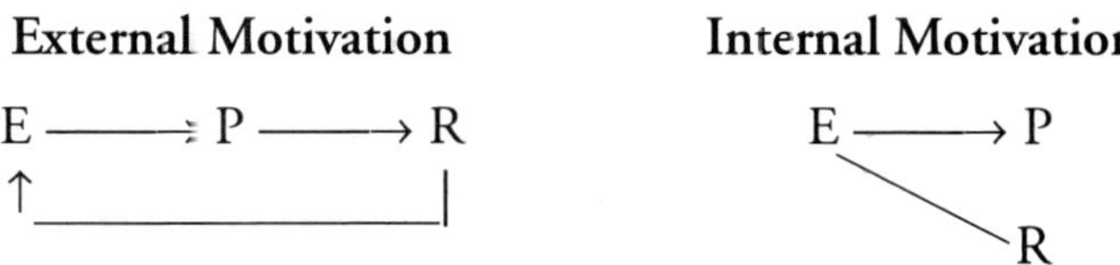

Where E = Effort, P = Performance and R = Reward

Explaining the model, the author states that most of us work on the basis of an 'external motivation model' wherein a 'reward' is essential to sustain the 'effort' which in turn results in 'performance'; the inference being, if there is no reward there is no effort and thus no performance. Rewards can be thought of as promotions, incentives or a pay rise. In essence, there being an external reward, the entire model depends on an external stimulation. Such a model, the author believes, should be replaced by an 'internal motivation model' wherein the performance or work undertaken is the reward itself. In this, the individual needs no external reward as he works with a better understanding of his self and thus requires no external motivation. In essence, he works for his higher self. On the basis of this understanding, the author has elucidated his 'Spiritual leadership theory' that is based upon intrinsic/internal motivation through vision, hope/faith and altruistic love. His enunciation clearly brings out that leadership more so strategic leadership is greatly enhanced and enabled when it draws upon spirituality. The drawback of this model is that it looks at an awakening of spirituality from a Western perspective by relying upon the building of altruistic love through the Church and Chaplain working together as an institution. Thus, while the concept and model can act as the base for the development of a spiritual leadership theory, it needs to be specifically adapted for the Indian military leadership.

Spiritual Leadership Indian Military (SLIM) Theory. This research has clearly established the necessity of spirituality for Indian military leaders and put forward ways in which spirituality will enable the Indian military leadership. It is therefore imperative that a theory be developed that would assist in institutionalizing the development of spirituality in the Indian military. I have also brought out that while Fry's Spiritual leadership theory is applicable in a Western context, its suitability without modification in an Indian context is suspect. There is therefore a need to adapt/modify it for the Indian military environment. Further, this chapter has already elucidated upon the methodology for development and practice of spiritual military leadership by utilizing the IDE concept (Imbibe High Values + Develop Right Attitude = Exhibit Positive Behaviour) which in itself draws heavily from Indian spirituality. Earlier in this chapter we have also discussed the ways in which spirituality has always been integral to Indian leadership to include Indian military leadership and brought out the traits that spirituality helps to develop which are suitable for Indian military leadership. The proposed theory of SLIM therefore looks to build upon Fry's spiritual theory model by incorporating into it the strengths of Indian spirituality. It is hoped that the SLIM theory would be utilized for developing future spiritual Indian military leaders. A proposed SLIM theory model is shown in Figure 2 below and its details are elucidated upon in the following paragraphs.

Environment and Stakeholders. The environment in which the SLIM theory has to work is the Indian military, that is, the three services primarily and includes all actions and activities taken by them within and without. The environment as shown is subject to various stresses and challenges that have been earlier enunciated in earlier chapters. The model has three stakeholders,

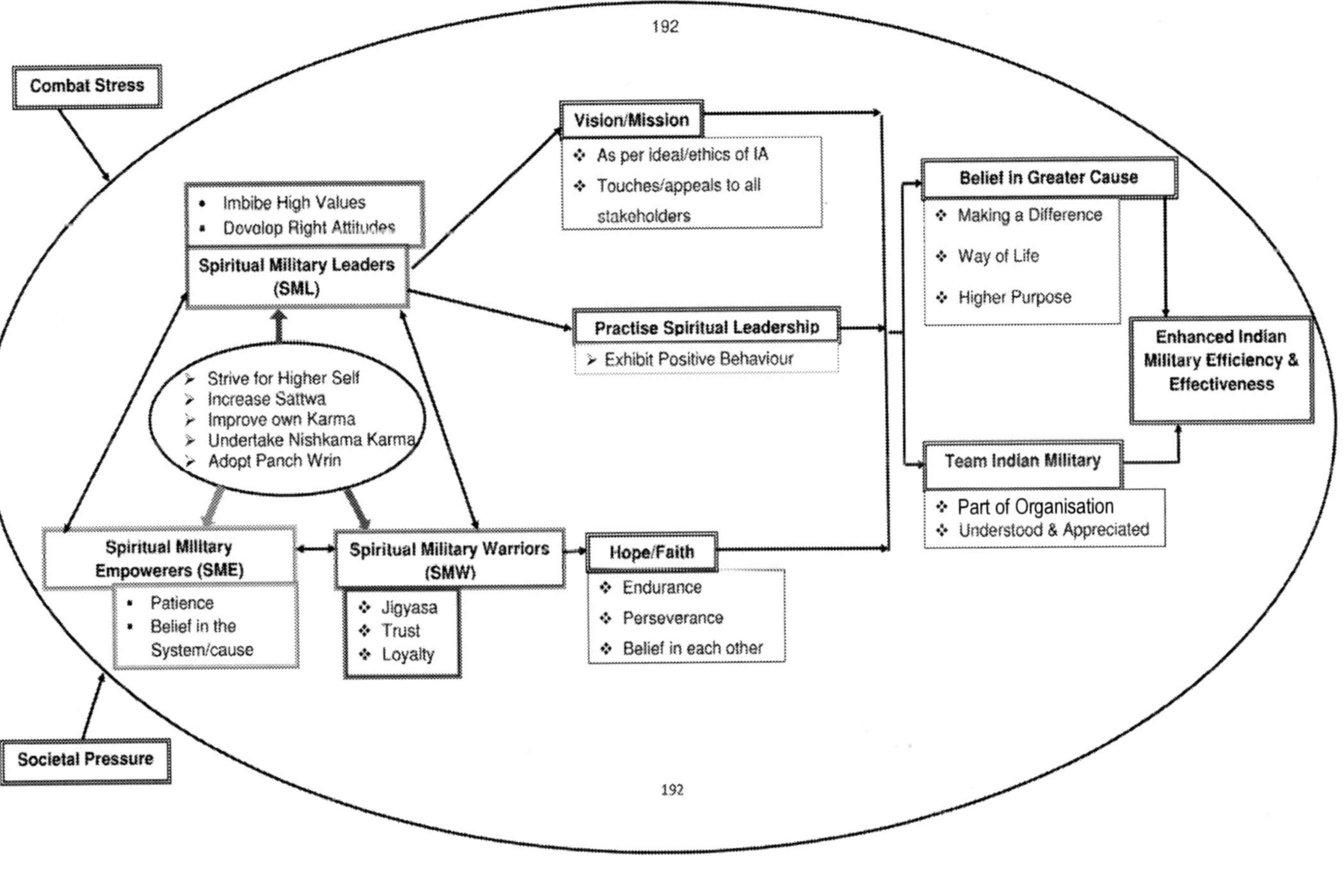

Figure 2: Spiritual Leadership Indian Military (SLIM)

namely, 'Spiritual Military Leaders (SML)', 'Spiritual Military Warriors (SMW)' and 'Spiritual Military Empowerers (SME)'. SML are all individuals of the Indian military who are in any position where they have to lead others. These range from junior, middle to senior/strategic leaders. While the necessity of following SLIM applies to all equally, it is well understood that the higher the leadership the greater its area of influence and thus more the necessity to adopt the SLIM theory. The second stakeholders are the SMW. These are individuals who are subordinates in any capacity. The roles of SML and SMW keep changing throughout the service and are not fixed. It is also well understood that the roles can be undertaken conjointly too, as all leaders while leading are subordinates to someone else too. While the first two categories of stakeholders are well understood and exist in various capacities in the Indian military presently, the third category of stakeholders, namely SME, are lesser understood and are being discussed in the following paragraph.

Roles, Functioning and Interplay. To some extent, instances of this theory already exist in the Indian military. These are however far and few and are individual based. Thus, it would be fair to say that the same is not institutionalized and there is an inescapable need for doing so. While institutionalizing of the SLIM theory would be dealt with in the next chapter, the said SLIM theory is being discussed briefly here. The SLIM theory in essence looks at awakening, inculcating and maintaining spirituality in the Indian military leadership so as to enable it in executing its tasks more efficiently and effectively. For the said theory, an important start point would be the creation of SMEs. These are spiritually inclined individuals who would have to be selected, trained and nurtured through well-designed processes. The SMEs would thereafter be responsible for awakening and spreading of spirituality in the Indian military by interacting with both SMLs and SMWs. It would therefore be essential for SMEs to have patience and a strong belief in the cause of spirituality as an enabler for Indian military leadership. SMEs are the spinal cord of the SLIM theory and their functioning is critical for the success of the said theory. As already brought out, the development of SMLs can be undertaken by undertaking two processes, 'Imbibe High Values' and 'Develop Right Attitude'. While the SMLs would undertake these two processes individually they would also be assisted in them by the SMEs. Both SML and SME would be responsible for spreading spiritual enlightenment amongst

SMWs. SMWs on their part would need to have unbounded '*jigyasa*' or curiosity to learn as also have trust and loyalty in their superiors and organization. Most importantly, though all the three stakeholders would need to faithfully uphold and execute the 'tenets of spiritual military leadership' these being – 'strive for higher self', 'increase *sattva*', 'improve own *karma*', 'undertake *nishkama karma*' and 'adopt *panch wrin* principles.'

Executing Spiritual Military Leadership. While executing the SLIM theory, SMLs would need to eschew a clear 'vision/mission' for the organization. The same would be based on the ideals and ethics of Indian military and should touch/appeal to all stakeholders. While the SMLs would practise spiritual leadership by 'exhibiting positive behaviour' (already discussed earlier), the SMWs have to have unbreakable hope/faith in the organisation and this essentially boils down to persevering and having belief in each other.

Benefits of SLIM Theory. Following and executing the SLIM theory would lead to a 'belief in a greater cause', wherein each member would function from a higher self and feel that he is making a difference and his life has a higher purpose. It would thus result in internal motivation and a lesser requirement of an external source of motivation. It would in addition lead to the building up of 'Team Indian Military' in which each member would feel that he is a part of the team on account of being understood and appreciated and thus be able to contribute in a larger measure. Cumulatively therefore, the adoption of the SLIM theory would lead to an enhanced Indian military efficiency and effectiveness.

I have no doubt whatsoever that the SLIM theory is the need of the hour and would do a world of good for the Indian military leadership. There is therefore an indisputable necessity of its institutionalization at the earliest. This aspect is dealt with in the next and concluding chapter.

Testing of the Hypothesis

Let me first recount the hypothesis of the present research, which is:

> ***"Spirituality will enable Indian military leadership to make it more effective and efficient in today's challenging environment."***

My research has clearly established the necessity of spirituality for Indian military leaders in today's challenging environment and elucidated ways in which spirituality will enable the Indian military leadership to make it more efficient and effective.

On the basis of the same it would be fair to state that the hypothesis stands proven right.

NOTES

1. Shardha Batra, *The Times of India*, Speaking Tree. 'Vaak Shakti, the power of creative speech.' 15 October 2021.
2. Ankur Rommel. Medium, 'Science, Art and Philosophy of War', 29 June 2023, https://ankurrommel.medium.com/science-art-and-philosophy-of-war-d7cd9584a562,
3. Louis W Fry. 'Towards a Theory of Spiritual Leadership', *The Leadership Quarterly*, pp. 693-727, 2003

Chapter Five

Present Level of Spirituality in the Indian Armed Forces

For this section too questionnaires were sent to respondents. The questions were: Are there formal structures available in the Indian Armed Forces for inculcation of spirituality? And, is there a need to include spirituality as an essential discipline in the curriculum of existing institutions? The response to these questions is presented through the following pie charts.

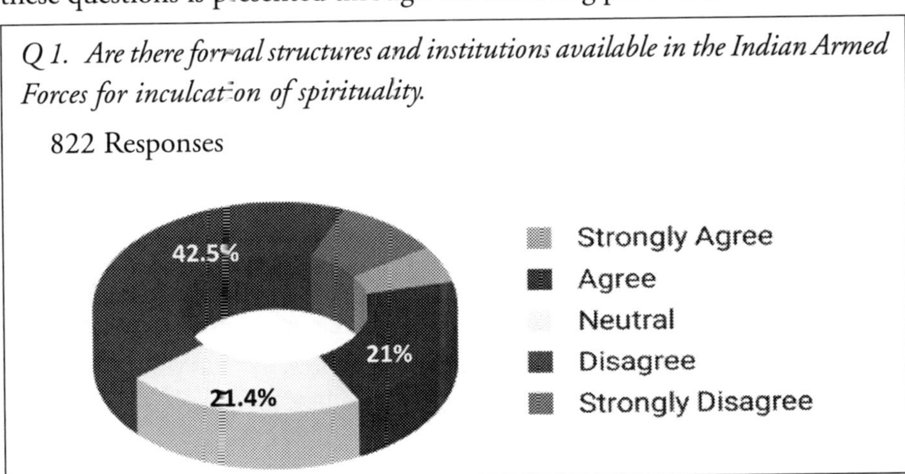

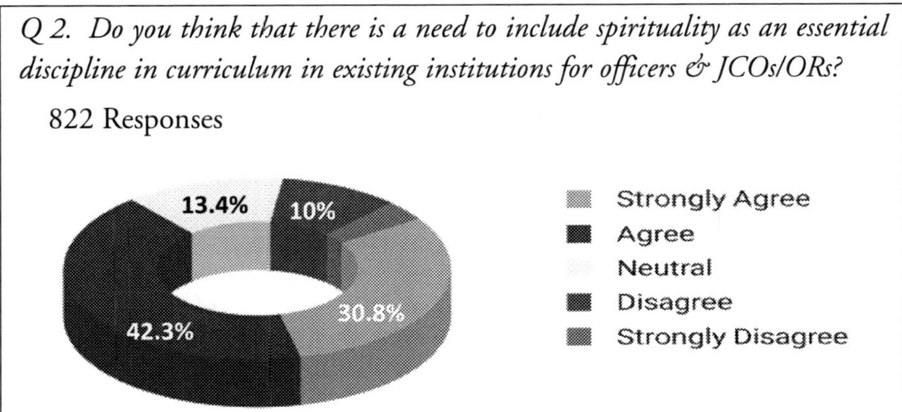

A brief analysis of the responses received in response to the questions posed in this section is as under:

(a) Sixty-three per cent of the respondents feel that there are no formal structures available in the Indian Armed Forces for inculcation of spirituality.

(b) More than half of the respondents feel that there is a need to include spirituality as an essential discipline in the curriculum of existing institutions.

Having seen the analysis of the survey, let us see the present levels of spirituality in the Indian Armed Forces.

In an earlier chapter we have examined in detail the rich Indian traditions and the vast pool of ancient wisdom. In our culture, we have age-old literature devoted to spirituality and wisdom. These include the four Vedas, the Upanishads, the Puranas, the *Bhagavad Gita* and the two great epics, the *Mahabharata* and the *Ramayana*. These holy books prescribe sets of principles that are applicable and relevant even in today's context. The *Bhagavad Gita* provides a metaphor for spirituality as a journey for man to understand his true Self. In the beginning of the battle of Mahabharata, Arjuna kneels at the feet of Lord Krishna who is represented as the embodiment of God; he claims, "I am the Self ... seated in the hearts of all beings. I am the beginning, the middle, and also the end of all beings." This statement of Lord Krishna conveys that each human being has in him the supreme presence but this is clouded by illusion or ignorance. The ego or 'I' believes itself to be the self. Once a person has a good understanding of the self, then only can he contribute effectively as a leader too.

I have already elucidated upon the methodology for development and practice of spiritual military leadership by utilizing the IDE concept (Imbibe High Values + Develop Right Attitude = Exhibit Positive Behaviour) which in itself draws heavily from Indian spirituality. While it has been clearly brought out in earlier chapters that embracing spirituality is an absolute essential requirement for modern-day military leadership, however, to put this theory into practical implementation would require creation of suitable structures and processes. What is important here to note is that this would be a completely new subject for most people; hence it is important that its acceptability by a larger section of the organization is a prerequisite for the smooth introduction of the concept. Before we discuss the aspects of institutionalizing the spiritual theory in the Indian Armed Forces let us discuss how certain other armies are implementing this aspect.

Spirituality in Foreign Armed Forces

The Emerging Study of Spirituality. In various militaries, increased interest is being shown to spiritual well-being of its personnel and its contribution towards motivation, resilience, and better operational preparedness. The study of spirituality with respect to military leadership is a new area of research. Also, this subject does not have much empirical data. There being no structured theory, the definitions in use are still in its nascent phases with terms such as spiritual intelligence, heightened awareness and elevated consciousness. Spirituality at the work place is also gaining much attention leading to a lot of efforts to find complete theories that focus on leadership concepts.

(a) Spirituality is being looked at to enable leaders to progress from having practical knowledge of leadership to become an emotionally intelligent and self-aware leader. Spiritual leaders are seen to be able to motivate their subordinates and help them understand the purpose, meaning and goals of the organisation. Hence, the core of effective leadership lies in the spiritual wellbeing of the leader. Such leaders create a vision and congruence of values across teams and at individual levels that translates into higher levels of organisational commitment and increased efficiency.

(b) Innate faith is the basic ingredient in the spiritual leadership model and is an essential aspect of the expression of the vision. It is the endurance of the hardship, facing of opposition and sense of conviction to fulfil the vision. Leaders who display spiritual values promote similar behaviours in others and create an enabling environment that promotes trust, ethical behaviours and positive relationships. In turn, the leader ensures that organisational goals are achieved with higher efficiency and greater sustainability.

(c) Spiritual leadership has a universal acceptance as subordinates normally follow such a leader who cares about positive relations with others.

Chaplain Model: Canadian Armed Forces. The Canadian Army has identified spirituality as one of the six aspects that contribute towards resilience, operational preparedness, performance and fitness of defence personnel (along with emotional, physical, social, familial and intellectual fitness). As per the Canadian Defence Academy, 'Ethos acts as the focal point for the defence profession and as a unifying spirit'. The Canadian Armed Forces are known worldwide to 'respect the dignity of all people, to serve Canada before self and to obey and support lawful authority'. Values such as duty, loyalty, integrity and courage, are the guiding force for all members of the Canadian Armed Forces. One of the definitions approved by the Chaplain Branch in the Canadian Army describes spirituality as a broad concept that is often confused with religion. While spirituality could be part of a particular religion, it could also be independent of religion. Spirituality connects us to our state of mind, being and place which lends us a sense of belonging and purpose. Though, spirituality is said to be practised, it is as much a part of humans as physical and emotional aspects. The main point of this definition is the understanding that we all have a spiritual dimension within us.

US Armed Forces. In 2009, the United States Army included spirituality as a part of its Comprehensive Soldier and Family Fitness Program (CSF2). This program was later expanded in 2012 to include family members. An attack helicopter squadron in Texas researched the efficacy of spiritual training in influencing response to vision, altruistic love, hope and faith among soldiers. They stated that the goal of spiritual leadership is to tap into the fundamental needs of both leader and followers for spiritual survival. It helps develop a vision that puts them on a path, which when undertaken, will give a sense of calling and make a difference to one's life. They found that those following spiritual leadership at the personal level will score high on life satisfaction in terms of happiness, peace and serenity. The research conclusively establishes the relevance of spiritual leadership in transformation of the army and recommends further research on outcomes of spiritual leadership on individuals and organisational effectiveness before it is widely applied.

Applied Spirituality Theories

A causal theory of spiritual leadership is evolved within an intrinsic motivation model that incorporates vision, hope, faith, altruistic love, theories of work place spirituality and spiritual survival. The goal of spiritual leadership is to create vision and values at personal levels and ultimately facilitate enhanced levels of organisational commitment and output. Spiritual leadership comprises the values, attitudes and behaviours required to intrinsically motivate an individual in order to have a sense of spiritual survival through calling and membership. The spiritual leadership theory given by Fry (2003) has the three essential components, namely, Vision, Altruistic Love, Hope and Faith.

These components yield positive outcomes such as employees' membership and sense of calling. The two aspects of spirituality, which are meaning (calling) and community (membership), are replicated in the basic definition of spiritual leadership by Fry (2003). Therefore, in the light of the above discussion, the literature supports the extensive connections between the constructs of spirituality and leadership.

It is evident that only a few armies in the world have a formal introduction of the concept of spirituality with limited structures. Moreover; when it comes to the practice of spirituality it should come more from within rather than as part of some organised event, in which case the sight of the very essence of the concept would be lost. The Indian Armed Forces are one of the largest in the world and has personnel of all faiths and beliefs. Therefore, institutionalising of spirituality in the context of the Indian Armed Forces is a delicate and challenging proposition. Hence, its planning and implementation requires due diligence and deep thought.

Present Level of Spirituality in Indian Armed Forces

The Indian Armed Forces have always been not only apolitical but also secular in nature in spite of having a system of regimentation. In order to prepare an organisation to imbibe spirituality, organisational structures play an important role. Spirituality has generally been mistaken with religion. While religion has rituals, spirituality focuses on principles, values, ethics, meaning, authenticity, purpose and presence. These values get enhanced when leaders are aware of their deeper selves. Spiritual fitness in the armed forces means the ability of the individual to believe in the importance, necessity and just nature of the mission; to have faith in the reliability of leaders; and to be prepared to encounter and cope with extreme danger and even death with confidence, dedication and courage. There is an aspect of courage which comes from a deep spiritual faith which, when prevalent in a unit, can result in uncommon toughness and tenacity in combat.

The Indian Armed Forces are internationally known for their ethics and moral values and have lived up to their tradition of valour, sacrifice and fortitude on numerous occasions. The concept of duty, selfless service and self-sacrifice has always been the basic foundation of our Armed Forces. Ethics, morals and values are the guiding force of the Indian Armed forces which has immensely assisted in structuring a soldier's character. As per spiritual sciences, character building and following virtues are considered to be more important aspects than following spiritual practices. Hence, taking into account the foundation of the Indian Armed Forces, each and every soldier to a large extent is aligned to spirituality. In view of this, it is imperative that the present-day soldier be integrated with spiritual training so as to make them more effective and efficient both at professional and individual levels.

Challenging Work Environment. The working environment in the Indian Armed Forces is becoming more challenging, fast-paced and professionally demanding, thereby subjecting leaders and the troops on the ground to extraordinary stress. We are witnessing an era where the Armed Forces are increasingly being deployed in challenging operational environments and simultaneously also undertaking an optimisation by downsizing its strength. Challenging work environments for the Indian Armed Forces comprise active field areas in counter-insurgency, line of control, line of actual control, varying terrains and peace areas with varied commitments including aid to civil authorities. The frequently changing operational environments coupled with prolonged deployment without relief prevents our troops with a clear break thereby resulting in increasing levels of physical and mental stress. Hence, by incorporating spirituality in the organisation, we can go a long way in reducing the present stress levels. Towards this end, the following steps can be undertaken:

(a) Connect your work to your value system.

(b) Look at things positively.

(c) Treat others well.

(d) Take some time for yourself.

(e) Get to know your co-workers.

(f) Speak with seniors about workplace spirituality.

(g) Be mindful of your words when interacting with others.

(h) Put people first.

(j) Get to know your co-workers.

Present Structures in the Indian Army

Very few countries in the world can boast of a cultural heritage as India which spans a period of over 5,000 years. Successive waves of immigration have enriched Indian culture and an Indian way of life has evolved. It is this variety which is in a way the uniqueness of Indian culture and is popularly referred to as unity in diversity. Indian culture is an excellent blend of diverse languages, religions and customs. The concept of the Nation being supreme is the common cause which binds the people in spite of our cultural diversity. This unity in diversity coupled with a 'Nation First approach always and every time' is the primary reason that makes the Indian Armed Forces a professional organisation.

Spirituality can be practised both at the individual and organisational levels. As discussed earlier, organised practices of spirituality in the Indian Armed Forces is limited to Sarv Dharm Sthal parades, classes on stress management and celebration of important festivals. While every soldier is free to practise spirituality at an individual level within the confines of military decorum, organised training to develop spirituality to meet organisational goals is only restricted to the religious teachers. To a large extent, the initiatives of the US Forces and Canadian Armed Forces illustrated earlier imitate the

Religious Teacher concept already existing in the Indian Armed Forces. Various structures existing in the Indian Armed Forces which provides an impetus to spirituality are as follows:

(a) *Institute of National Integration (INI).* The Institute of National Integration was established by the Indian Army at Dapodi, Pune, in 1985 to foster a sense of brotherhood for a common cause and integrate people of diverse faiths, religions, regions and languages under one National Flag. The Institute of National Integration was an outcome of exchange of ideas between the then Prime Minister and the Chief of the Army Staff in 1980 and launched as a project for giving depth to the cohesion and inter-faith harmony which exists in the Armed Forces. The primary role of this institute was to train religious teachers in developing secular ideology amongst troops at the unit level and accordingly conduct various teacher training and refresher courses. The Institute consistently strives for excellence in behavioural and social sciences. In addition to the recruit training, it also trains the religious teachers for performing an effective role in promoting the ethos of national integration in the organisation. The focus of training is:

   (i) Impart soldierly qualities, secularism, security and health counselling.

   (ii) Knowledge of other religions and working in a mixed environment.

   (iii) Psychological aspects and underpinnings of military behaviour and counselling.

(b) *Conduct of Mandir Parades & Celebration of Religious Festivals at Sarv Dharm Sthals.* The Indian Armed Forces are known for following secularism in the most appropriate manner through the concept of *Sarv Dharm Sthals.* The primary role of establishment of *Sarv Dharm Sthals* is to uphold the individual spirit and religious sentiments of all ranks with the aim of National Integration. All formation/units have Sarv Dharm Sthals which is one of the most important regimental institutes where all ranks belonging to various religions, regions and languages worship the Almighty together under one common roof. It is a symbol of harmony in the Indian Armed Forces which binds troops together irrespective of their religions and faiths. The unit *Sarv Dharm Sthal* is considered one of the most important regimental institutions and the place of common worship. Similar to any official function, mandir parades are regularly conducted in the units where all ranks, irrespective of their religion, caste and region come together and offer their prayers to the Almighty as per regiment customs. Festivals bring a wave of excitement and happiness breaking the monotony of daily routine and reflect our rich traditions and culture. Religion is an important part of a soldier's life as troops have deep-rooted faith in their religion. Celebrating religious festivals at unit *Sarv Dharm Sthals* regularly fosters the feeling of oneness amongst all ranks. Organising collective celebrations of religious festivals helps in implementing a stronger feeling for national integration. Festivals are celebrated in the unit to keep the troops spiritually and emotionally connected to their respective cultures.

(c) *Religious Teacher at Unit Level.* Religious teachers have been authorised units to meet the religious and spiritual needs of all ranks during peace and motivate them during war. The qualification and awareness level of the present religious teachers is high which can be of immense help to the unit if employed judiciously. The trainees are selected through a selection process and undergo a three-month long course at the Institute of National Integration after which they are commissioned as junior commissioned officers with designations like maulvis, pandits, priests, monks or granthis. They play a pivotal role in identification of troops under stress due to various issues like health, family, finance and job-related stress. The religious teachers have been able to bridge the gap between the officer-men relationship in establishing unknown facts during routine functioning of the unit. They continuously act as spiritual mentors in the unit for guiding and motivating all ranks on the path of Truth. Their presence with the troops in peace and field has reinstated faith and positivity among troops during adverse and stressful conditions. They are also responsible to organize religious functions and deliver talks to strengthen spirituality, morality and ethics amongst all ranks and their families.

(d) *Yoga*. Yoga is regularly practised in the unit as part of training activities. It has assisted all ranks in dealing firmly with various complex situations in daily lives. Yoga improves strength, balance and flexibility of mind, body and soul. It helps troops to enhance their mental and physical energy thereby boosting their alertness and enthusiasm in performing their duties. Practising *pranayama* as part of morning parades has been implemented to benefit all ranks serving in peace, field and extreme weather conditions. Scientific evidence has proven that yoga has been immensely helpful in stress management, managing mental health, improving mindfulness, following healthy eating habits, weight loss and gaining quality sleep.

(e) *Central Lectures and Seminars*. The aim of central lectures and seminars is to continuously train and motivate all ranks in the organization on professional, intellectual, physical and moral aspects. Troops are given an opportunity to participate in various central lectures and seminars conducted at formation levels. Various leadership development programs are conducted to imbibe the qualities of devotion to duty, selflessness, loyalty, integrity, discipline and esprit-de-corps. It also assists in development of military leadership qualities to include high moral and physical courage. Lectures on intellectual development enhance the power of analysis and creative thinking.

It is however important to note that the concept of spirituality being followed in the Indian Armed Forces is at a very basic level and there is an inescapable need to institutionalise inculcation of spirituality to the level that this research has shown to be necessary by the way of creation of organisations/structures for the same. For introduction of formal spiritual training in the Indian Armed Forces, we would have to examine the issue with more deliberation. The next chapter will look to giving certain recommendations for the same.

Chapter Six

Recommendations for Institutionalising Spirituality as an Enabler in the Indian Armed Forces

A questionnaire was circulated to obtain data for this section. The questions in it were the following: Should training in spirituality commence from the pre-commission period and continued throughout service? What is more important: Formal teaching in schools of instruction on existing curriculum, adoption and leveraging of spirituality or continued focus on traditional ways of man management? The responses to these questions are presented through the following pie charts.

Q 1. Training in spirituality, whose foundation should be laid in pre-commissioning training institutes and regimental centres, must be a continuum with raised levels in higher institutes of learning, besides suitably incorporating it in our regimental life and ethos.

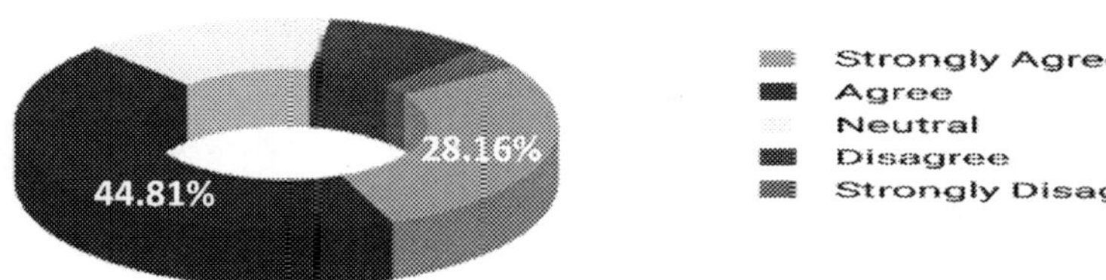

Q 2. *Rank Order them (1, 2 or 3, with '1' being most important and '3' the least) with the changing socio-economic milieu, aspects that can be adopted in the Indian Armed Forces in order to enhance the quality of military leadership are:*

822 Responses

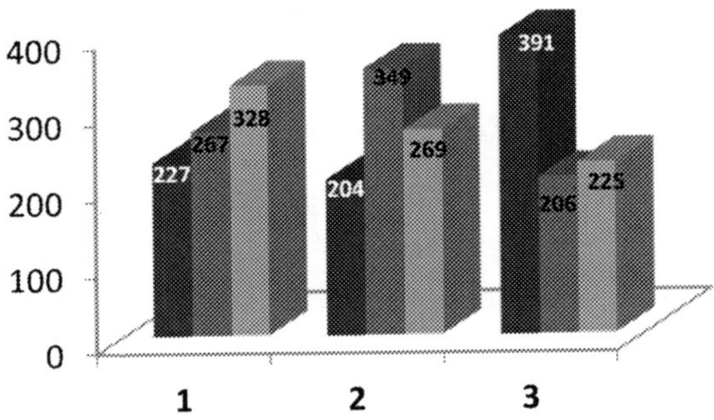

1 - Formal teaching, in schools of Instruction, on corporate leadership
2 - Continued focus on traditional ways of man management in the Armed Forces
3 - Adoption and leveraging of Spirituality to enhance aspects like forgiveness, empathy, integrity, courage, gratitude, fearlessness in a Leader

A brief analysis of the responses received in response to the questions posed in this section is as under:

(a) A resounding 97 per cent majority feel that training in spirituality should commence from the pre-commission period and continued throughout service.

(b) The order of importance as regards the methods to enhancing the quality of Indian military leadership is: Adoption and leveraging of spirituality, continued focus on traditional ways of man-management and formal teaching in schools of instruction on existing curriculum.

Having seen the analysis of the survey, in this concluding chapter, the researcher aims to suggest certain recommendations that will help to institutionalise spirituality as an enabler in the Indian defence forces.

Construct of Military Leadership

Before we come to the detailed aspects related to institutionalising spirituality in the Armed Forces, it would be pertinent to spell out the core construct around which the development of spiritual military leadership would hinge. This would then facilitate further evolution of the various organisational policy guidelines and structures for enabling institutionalising spirituality in the Armed Forces. These are elucidated in the following paragraphs.

Tat Tvam Asi. Development of the highest state of spiritual military leadership could be said to be achieved when one realises the 'self'. This is what spirituality is all about as preached in our various scriptures. It is in this context that we must understand the concept of *Tat Tvam Asi* which is used within Hindu and yoga philosophy to refer to the unity of *Atman*(the individual self or soul) with *Brahman* (universal consciousness or the Absolute). The translation 'I am that' unites the macrocosmic ideas of God and universal consciousness with the microcosmic individual expression of the Self. Understanding this is believed to be the ultimate form of compassion, in which individuals recognize one another as part of the same whole. The aim of development of spiritual military leadership is to understand this concept and strive to progress on this path. This core construct could further be broken down into various aspects the understanding of which will facilitate development of the desired institutions.

Knowledge of Spiritualism/Real Self. Identifying and ability to discriminate 'Real Self' from 'Gross Self' is the knowledge called '*Vidya*', that makes a person understand spiritualism. Lack of knowledge or ignorance of *vidya* causes fear, overconfidence, and inflated egos. Wrong knowledge or '*avidya*' will result in a destructive mindset, and if endowed with physical and mental prowess, such individuals will have devilish tendencies. In the Armed Forces, individuals that are able-bodied, morally upright and possess right knowledge are endowed with spirituality. Understanding 'Service before self' or performing duty without attachment and fruits thereof as a consequence of spirituality develops true leaders. Such leaders understand the 'Self' better, understand others better, have greater awareness of the conscience, are fearless and are decisive. Such leaders will be extremely compassionate but will not tolerate immorality and can unleash desired violence when necessary. Understanding self or such knowledge is very difficult for all to attain:

(a) A few who understand and pursue the truth purely by knowledge, follow '*Gyan Marg*' and become '*sanyasis*' at an early age.

(b) Some have knowledge and are physically well endowed, they follow *Karma Yog*. They follow the dictum 'Doing duty without expecting any returns.'

(c) Most do not comprehend this knowledge, but are aware of the truth, are good, compassionate people, obedient, disciplined and well meaning. Such people follow 'Bhakti Marg' and are more ritualistic.

(d) In the Armed Forces we have soldiers following *Karma Yog* and *Bhakti Yog*.

Physiological and Psychological Constructs

The personality, thought process, psychology, interest and orientation of an individual is dependent on various factors. Interaction of an individual with parents, siblings, relatives, teachers, friends, nature and influences from experiences develops an individual. As per the natural scheme of existence, an individual's primary aim is survival and secondary aim is to create progeny to ensure survival of the species. It is therefore necessary to understand the physiological, social and psychological influences on an individual in various stages of life. This will then lead to the aspects that need to be addressed at each stage of life of an individual to enhance spiritualism. Armed Forces personnel are trained on the model of 'operant conditioning' that focuses on behaviour based on 'rewards and punishment'. It is out of fear of punishment or insult and fear of failure that the Armed Forces operate. In the Indian context, a mix of regimentation and scriptures mould soldiers along with operant conditioning to be the finest soldiers in the world. Most of the regimental mottos are from the scriptures, so there is a certain amount of spiritualism inculcated in the Armed Forces.

Physiological, psychological and social constructs that need to be considered to address imbibing of spiritualism in the Armed Forces are enumerated in the following sub paras.

(a) *Purusharth.* Refers to the four goals in Hinduism – *Dharma, Artha, Kama* and *Moksha. Dharma* is the most important, and to understand it, understanding *Vidya* is important. An individual, during youth, should attain profitable goals (*artha*) such as learning, in his prime, pleasure (*kama*) and in his old age, nirvana (*moksha*). *Dharma* is to be observed during the entire life.

(b) *Ashram.* Part of an indigenous development psychology that shapes the orientation and goals of individuals. What an individual should focus on in various stages and ages of life to attain *Moksha*, be a better individual and pursue the four goals of *Purusharth* is dependent on his physiological and psychological development at each stage. The four ashrams lay down very aptly and scientifically how an individual should live his life and be closer to reality and spiritualism.

Purusharth and *Ashram* are inter-related and have to be addressed together while creating a training schedule for the soldiers.

***Gunas*: Matter Attributes.** *Sattva, Rajas* and *Tamas* are the three attributes of matter. While reality or true self or *atman* is unchangeable, *maya* or matter is changeable. And this matter has the three attributes of the gunas. *Sattva* takes an individual closer to spirituality, but *rajas* is required to operate *sattva* and *tamas*. Matter cannot be complete without three gunas in various proportions that determine the orientation and personality of an individual. Focusing only on *Tamasic* or gross body will not lead to spirituality.

Soldiers and Food. As a soldier, *sattva* and *rajas* have to be most predominant, that is, knowledge and movement/action. *Shastra and shaastra* are essential for a soldier to understand the difference between the real and the ephemeral to be able to take correct or righteous action. Food is also matter and has the three gunas. *Sattvik, Rajsik* and *Tamsik;* it will evoke responses in an individual accordingly. It is not necessary that only *sattvic* food should be fed to soldiers but has to be a healthy mix of all three types of food depending on various stages of *Purusharth* and *Ashram*.

***Pancha Kosha*.** The body is made up of five sheaths or *koshas*. The focus or orientation towards one or more *koshas* determines one's personality and inclination towards or away from spiritualism.

(a) ***Annamaya Kosha*.** The food body, the physically seen body, the glorified body is a body made up of the food that we eat and is manifested as hair, nails, bones, tissue and fluids. An individual who believes this is the self, lives in ignorance of spirituality as this body is '*Nashwant*' or destructible or non-permanent.

(b) ***Pranmaya Kosha*.** The energy body that breathes life in the '*tamasik*' body consisting of '*Panchpran*', concentrating on *Pranmaya kosha* keeps the physical body and the mind body or *Manomaya kosha* stable and healthy. This is the bridge between *Annamaya Kosha* and *Manomaya*

Kosha. This body is kept healthy by pranayama and breathing exercises.

(c) ***Manomaya Kosha.*** It is a subtle body like the *Pranmaya Kosha,* also called the 'mind body'. It is fed by the sources of the *Annamaya Kosha* energised by the *Pranmaya Kosha* and controlled by the *Vigyanmaya Kosha* or the intellect. Therefore, to control the mind, right knowledge or *vidya,* equitable energy and a healthy physical body is essential.

(d) ***Vigyanmaya Kosha.*** A subtle body of intellect, the right knowledge or *vidya* that is the inner voice. Right knowledge will control the mind; wrong knowledge will lead to destructive tendencies of the mind. Investing in the *Vigyanmaya Kosha* will lead to spiritualism.

(e) ***Anandmaya Kosha.*** The causal body that houses the '*atman*', can be experienced when the other four bodies are calm, controlled and steadied. The experience is *nirvana.* The process of aligning the four bodies and the desire to attain *moksha* is '*Mumukshatwa*'.

Indian Philosophies. While the six *astik* philosophies called *shad darshana* divulge in ways to attain *moksha* in six different ways, yoga philosophy is an experiential philosophy that elaborates on how to align the body, energy, mind and intellect towards *moksha,* enabling spiritualism. The six philosophies are:

(a) Vaisheshikha by Kanad

(b) Nyaya by Gautama

(c) Purva Mimansa by Jaimini

(d) Sankhya by Kapil

(e) Yoga by Patanjali

(f) Vedanta by Badarayan

Ayurveda. It was compiled by Atreya and encompasses the complete knowledge of the gross body, effect of behaviour, food and matter that the body is made up of. Hence the knowledge of Yoga and Ayurveda in the training curriculum of the Armed Forces will inculcate spiritualism in them and make officers better leaders with better intellect and spiritualism.

Ayurveda and Food. The possession of a healthy body is extremely important to achieve spiritual thought. Therefore, the *Annamaya Kosha* or the food body has to be suitably fed and nurtured. The food should be *Satvik, Rajsik* and *Tamasik* and should invoke the respective *gunas* accordingly in the mind and the body. The abnormal consumption of the types of food leads to '*tri dosha*' of *Waat, Kaff* and *Pitta* caused by abnormalities of air, water and earth in the body. Therefore, diet plays an important role in building spirituality and has to be suitably incorporated in the curriculum.

Suggested Structural & Organisational Reforms for Institutionalizing Spirituality in Indian Armed Forces

Broad Contours. As discussed earlier, the introduction of the concept of spiritual training in the Indian Armed Forces needs due diligence. This concept needs to be understood more as a science and not confused as some religious belief. This aspect, if well understood, would usher proper implementation of the central theme and would benefit the organisation in the long run. Hence, it is essential to discuss the contours of the implementation plan and lay down certain guidelines which will help evolve the organizational structures that are required for introduction and institutionalising of this important subject in the Indian Armed Forces. As brought out in Chapter IV, it has clearly been enunciated that the methodology for development and practice of spiritual military leadership should be by utilizing the IDE concept (Imbibe High Values + Develop Right Attitude = Exhibit Positive Behaviour) which in itself has been drawn primarily from the Indian way of life. Hence, in a large measure, the implementation plan will draw its essence from the age-old wisdom of our scriptures. However, before we do that, let us lay down the broad contours of the implementation plan so that it would help in formalizing the structures and the curriculum at various levels.

(a) *Innate Sense of Spirituality.* Every person by birth is innately spiritual. Its manifestation may vary depending on various factors. Conversely, if given the right direction and guidance, it may help a person explore one's spiritual domain and guide him/her on the path of self-discovery. While on that path of self-discovery, one would imbibe the IDE concept which in turn will further help every individual to evolve as a better military leader. Hence, with this as a primary assumption, the implementation plan looks at encouraging all individuals to follow the path of spirituality.

(b) *Measurability of Spirituality Quotient.* While introducing any concept, the aspect of measurability or standards achieved is always given prime importance. However, in the context of spirituality, this aspect needs to be handled in a subtle way, lest the measurability aspect itself creates unwanted anxiety in the environment. It is essential that the concept be acceptable to all rather than it being pushed down as mandatory learning.

(c) *Requisite Flexibility in Conduct.* A spiritual seeker may be from different faiths. Accordingly, the programs that are planned to be introduced need to cater for a secular audience and should be designed in a scientific manner that lends itself to easier acceptance. Further, some flexibility, depending on one's faith, needs to be factored in while following certain procedures (*Kriyas*) that are planned to be introduced as a part of the curriculum.

(d) *Time Plan.* It needs to be understood that for a subject of this nature to be introduced and mature would require time. The structures would evolve with experiential feedback and the same would be an ongoing iterative process that would take time to stabilize. Hence, the time plan needs to be prepared with achievable deliverables.

(e) *Outside Expertise.* The Indian Armed Forces would need to rely heavily on outside expertise available within the country in the initial stages for implementing the planned curriculum. Over the years however it would develop in-house expertise that would then be able to steer and conduct this process.

We have already examined the age-old wisdom provided to us through our scriptures which states that on the spiritual journey a person may choose many of the available paths. The *Bhagavad Gita* talks of Karma Yoga, Dhyana Yoga and Raj Yoga as the various paths for self-realisation. Thus, adopting yoga in some form or the other is the key to one's spiritual journey. As a nation, India over the last decade has promoted the idea of yoga to the whole world. As a result, the UN has adopted 21 June every year as Yoga Day. We, in the Indian Armed Forces, have been very actively celebrating Yoga Day right from the heights of Siachen Glacier to the naval platforms deployed on the blue waters of the oceans. Hence, the concept of yoga is more acceptable and its benefits are well understood by all ranks. Therefore, the concept of Ashtang Yoga as enunciated by Maharshi Patanjali seems most appropriate to be adopted as the guiding document for implementation of the process of spirituality in the Indian Armed Forces.

Understanding Yoga Sutra. Yoga as a system of Indian philosophy was developed by the great sage, Maharishi Patanjali, in his classical work, the "*Yoga Sutras.*" The system of yoga teaches the means by which the *jivatma* can be united to or be in communion with the *Paramatma* and so secure liberation (*moksha*). The *Bhagavad Gita* gives various explanations of the term 'yoga' and lays stress upon *Karma Yoga* (Yoga by action).

The Stages of Yoga. While following the spiritual path, the correct process is just as essential as the end state in mind. Maharishi Patanjali explains this process as the eight stages of yoga. These are called *yama, niyama, asana, pranayama, pratyahara, dharana, dhyana* and *samadhi.*

Following *Ashtang Yoga* of Yoga Philosophy that encompasses all the physiological and psychological constructs of *Purusharth, Ashram, Guna* and *Panchakosha* will be extremely beneficial. *Ashtang Yoga* sequentially inculcated in the training curriculum will enable spiritualism. A further elaboration of the eight limbs that are to be followed in sequence are:

(a) **Yama: The External Disciplines**

(i) *Ahimsa.* Approach or behaviour to any object, animate or inanimate should be that of compassion and love and not violent. But, in spite of good intent and compassion, if the subject displays violence then violence should be used to destroy the subject. Ahimsa does not mean 'no violence' as people commonly believe as all the gods carried weapons and had killed after giving ample opportunities to offenders to mend their evil ways.

(ii) '*Satya*' or non-falsehood.

(iii) '*Asteya*' or non-stealing.

(iv) '*Brahmacharya*' or sexual restraint.

(v) '*Aparigraha*' or non-possessiveness.

(b) **Niyam: External Disciplines**

(i) '*Shaucha*' or cleanliness of body and mind.

(ii) '*Santosha*' or contentment.

(iii) '*Tapas*' or perseverance.

(iv) '*Svadhyaya*' or study of self, self-reflection.

(v) '*Ishwarpravidha*' or contemplation of the true self.

(c) **Asana.** Posture that should be stable and that requires a strong body that is agile, healthy and complete. This addresses the *Annamaya Kosha.*

(d) **Pranayam.** Control of breath to enable equitable energy in the body to keep the gross body and the mind body stable. This addresses the *Pranamaya Kosha.*

(e) **Pratyahara.** Retracting the senses having controlled the body and *pran.* It is about controlling the *Manomaya kosha* or controlling the mind.

(f) **Dharana.** Having control on the behaviour, possessing a healthy body, control on the *pran* and control on the mind, one can hold the mind towards inner state to keep focus. This is the first step to meditation by the intellect or knowledge of *Vigyanmaya kosha.*

(g) **Dhyana.** It is profound abstract meditation towards *Anandmaya kosha.*

(h) **Samadhi.** It is the experience of the '*atman*' or true self to achieve *moksha.*

***Yoga Sutras* and Indian Armed Forces.** The core ethos of the Indian Armed Forces has always laid stress on ethical and moral behaviour. As soldiers and leaders of men, we have a set of 'Dos' and 'Don'ts' in our daily lives. Being utmost truthful to one's profession, displaying impeccable integrity to organizational goals and being ready for the ultimate sacrifice for the nation are some of the hallmarks of our organizational culture. Most aspects of *yama* and *niyama* as explained in the above paras form the core of our teachings to all ranks. As discussed earlier, the importance of *asanas* and *pranayama* in India now needs no further deliberation as the benefits accrued are well understood at the grass root levels. Most individuals and the organization itself have informally started adopting the practice of *asanas* and *pranayama.* It can therefore be safely concluded that, the first four limbs of Ashtang Yoga are being followed in the Indian Armed Forces in some way or the other. It is only the latter four limbs that need to be suitably introduced so that the adoption is complete. Hence, it would be most befitting to state that the Ashtang way of yoga implementation would be the right approach for the Indian Armed Forces.

Let us now examine as to whether Ashtang Yoga would enable the military leadership to develop the qualities that we enunciated as part of the SLIM in Chapter IV which are again depicted in the table below:

Values	*Attitudes*	*Behaviour*
Loyalty	Non-Judgemental	Understand Self/Self Awareness
Integrity	Maturity	Understand job & environment
Honesty	Forgiveness	Nurturing Leader
Courage	Kindness	Selflessness
Morals	Trust	Equanimity
Character	Compassion	Self-Actualisation
Will Power	Gratitude	Transcend BMI

We have analysed the eight stages of Ashtang Yoga above and it is evident that most of the qualities that the SLIM has enunciated closely match the desired outputs of the Ashtang Yoga way of life. Hence, while formulating the implementation plan for the Indian Armed Forces, the core concepts of the SLIM and that of the Ashtang Yoga way of life need to mesh to generate a comprehensive implementation plan for the Armed Forces.

Proposed Structures: Indian Armed Forces. Presently, no dedicated organisational structure exists in the Indian Armed Forces to conduct and monitor spiritual training. At present, spirituality is being practised at an individual level in the Indian Armed Forces. It is strongly recommended that organisations and structures be created at various levels to conceptualise, execute and monitor various aspects related to institutionalization of spirituality in the Indian Armed Forces. A dedicated team of spiritual strategic leaders per command is recommended to be created and established for systematic implementation of spiritual training at all levels. At corps/division/brigade level, a team of qualified officers (Spiritual Empowerers) assisted by a team of officers/JCOs from within the formation can be formed for seamless implementation of all recommended practices at the ground level. The above recommended concept will need continuous evaluation at all levels to monitor the implementation process, identify challenges and recommend changes to achieve the desired transformation of the Armed Forces. All ranks in the organisation must constantly strive to improve the suggested model of spirituality.

Suggested Organisational Model. A suggested model for implementation of spiritual training in the Indian Armed Forces is as follows:

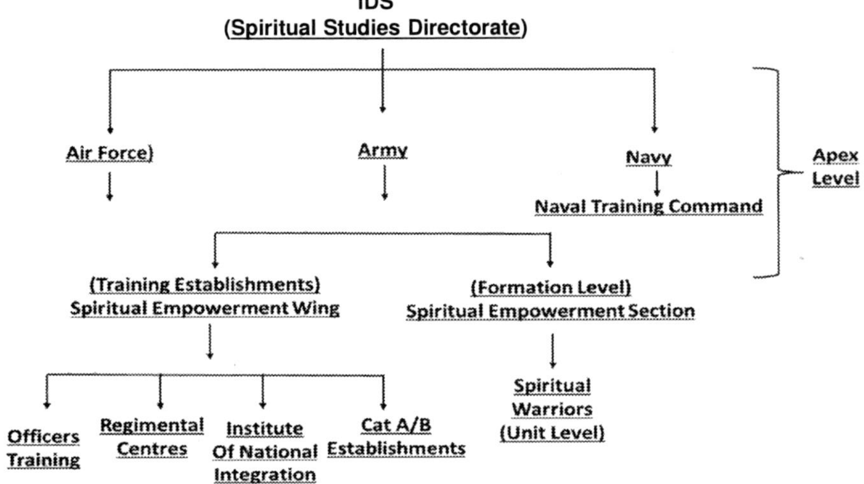

Roles of Various Branches

(a) **Spiritual Studies Directorate.** This should be created at the apex level first and subsequently organisations at the lower formations can be created. This would be created at the apex level (Headquarters Integrated Defence Staff (HQ IDS)) and at individual service levels, respectively (Headquarter ARTRAC in the case of the Indian Army) and would be responsible for conceptualising, execution and overall management of the training philosophy to include creation and management of Spiritual Empowerers and Spiritual Warriors at all levels.

(b) **Spiritual Empowerment Wing (Training Establishments).** The Spiritual Empowerment Wing at training establishments will play a pivotal role in pacing training programs from basic to advance levels at the training centres and academies.

(i) *Staff.* Spiritual Empowerers.

(ii) *Tasks.* The Spiritual Empowerment Wing will be responsible to understand the scope of curriculum, impart training and develop the Spiritual Warrior in a spiritually-awakened soldier. They will create specific course content for all Spiritual Warriors depending upon their rank, service and primary courses they have come to attend in the schools of instruction as prescribed by the Spiritual Studies Directorate at Service Headquarters.

(c) **Spiritual Empowerment Section.** This section at formation and lower levels will play a vital role in execution and monitoring of the training philosophy and management of Spiritual Empowerers and Spiritual Warriors at all levels.

(i) *Staff.* It will primarily comprise of Spiritual Strategic Leaders including Spiritual Empowerers as the support staff.

(ii) *Tasks.* This section at the formation level will ensure successful implementation of various training programs issued by Spiritual Studies Directorate. They will also analyse the progress of spiritual training based on a realistic feedback mechanism and suggest/ recommend amendments to the curriculum to achieve the desired results.

Training Methodology and Curriculum

Training Methodology. Though spirituality has been practised since ages in Indian culture, no formal training for it has been incorporated in the Indian Armed Forces till date. The primary reason can be attributed to the lack of availability of personnel qualified/trained in spirituality. Hence, the need for exploiting the benefits of spiritualism for overall development of men in uniform is an urgent and inescapable one. As the first step towards institutionalising spirituality in the Indian Armed Forces, there is a need to identify people from all ranks who have some sort of inclination, prior knowledge of spirituality and are forthcoming to enhance their knowledge on this subject, as well as are ready to share their experiences for overall development of the organisation. Knowledge about spirituality in their case could have been obtained either at individual or at collective levels earlier. Depending on their knowledge of spirituality and period of service, they can be categorized as Spiritual Strategic Leaders (SSL), Spiritual Empowerers (SE) and Spiritual Warriors (SW). With this as a broad spectrum, every soldier who is spiritually aligned must possess the following qualities:

(a) Trust.

(b) Loyalty.

(c) Integrity.
(d) Honesty.
(e) Courage.
(f) Understanding of self.
(g) Moral character.

Spiritual Strategic Leaders (SSL). Selection of SSL with a high spiritual quotient is an inescapable requirement of the Indian Armed Forces for conceptualising, planning and execution of various policies and directives on the subject at hand. The final selection of the team should be deliberately carried out on merit irrespective of rank/profile of the officer in the organisation. The minimum rank under this category is recommended to be brigadier and above. SSL will be the think tanks of the organisation at the highest level and would be involved in evolving policies and oversee implementation. They will play a vital role in conceptualising the training philosophy, execution and management of Spiritual Empowerers and Spiritual Warriors at all levels. As an initial step, volunteer applications from serving/retired officers with an understanding of spirituality should be invited for forming the team of Spiritual Strategic Leaders. For training of Spiritual Strategic Leaders, a foundation course at the Army level for a period of 2 to 3 weeks can be structured initially which will include operational, administrative and organisational applications of spirituality in the Indian context. Advance courses for selected officers can be planned in the future for broadening and strengthening understanding of the subject. Certain qualities which spiritually aligned SSL should possess are as follows:

(a) Nurturant Leader
(b) Self-Actualisation
(c) Maturity
(d) Forgiveness
(e) Kindness
(f) Non-Judgmental
(g) Compassion.
(h) Ability to transcend BMI

Spiritual Empowerers. Spiritual Empowerers will be responsible for imparting training and implementing various policies at various levels. The rank structure under this category is recommended to be colonel and below. The primary role of Spiritual Empowerers is to impart spiritual training from basic to advance levels at training centres, academies, formation headquarters and units. Here too, initially, volunteer applications from serving/retired officers with an understanding of spirituality should be invited for putting together the initial team of Spiritual Empowerers. For training of Spiritual Empowerers, there is a requirement of an advance course of 3-4 months, which will include training on various aspects with respect to understanding the scope of curriculum, inculcating instructional capabilities and strengthening a spiritual bent of mind.

Spiritual Warriors. All officers, JCOs and ORs undergoing spiritual training fall under this category. They are the seekers, who should have the desire to acquire spiritual knowledge and will be imparted spiritual training by the Spiritual Empowerers. A basic course of one week duration is recommended initially for training of Spiritual Warriors in every Army course of instructions at Cat A and Cat B establishments. Subsequently, once they have developed adequate interest in this field, they can be nominated for advance courses on spirituality to become Spiritual Empowerers based on their potential and capabilities.

Validation of Spiritual Quotient. The process of identification, selection and validation of efficient Spiritual Strategic Leaders, Spiritual Empowerers and Spiritual Warriors can be carried out by a combination of the following methods. These methods are just indicative and more deliberate thought will have to be given to formalize the process of selection of these personnel so that they become the fountainhead for the institutionalising of spirituality in the Armed Forces:

(a) Psychological assessments
(b) Peer ratings
(c) Written evaluations
(d) Formal education acquired on spirituality
(e) Association with reputed spiritual organisations
(f) Evaluation of personality traits with special emphasis on ethics and moral values

(g) Ethical past record
(h) Personal Interviews
(j) Instructional capabilities
(k) Past experience in spirituality

Training Curriculum. Faith is an extremely important aspect for all ranks in the organisation. In a highly challenging profession like the Indian Army, all ranks tend to repose greater trust in the leadership than almost in any other profession. Troops launch operations in highly sensitive counter-insurgency/counter-terrorism areas with extremely sound faith on their leadership. The concept of *Sarv Dharm Sthal* has imbibed a sense of belonging among all ranks that stand shoulder to shoulder under one roof and offer prayers to all religions irrespective of their individual faiths. Similarly, spirituality is a lifestyle that needs to be inculcated by practice of yoga, meditation, character building and following virtues that deepens our life experiences and understanding of how to live a more fulfilling life. Its practice provides useful skills to be successful, healthy and happy. Research has also proven that the practice of spiritual techniques significantly enhances focus, mental clarity, higher energy levels and improved productivity. It not only makes a person psychologically stronger but helps him explore the untapped wisdom for better decision making to achieve higher goals in life. There have also been cases where a considerable improvement in overcoming various physical ailments was observed by practising spirituality consistently. Keeping all these factors in mind, spirituality can definitely enhance the quality of life by shaping the present structure of the Indian Armed Forces. Hence, a recommended training curriculum can include the following topics:

(a) Spiritual essence of all religions
(b) Belief in the Supreme Power
(c) Classification of esoteric principles
(d) Amalgamation of core military values and ethics
(e) Change in personality for higher benefits
(f) Emphasis on importance and benefits of yoga in daily lives
(g) Yoga and meditation exercises as prescribed by experts of yoga
(h) Regular seminars, central classes by qualified instructors and renowned speakers

Selection and Training Methodology. After having analysed the need for introducing spiritual training in the Armed Forces, it is important that we categorise the training content as per the service and rank of an individual. Formulation and adoption of any policy takes the cumulative efforts of the organisation and leaders at all levels. Hence, developing a spiritual training programme with an objective would require deliberate brainstorming by spiritual strategic leaders. The training methodology will be different for each category/level in the organization as under:

(a) **Inception Level.** At this stage, the basic tenets of spirituality should be inculcated among all ranks right from the training phase. Understanding the importance of *Yama* and *Niyama* will make them mentally prepared for progressing to the next levels of Ashtang Yoga in a smoother way. Practising of *asanas* and *pranayama* regularly will align their thought process to 'higher than life' purpose and to the 'Supreme Being'. At such a time when they are being initiated to the 'military ethos', 'the Army's Way of Living' and other core values, if the same is coupled with spirituality, it will not only add value to their personal life but also to the professional service that they will render to the nation in the future. A small step taken at the right time will definitely fructify into bigger gains. The formative years have a major impact on human personality and also shape the character of a person. Young cadets and recruits are exposed to military discipline, inculcation of integrity, loyalty and other such qualities besides developing physical robustness and mental steadiness. Presently, the two aspects of human interface, that is, Body and Mind, are being addressed adequately; however, the soul or spirit is not addressed since the existing curriculum does not cater for arousing spiritual consciousness. It is therefore imperative to do so. In fact, when spiritual content is included in the syllabus, it will facilitate the body and mind also. This stage should comprise all ranks from the inception stage till they reach 10 years of service.

(b) **Intermediate Level.** With an increase in one's spiritual level, one's altitude and perspective to life changes. At an intermediate level, a deeper look into the conceptual understanding and application will be focused upon. Besides following the aspects of *Yama, Niyama, asanas* and *pranayama*, which by now would have been deeply ingrained in their psyche, at the intermediate stage, the spiritual leader needs to be exposed to the various aspects of *pratyahara* and how one can advance further to the higher stages of *Dharana, Dhyana* and *Samadhi*. The content of these courses will enable middle-level officers to have adequate exposure to spirituality. This stage should comprise all ranks in the service bracket of 10-25 years. The following activities are recommended:

(i) *Cat A and Cat B Establishments.* Basic and advanced level training courses must be conducted at all Cat A & B establishments to adequately cover the spiritual training curriculum by amalgamating it with all army courses being conducted in the respective institutes.

(ii) *Formation/Unit Level.* Basic and advanced level refresher courses must be conducted at regular intervals for all ranks to achieve consistency in achieving spiritual training objectives.

(c) **Advanced Level.** This level is the most crucial level as it deals with the highest level of military leadership that is generally above 25 years of service. It is the stage of self-realisation and would be making crucial contributions towards organisational growth. By this time, the initial stages of Ashtang Yoga till *Pratyahara* would be well known to all spiritual warriors. They now need to progress to higher levels where they understand and practise the stages of *Dharana* and *Dhyana*. These practices will expand their energy levels and make them calmer and focused to deal with the larger issues of the organisation. It is the stage of full awakening, inner peace and tranquillity. They will be called upon to provide a nurturing leadership to all subordinates. Senior strategic leadership can imbibe lessons from rich Indian culture and spiritual warriors like Guru Gobind Singhji, Chanakya, Arjuna and Bhishma.

(i) *Institute of National Integration.* Basic and Advanced Spirituality courses to be conducted apart from religious teachers training at the Institute of National Integration. The spiritual strategic leaders initially can be imparted an orientation course on spirituality of about two weeks to bring them onto a level platform.

Subsequently, basic courses of two weeks and advanced courses of three weeks can be conducted for spiritual strategic leaders and spiritual empowerers.

(ii) *National Defence College.* Advanced courses for spiritual strategic leaders can be conducted at the National Defence College. A capsule of 1-2 weeks as part of the regular National Defence College course may be incorporated so as to give a perspective on spirituality to all senior officers attending the course.

Proposed Curriculum

The following few paragraphs will cover the proposed way in which the curriculum and various activities can be planned at various levels. This is an indicative proposal and can be further refined and improved with suitable feedback from the environment. This proposal covers aspects/activities that can be introduced at training centres, at the formation levels and also introduces the Southern Command model of institutionalising spirituality that has now taken off and begun to mature with positive feedback from the environment.

Suggested Training Curriculum. The suggested training curriculum in the Armed Forces towards spiritualism will encompass all the constructs discussed and sequenced based on the philosophy of yoga. It will also include training that is based on operant conditioning. The imperative and non-negotiable attributes a soldier should have, especially the officers, are based on *Yama* and *Niyama* are as follows:

(a) Physical fitness as per desired standards

(b) Honesty, integrity and non-possessiveness

(c) Self-study and perseverance

Aspects recommended in training curriculum organised in various categories are in subsequent paras.

Soldiers and Officers having Service less than 10 years: Attributes and Orientation

Attributes and Orientation. Energetic, daring, willingness to learn, adventurous and agile – ripe to be moulded.

(a) ***Purushartha.*** *Dharma* and *Artha* – focus on learning.

(b) ***Ashrama***. *Brahmacharya* – hearing and celibacy.

(c) **Prominent *Guna***. *Rajas* – activity and motivation.

(d) ***Panchakosha***. *Annamaya* and *Vigyanmaya* – body and knowledge.

(e) ***Ashtangyoga***. *Yam, Niyam, Pranayam* and *Asan*.

Training Curriculum Aspects to be included:

(a) **Yoga**. Yama, Niyama, Asana, Pranayama and Dharana.

(b) **Food**. 25% Satvik, 50% Rajsik and 25% Tamsik.

(c) **Knowledge**. Apart from professional subjects:

  (i) The first four chapters of *The Bhagavad Gita*.

  (ii) *Itihaas*: The *Ramayana* and the *Mahabharata*.

  (iii) *Vivekachudamani*.

  (iv) Works of Tirukural.

  (v) *Arthashastra*.

(d) High level of physical fitness.

(e) Forgiveness towards adventurous and daring acts that do not involve immorality but non-forgiveness towards infringement of *Yamas*.

(f) For officers, knowledge could be more elaborate and extensive as compared to the soldiers.

Soldiers and Officers having service from 10 to 25 years: Attributes and Orientation

Important and formative years of any individual as he becomes an adult, takes responsibility, develops relationships, physiological, social and psychological needs arise:

(a) ***Purushartha***. *Kaama* and *Dharma*.

(b) ***Ashrama***. *Grihastha*.

(c) ***Guna***. *Rajas*.

(d) ***Panchakosha***. *Annamaya* and *Manomaya; Vigyanmaya,* if inclined.

(e) ***Ashtang Yoga***. *Yama, Niyama, Pranayama, Asana, Dharna*.

Training Curriculum aspects to be included:

(a) **Yoga**. *Yama, Niyama, Pranayana, Asana, Dharna, Dhyan*.

(b) **Food**. 25% Satvik, 50% Rajsik and 25% Tamsik.

(c) **Knowledge**.

(i) *The Bhagavad Gita*.

(ii) Yoga philosophy

(iii) *Purushartha* and *Panchkosha*.

(iv) *Arthashastra*.

(v) Introduction to Sankhya philosophy

(vi) *Vivekchudamani*.

(vii) Works of Tirukkural.

(d) Required standards of physical fitness.

(e) No forgiveness on any immoral acts.

(f) Self-study to be inculcated, especially for officers.

Officers with service above 25 years: Attributes and Orientation

Practical experience and knowledge make an officer wise if he has followed the path of *purusharth* and gained '*vidya*'. The officers will be senior officers holding very important and responsible appointments. These officers need to be spiritual to be extremely effective leaders.

(a) ***Purushartha***. *Kaam* and *Dharma*.

(b) ***Ashram***. *Grihastha* and *Vanaprastha*.

(c) ***Guna***. *Rajas* and *Satwa*.

(d) ***Panchakosha***. *Pranamaya, Manomaya, Vigyanmaya*.

(e) ***Ashtang Yoga***. *Pranayama, Asana, Dhayna, Dharna*.

Training aspects to be included:

(a) **Yoga**. *Pranayam, Asana, Dharma* and *Dhyana*.

(b) **Food**. 60% *Satvik*, 25% *Rajsik* and 15% *Tamsik*.

(c) **Knowledge**

(i) *The Bhagavad Gita*.

(ii) Yoga Philosophy.

(iii) Sankhya Philosophy.

(iv) Vedanta Philosophy.

(v) *Arthashastra.*

(vi) *Isha, Kena, Katha* and *Prashna Upanishads.*

(vii) *Vivekachudamani.*

(viii) Bheeshma's advice to Yudhishthira.

(ix) Works of Tirukural.

(d) Required standards of physical fitness.

(e) Self-study and meditation.

Implementation Strategy. The salient aspects that need consideration prior to putting in place the implementation strategy are discussed below:

(a) The implementation of the Ashtang way of Yoga needs to be structured in the daily curriculum of all ranks. All ranks need to understand the science behind this way of life and what is the desired end state that is being targeted. Its essence needs to be condensed into a Chetwood kind of motto of the Indian Military Academy, and it should become the guiding way of life for all those who don the Indian military uniform.

(b) A detailed syllabus needs to be evolved that can be introduced at the various Cat A and Cat B establishments of the Indian Armed Forces for covering various aspects of Ashtang Yoga. This aspect needs to be handled at the Services Headquarters and an institute of excellence like the Institute of National Integration can be nominated to evolve the syllabus.

(c) HQ ARTRAC needs to plan introduction of Yoga for all courses. The aspect of what content needs to be included as part of the syllabus with achievable standards needs to be clearly enunciated. For courses at higher levels, namely, Higher Command and National Defence College, suitable exposure in the form of a capsule needs to be introduced. Similar activities need to be carried out by the other two services as well. Being a tri-services implementation plan, HQ IDS will have to play the role of overall coordination and issue of policy guidelines.

(d) The daily routines that are to be followed at the unit, formation and station levels need to be enunciated so that it becomes a guideline for conduct of various events and programs pertaining to spiritual training. Based on the type of terrain and climatic conditions necessary modifications would have to be factored into the plan.

(e) The strategy for creating a pool of trained manpower who can then implement the spiritual development programs at all levels needs to be clearly enunciated.

(f) *Memoranda of Understanding (MOUs).* To tap the expertise of the existing wisdom in the field of *Ashtang Yoga*, the Indian Armed Forces need to enter into MOUs with organizations like Isha Foundation, The Art of Living, The Iyengar School of Yoga, etc., to seek expert guidance on framing the syllabi, provision of trainers and training the personnel of the Indian Armed Forces to acquire the requisite qualifications.

(g) *Concept Note.* However, prior to addressing all the above issues a tri-services core team needs to be nominated which will work out the modalities of charting out the plan for introduction of this subject in the Indian Armed Forces. This team will prepare the vision, mission and implementation plan with recommendation on the policy guidelines that need to be adopted. A comprehensive concept note can be prepared and presented at the Combined Commanders Conference for debate and discussion. The outcome of this discussion will enable ironing out of various issues and make a comprehensive and acceptable implementation plan.

Implementation Plan

(a) Once the planning and approvals for the proposed structures have been completed, then new verticals need to be established under the existing organisation. Thereafter, requisite policy guidelines need to be issued for time bound implementation.

(b) The stated desired end state of the proposed training would be the *Code of the Warrior* as promulgated by the Additional Director General Public Information (ADGPI)[1] as given below:

"I am a Warrior, Defending my
Nation is my Dharma"

I Will
Train my Mind, Body and Spirit to
Fight
Excel in all Devices and Weapons
Of War – Present and Future
Always Protect the Weak
Be Truthful and Forthright
Be Humane, Cultured and
Compassionate
Fight and Embrace the
Consequences Willingly.
God, Give me the Strength that I ask
Nothing of You"

(c) Once the new verticals have been raised, it is essential to form a core group of spiritual strategic leaders. This core group will thereafter steer the implementation plan in various command theatres.

(d) Based on the directions of the core group, training curriculum and training methodology would be formulated and approved. Once this action is completed, the courses at various levels can commence.

(e) For simultaneous and smooth implementation at all levels, it is imperative that HQ Commands steer the process with HQ Corps being the lead execution agency.

Southern Command Spiritual Leadership Model: A Working Model for Implementation at Command Level. As brought out above, HQ Commands are the right level from where the entire implementation plan could be steered. An example of this is the Southern Command Spiritual Leadership Model. The Southern Command at Pune under the guidance of the spiritual strategic leadership of Lt. Gen. Ajai Kumar Singh, PVSM, AVSM, YSM, SM, VSM of General Officer Commanding in Chief, Southern Command has embarked on a journey of creating the requisite environment for Indian Army personnel to get exposed to the various facets of spirituality and Indian way of life. As per the model, the following initiatives have been taken at various levels:

(a) **Talks by Eminent Personalities.** Spiritual gurus like Shri Vasudev Jaggi Sadhguru of Isha Foundation and Sri Sri Ravi Shankar of the Art of

Living Foundation were invited to deliver talks on various aspects of spirituality. These talks were open to all the ranks including their families. These talks generated a lot of interest in the personnel who were keen to get acquainted with the ways to address modern-day stress-related problems. This initial exposure was followed up with the Isha Foundation conducting a four-day Inner Engineering Program for about 60 volunteers. In this program, the volunteers were introduced to the concept of inner engineering of the body and mind and mind and soul. The volunteers were initiated to the famous *Shambhavi Mahamudra Kriya* of Sadhguru which is aimed at creating a calm and composed mind with end result being to achieve a certain degree of equanimity and ability to have an enjoyable life. The entire program was sponsored by Headquarters Southern Command and the feedback from the volunteers who underwent the initiation was extremely positive and encouraging. There are plans to introduce more such volunteer programs for Indian Army personnel so that there is a greater generation of interest to embrace the Indian way of life.

(b) **Southern Command – Prakriti Centre**. To move towards a holistic lifestyle and address various routine ailments through our age-old wisdom, a Prakriti Wellness Centre has been established at Southern Command, Pune. This is a one of its kind facility centre, probably the first in the Armed Forces, which aims at creating various facilities with a view to ensure holistic wellness amongst all ranks and their families. This centre has facilities to provide Naturopathic ways of healing, a yoga and meditation centre and provision of Ayurvedic medicines as part of the Jan Aushadi program of the Government of India. Tie-ups have been done with experts in their respective fields, namely, The Naturopathy Centre in Pune and the Iyengar School of Yoga who have readily agreed to offer the help of their experts in providing the requisite guidance. This centre has attracted a lot of enthusiasts who start their morning with meditation and yoga under the supervision of experts. The 'footfalls' since starting this centre has been substantial and clearly indicates that this is the need of the hour and points to the necessity of creating more such facilities all over the country for all ranks and their families.

(c) **Yoga Day Celebration.** 21 June every year is celebrated as International Yoga Day and is a day for all Indians to feel proud as the whole world now celebrates this day after accepting the benefits that yoga provides. As a part of it, Southern Command took it upon itself to celebrate this event on a grand scale with about 30,000 personnel joining from 34 stations across Southern Command to celebrate the event. Children and families also joined enthusiastically in the event. Expert yoga teachers from the Iyengar School of Yoga graced the event with their expert views on the importance of Yoga in our daily lives. Lt. Gen. Ajai Kumar Singh, PVSM, AVSM, YSM, SM, VSM, General Officer Commanding in Chief, Southern Command took it upon himself to explain the relevance of yoga in everyone's lives. He further compared the soldiers' lives and how many aspects of yoga are ingrained in the character of a soldier and how the organization would benefit from adopting it as part of daily routine.

(d) **Visit to Iyengar School of Yoga.** Regular visits are being organised to local yoga institutes for all ranks and their families to expose them to the expert resources that are available for learning Yoga. Expert yoga teachers are also imparting instructions on utility of yoga in arresting modern-day ailments caused due to present-day stressful lifestyle. Such an initiative has created a positive environment and lot of persons are getting motivated to follow these programs.

Highlights of the Southern Command Spiritual Leadership Model. As already discussed in the earlier chapters, the path of spirituality is an individual's personal choice and should never be enforced. Hence, the correct way of motivating someone is done best by creating the right atmosphere that arouses natural interest. Making such programs compulsory would defeat the very purpose of stoking the innate sense of spirituality of an individual. Hence, the methodology adopted by the Southern Command Spiritual Leadership Model is to provide various means and support system and let natural interest be generated towards yoga, meditation, healthy and happier living for Indian Army personnel and their families. Such initiatives, if well planned and introduced at various formation levels, will certainly yield the desired results.

Execution of Spiritual Education for Troops

While the Command Spiritual Leadership Model is one suggested way of steering the implementation plan, the first pre-requisite of an education programme of any sort would be to have well-qualified teachers. To that end, there needs to be a two-pronged approach as under:

(a) **Train the Trainers**: Focused spiritual education for the higher leadership, with an aim of empowering them to fulfil their role as spiritual strategic leaders and train the next generation of spiritual warriors.

(b) **Outsourcing Model**. In order to keep the curriculum current and infused with fresh vitality, at least 50 per cent of spiritual empowerers should be outsourced for the short term. This will also ensure that the spiritual education efforts do not become stale and templated over time. The suggested percentage can be reduced over the years as the spirituality level in the Indian Armed Forces matures.

The starting point of spiritual education for troops will have to be with the training of spiritual strategic leaders, so that they can subsequently oversee the training of their subordinates at all levels. This may be done with the following methodology:

(a) Infusion of spirituality in military courses for potential spiritual strategic leaders, such as higher command and NDC courses.

(b) Organise specific, short duration courses/cadres for senior officers, who in addition to professional competence, also show promise of becoming good spiritual strategic leaders.

(c) Encourage group and individual *retreats* at spiritual camps in order to enhance their own spiritual growth.

(d) Encourage study and research on matters related to spirituality by spiritual strategic leaders.

(e) Make them capable to selecting in-house spiritual empowerers and outside experts who would undertake the process of imparting spiritual education to spiritual warriors.

Training of Spiritual Warriors. Spiritual warriors form the *cutting edge* of any military force. In the Indian context, our soldiers are already at least aware of the spiritual roots of the Motherland, if not spiritually advanced themselves. This makes the work of training them that much easier. In fact, the *'Code of the Warrior'*, highlighted above by itself lays down the desired end state as far as spiritual warriors are concerned. This also forms the basis towards which spiritual education of troops may be channelized. In order to achieve the same, the following steps may be undertaken.

Battalion Level. Battalions are the key when it comes to spiritual education, because they are the cutting edge that the nation employs in battle. A typical battalion of the Indian Army is already a closely-knit entity of soldiers and their families. It would not be wrong to say that a battalion by itself can be compared to a living and breathing *being*. However, as is true of all living beings, different battalions have different 'personalities' as well. Hence, after giving broad guidelines, higher headquarters should ideally leave the execution to the commanding officers, while themselves keeping track of the progress via periodic audits. Suggested broad guidelines towards conduct of spiritual education at the battalion level may be as under:

(a) Enhance the scope of weekly *mandir parades* to include discourses on spirituality by the religious teacher (RT) JCOs.

(b) Introduce spiritual education as a subject during the mandatory promotion cadres for NCOs and JCOs.

(c) Modify the monthly *Sainik Sammelan* drill to include a discourse by the RT JCO to the battalion.

(d) Utilize *Family Welfare Meets* to introduce wives of soldiers to the concept of spirituality.

(e) Excursions to local places of spiritual importance may be organized for troops and their families.

(f) Introduce troops to the unmistakable linkage between spirituality and warriors from own history, by anecdotal references as under:

- (i) Lord Rama praying to Lord Shiva before the attack on Lanka.
- (ii) Lord Krishna giving the *Bhagavad Gita updesh* to Arjun before the battle against *Adharma*.
- (iii) Guru Gobind Singh invoking the blessings of Lord Shiva to help him fight the war in the defence of righteousness.

(iv) Commanding officers and troops of 18 Grenadiers performing a Havan before the successful attack on Tiger Hill during the 1999 Kargil War.

(g) Rudimentary study of Indian scriptures which themselves are full of references towards the strong bonds between spirituality and war-fighting.

(h) Introduce yoga as part of routine physical activities for troops.

(j) Culminate all routine training activities with a short, five-minute meditation session.

(k) Troops proceeding on leave be compulsorily issued books on various facets of spirituality, for them to read while travelling to their homes.

(l) Creation of *Wellness Centres* at all military stations that can, in addition to providing holistic healing, also act as informal retreats outside battalion premises.

Levels Higher than Battalions. Requirements of personnel serving in higher headquarters with respect to spiritual education are much different. This is due to the fact that they are unlikely to be directly involved in fighting an enemy, but instead their primary task is to guide and facilitate battalions that actually go into battle. In addition, these are the levels wherein spiritual grooming of current and future spiritual strategic leaders will also need to be undertaken. Suggested methodology for the same is as under:

(a) Short, 2-3 day retreats every quarter in order to take away selected personnel from their demanding jobs in higher headquarters for spiritual education.

(b) Guest lectures/talks by noted spiritual gurus for officers and men of higher headquarters.

(c) In-house seminars on aspects related to spirituality and spiritual education.

(d) Encourage personnel in higher headquarters to pursue research/PhD on topics related to spirituality in the Armed Forces while on study leave.

(e) Organise *TED TALKS* or similar events wherein not only can they deliver talks, but at the same time, also become a repository for further promulgation within the organisation.

(f) Posting selected RT JCOs as 'spiritual advisors' to strategic spiritual leaders on a trial basis. The same to be expanded based on feedback of the proposal.

(g) At the highest level, that is, service headquarters, create a post for a subedar major (RT) who can act as the spiritual advisor at the very highest echelons of the services and also help the Spiritual Studies Directorate oversee the aspect of spiritual education throughout the Services.

Objective Assessment of the Efficacy of Institutionalising of Spirituality in the Indian Army

Objective assessment can be done by formation HQs at all levels by carrying out realistic surveys. Genuine feedback mechanism practices must be ensured post termination of all training cycles to analyse the future course of action. Imparting online spiritual counselling sessions can be an excellent option for geographically separated entities in the context of the Indian Armed forces. Commanders at all levels must religiously inculcate a robust and realistic feedback mechanism for actual assessment and evolving the future courses of action. In addition, the following practices should be continued:

(a) **Regular Feedback.** A detailed feedback mechanism must be instituted in order to bring required organizational changes and improve satisfaction levels of all the participants.

(b) **Regular Reports and Returns.** Reports from commanders at all levels will enhance the scope of improvement in the training parameters.

(c) **Assessment of Test Bed Formation.** After having imparted spiritual training to all ranks for a duration of about a year, there will be a need to earmark units/formations in field/peace/CI to validate the efficacy of institutionalizing spirituality. These test bed units/formations can be assessed based on special parameters developed by the spiritual studies branch at headquarter ARTRAC. Certain suggested parameters can be as follows:

  (i) Reduction in number of battle casualty/physical casualty cases.

  (ii) Improvement in overall discipline and reduced discipline violation cases.

(iii) Reduction in cases of personnel suffering from occupational stress and life style diseases.

(iv) Increase in number of successful operations.

(v) Overall enhancement of morale and happiness quotient amongst all ranks.

(vi) Reduction in premature retirement cases.

Timelines

Short-Term. The short-term objectives should be achieved within one year of commencement of institutionalizing of spirituality in the Armed Forces. It will require dedicated establishment of organisational structures in the Indian Armed Forces at all levels. It would also include creation of the core spiritual strategic leaders. These leaders will be responsible for overall formulation and implementation of various policies in conceptualising the training philosophy, execution and management of spiritual empowerers and spiritual warriors at all levels. Formulation of training curriculum for all ranks in the organization would also be undertaken in this phase. Selection and training of spiritual strategic leaders and spiritual empowerers at various training institutes must be deliberately planned and executed. The spiritual strategic leaders must constantly make an endeavour to continuously evolve the standards of training curriculum and its training methodology. Capacity building of training institutions should be undertaken so as to enable them to commence basic level courses.

Mid-Term. The mid-term objectives should be achieved within two years of commencement of institutionalizing of spirituality in the Armed Forces. It is recommended to fully establish all related training in Cat A and Cat B establishments and units by this time. Training establishments should commence intermediate level courses. A significant pool of spiritual strategic leaders and spiritual empowerers should be created by this time. Initial evaluation of units in peace and fields should be carried out for constant improvement and enhancement of spirituality levels. It should lead to reduction of organizational stress, physical casualties and life style diseases. Preparation of case studies will go a long way for all subsequent courses being run at various training institutes. In addition, the Defence Institute of Psychological

Research must constantly recommend changes in the training curriculum at different levels to achieve the desired goals envisaged in the Indian Armed Forces.

Long-Term. The long-term objectives should be achieved within five years of commencement of the institutionalizing of spirituality in the Armed Forces. Advanced and refresher courses should commence for all spiritual warriors in the organisation at various training institutes and the Institute of National Integration. It is strongly recommended to implement changes based on progress, environmental feedback and achievement of specific goals. Test bed a formation and systematically analyse the effects of institutionalizing of spirituality in the Indian Armed Forces. Post this, incorporation of spiritual training aspects in training, administration inspections, tactical exercises with troops and exercises with troops at all levels in the Indian Armed Forces should be undertaken. Evaluation of benefits accrued from spiritual training will enhance performance and motivation levels of individuals/units in the Indian Armed Forces. Spiritual training should have enhanced job satisfaction and improved physical and psychological health of troops serving in different terrain and weather conditions. Spiritual training will play a pivotal role in reduction of disciplinary cases which will further strengthen the moral and core values of the Indian Armed Forces. It should result in reduction of physical casualties and lifestyle diseases of all ranks which in turn will directly lead to improvement of efficiency of troops.

Conclusion

Spirituality is emerging as a crucial necessity for leadership in the emerging competitive and challenging environment. The spiritual culture prevalent in the organization recognises the crucial aspect of the quest of every individual to know the purpose of their actions. Such organisations lay great emphasis on the spiritual aspects such as mindfulness, empathy, associations, ethics and beliefs. Once the importance of spirituality is understood and an organization adopts it as its regular practice, the results would be highly beneficial and they could be found in terms of joy, fulfilment, togetherness, creativity, job satisfaction, and deep commitment. Every member finds himself fully relevant. A spiritually inclined leader inspires dedication in them, substantially improves the work culture and the overall performance of the organization thus gets enhanced manifold.

Spirituality is a broad and multifaceted concept that encompasses various beliefs and practices related to the human spirit and its relationship with the universe. In the context of leadership, spirituality can substantially enhance a leader's effectiveness and the overall success of an organisation. Spirituality can provide a moral compass for leaders to guide their decisions and actions based on principles such as compassion, empathy, and integrity. When leaders are enabled by spirituality, they are more likely to make the right decisions that align with their values, which can inspire trust and loyalty among team members. This helps a leader to understand own and other's emotions better and therefore understand responses better and more maturely. Resultantly, they can create a positive work environment that fosters collaboration, creativity, and innovation. It significantly helps leaders to connect with their purpose and inspire their team members to do the same. When leaders lead with a sense of purpose, they are more likely to create a vision that inspires and motivates their team members to achieve their goals. Spirituality can help leaders cultivate resilience in the face of challenges and setbacks. When leaders are grounded in their spiritual beliefs, they are more likely to bounce back from adversity and maintain a positive outlook in difficult situations. Spirituality enables leaders to focus on serving the needs of others rather than seeking personal gain. When leaders prioritise the well-being of their team members, they create a culture of respect, trust, and collaboration that can enhance the overall success of an organization.

My research has conclusively highlighted that there is a great degree of co-relation between the constructs of spirituality and military leadership. Based on the same, it would be fair to conclude that spirituality and its important tools of yoga and meditation can effectively bring transformation in any organization to include the Indian defence forces. It helps leaders to create an atmosphere of trust and give meaning to every action, where a fine balance of work-life is maintained. Leaders develop the required control over their bodies, mind and thoughts and remain unfazed in tense situations. Our rich literature and culture clearly illustrate that leaders who have a good understanding of their self are able to understand others well, be good at inter-personal relationships, be more compassionate and are therefore more acceptable to their subordinates. They lead from the front and are able to generate the loyalty of their subordinates. Further, belief in the cause and justness of action leads to greater and conclusive actions, be it by a normal organisation or a military one.

While the introduction of spirituality in the domain of military leadership in contemporary times has its challenges, the need for its implementation is well established and cannot be doubted. Some armies have commenced the process by introducing it in their curriculum. However, the Indian defence forces have not attempted the same formally till date. This research has attempted to evolve a theory called Spiritual Leadership Indian Military (SLIM). Further, the research has recommended certain implementation strategies, one of them being the introduction of yoga, by which spirituality can be introduced in the Indian defence forces. This approach also gets credence from the fact that, world over and within the country, the benefits of yoga are now well understood and practised by an ever-increasing group of people. Hence, it is felt that the recommended implementation strategy would receive greater acceptability.

That said, it is also well understood that creating organised structures, policies and training curriculum related to spirituality require due diligence. Hence, various models for implementation have been suggested. This aspect would need to be deliberated and debated both at apex, middle and lower echelons to get a correct feedback so that the implementation is smooth and corrective mechanisms are introduced based on feedback. Needless to say, this would be an evolving subject and the structures, policies and procedures would take time to stabilise. Thus, there is no gainsaying the fact that the road to institutionalising spirituality in the Indian defence forces would be long and winding. This notwithstanding, there is also no doubt that spirituality would enable the Indian military leadership in more ways than one. The need of the hour therefore is to embrace this concept wholeheartedly so that tomorrow's military leadership is well evolved and capable of leading the Indian Armed Forces effectively through all kinds of challenges and situations that we may face in the ongoing Amrit Kaal!

NOTES

1. ADGPI on Facebook, 12 July 2014.

Bibliography

Ahmad Iftakud-din, Maj. (retd.). *Memories of a Lacerated Heart* (1971), Trafford, 2017.

ARTRAC, Leadership, 1999.

Bhaktivedanta, A.C. (1995) *Srimad Bhagwavetam*, Bhaktivedanta Book Trust.

Bhatia, Ved Prakash. *Ethical & Spiritual Values in India Scriptures*, 2016.

Bhattacharyya, Haridas. *The Cultural Heritage of India: The Philosophies*,1953.

Bhawuk, Dharam P.S. *Spirituality and Indian Psychology*, 2011.

Bladon, Lee. *The Science of Spirituality*, 2007.

Chacko, Johnson, Gp. Capt. (retd.), Chapter 23: 'Nurturing strategic leadership' from the book, *A Campaign called Victory India*, edited by Col. Vinay B. Dalvi (retd.),Pentagon Press, New Delhi, 2016.

Cloughley Brian. *A History of the Pakistan Army: Wars and Insurrections*, Skyhorse Publishing, Inc., 2016.

Dalvi, Vinay, Col. (retd.). *Victory India A way to quality military leadership*, Pentagon Press, New Delhi, 2013.

Elizabeth Scott. 'What Is Spirituality? Spirituality Can Benefit Your Health and Well-Being'.

Frawley, David. *What is Hinduism? A Guide for The Global Mind*, 2018.

Frederic and Mary Ann Brussat. *What is everyday spirituality?*

Fricker, John. *Battle for Pakistan: The Air War of 1965*, 1979.

Gardner, W.L. & Schermerhorn, J,R. 'Performance gains through positive Organizational Behaviour and Authentic Leadership', *Organizational Dynamics,* 2004.

Giacalone, R.A.; Jurkiewicz, C.L. & Fry, L.W. *From advocacy to science: The next steps in workplace spirituality*, 2005.

Grint, Keith. *The Arts of Leadership*, Oxford University Press, New York. 2000.

G.S. pamphlet on 'Leadership and Military Command'. Controller of Publications, Delhi, 1976.

Gupta, Das; Amit, R. & Lorenz. M. Luthi. *The Sino-Indian War of 1962: New Perspectives*, Routledge India, 2017.

Houston, George Gregory. 'Spirituality and Leadership: Integrating Spirituality as a Developmental Approach of Improving Overall Leader Effectiveness,', 2014.

Kala, H.B., Lt. Gen. (retd.). *Demystifying Military Leadership*, Manas Publications, New Delhi, 2005.

Khanna, K.K., Lt. Gen. (retd.). *Art of Generalship*, Vij Books India Pvt. Ltd.

Kirkland, Faris R. Combat Leadership Styles: Empowerment versus Authoritarianism.

Lal, P.C., Air Chief Marshal (retd.), *My Years with Indian Air Force*' 2009.

Lyon, Peter. Conflict between India and Pakistan: An Encyclopaedia, India's decisive victory over Pakistan in the 1971 war and emergence of independent Bangladesh dramatically transformed the power balance of South Asia, 2008.

Mclynn, Frank. *The Burma Campaign, Disaster into Triumph*, 2010.

Mishra, Sushanta Kumar and Varma, Arup. *Spirituality in Management, Insight from India*, 2019.

Nye, Roger. *The Challenge of Command*, 2001.

Palit, D.K., *The Lightning Campaign: The Indo-Pakistan War, 1971*, Lancer Publishers, 2012.

Palit, D.K. *War in High Himalayas: The Indian Army in Crisis, 1962*, C. Hurst & Co. Publishers, 1991.

Paloutzian, R.F. & Park, C.L. *Handbook of Psychology and Religion.*

Pande, G.C. *Foundation of Indian Culture*, 1995.

Pillai, Radhakrishnan and Sivanandhan D. *Chanakya's 7 secrets of leadership*, Jaico Publishing House, Mumbai, 2016.

Piryear, Edgar. *Nineteen Star, A Study in Military Character & Leadership*, 2003.

Pradhan, R.D., *1965 War: The Inside Story*, Atlantic Publishers & Distributors (P) Ltd., 2007.

Precis on Organisational Behaviour.

Rao, K.V. Krishna, Gen. (retd.), 'Prepare or Perish: A Study of National Security, *Jul* 2021.

Robert, L. and Rosenbach, William E. 'Military leadership in pursuit for excellence,' in *Ethics of Leadership* by Colonel Malham M. Wakin, Jupiter

Boulder, Westview Press, Published in India by L.D. Dewan, Jupiter Publications, Pathankot.

Sardeshpande, Lt. Gen. (retd.). Op PAWAN, some reflections', *The Custodian,* January 1993.

Scudieri, James D. *The Indian Peace-Keeping Force in Sri Lanka 1987-90, A Case Study in Operations Other Than War*, 1994.

Sharma, Y.N., Lt. Gen. (retd.). 'Military Leadership: Contemporary Challenges,' *Defence Management*, October 1995.

Sheldrake, Philip. *Spirituality: A Very Short Introduction*, 2012.

Shirish Shinde. *Guru Tegh Bahadur*, Kalyani Corporation, 2021.

Siddhantalankar, Satyavrata. *Heritage of Vedic Culture*,1972.

Singh, Amrinder, and Lt. General Tajinder Shergill, PVSM. *The Monsoon War: Young Officers Reminisce – 1965 India-Pakistan War*, Roli Books.

Singh, Jasjit. *Military Leadership for tomorrow, An article on 'Military Leadership: An Introductory essay*, KW Publishers, New Delhi, 2009.

Singh, V.K. *Leadership in the Indian Army*, 2005.

Singh, N.K. *Bangladesh: Causes of Liberation War*, Anmol Publications Pvt. Ltd,, 2003.

Slim, William. *Defeat into Victory*, 1956.

Sundararajan, K.R. and Bithika, Mukerji. *Hindu Spirituality*, 1997.

Swami Prabhavananda. *The Spiritual Heritage of India*, 2003.

Swami Ranganathanda. *The Message of the Upanishads'* Advaita Ashrama, 1980.

Swami Rangathananda. *The Spiritual Life of Indian People*, 2019.

Taylor, Robert L. and Rosenbach William, E. 'Military Leadership in pursuit for excellence,' in *'Leadership as an art'*, by Colonel Malham M. Wakin, Jupiter Boulder, Westview Press, Published in India by L.D. Dewan, Jupiter Publications, Pathankot.

Tzu Sun. *The Art of War Illustrated*, 5th century BC.

Research Papers/Publications

Aiyengar, S.R.R. 'Ethics & Military Leadership,' *Journal of Defence Studies*, IDSA, https://www.idsa.in/journalofdefensestudies

Bass, Bernard M. 'Re-examining the components of transformational and transactional leadership,' *Journal of Occupational and Organizational Psychology*, 1999.

Burack, Elmen H. 'Spirituality at work place,' *Journal of Organisation Change Management*, August 1999.

Canadian Forces College. Strengthening the Military by way of the soul. The role of spirituality in the Canadian Armed Forces.

Chawla, V. and Guda. 'Individual spirituality at work and its relations with job satisfaction, prosperity to leave and job commitment,'. *Journal of Human Values,* 16 (2), 157-167, 2010.

Descent Into Danger. The Jaffna University Helidrop, Archived 2011-06-09 at the Wayback Machine. Bharat-rakshak.com

Dissertations & Thesis. Accessed on 10 June 2021 at https://aura.antioch.edu/etds/87/ http://aura.antioch.edu/etds/8

Hindu Janjagruti Samiti 'Why is man interested in Spirituality?' Accessed on 10 June 2021 at https://www.hindujagruti.org/hinduism/knowledge/article/why-is-man-interested-in-spirituality

Howell, Ryan T. 'Why Be Spiritual? Five Benefits of Spirituality', February, 2013. Accessed on 16 July 2021 at https://www.psychologytoday.com/us/blog/cant-buy-happiness/201302/why-be-spiritual-five-benefits-spirituality

http://www.harekrsna.de/artikel/bhisma.htm

http://www.hinduwebsite.com/hanuman.asp

http://www.hinduwisdom.info/War_in_Ancient_India.html

http://www.joebm.com/papers/127-L00017.pdf

http://www.sanatansociety.org/indian_epics_and_stories/the_life_of_hanuman.html

http://www.sssbpt.info/summershowers/ss1996/ss1996-06.pdf

https://books.google.co.in/books/hanuman+as+a+leader&source

https://www.thequint.com/lifestyle/books/operation-pawan-sushant-singh-book-review-op-pawan-87-surgical-strike-that-went-horribly-wrong

India-Pakistan War, 1971, Western Front, Part I; acig.com. Retrieved 22 December 2011.

Joanna Barsh, Susie Cranston, and Rebecca A. Craske, 'Cantered leadership: How talented women thrive', *Mckinsey Quarterly,* 1 September 2008. Accessed at https://www. mckinsey.com/featured-insights/leadership/centered-leadership-how-talented-women-thrive

Kaur, Navneet. 'Leadership: The Essence of Sikhism,' *International Journal of*

Trends in Scientific Research and Development, (IJTSRD) @ www.ijtsrd.com|volume 2|issue 2|Jan-Feb 2018

Korac, Kakabadse and N. Kouzmin. 'Spirituality and leadership praxis,', *Journal of Managerial Psychology,* vol. 17, no. 3 (2002).

Kuldip Singh, *The Tribune*.' Battle of Sehjra that secured Harike Barrage', 4 December 2021, https://www.tribuneindia.com/news/comment/battle-of-sehjra-that-secured-harike-barrage-346053

Louis W. Fry. 'Towards a Theory of Spiritual Leadership', *The Leadership Quarterly*, 2003.

Manikutty, S. 'Why should I be ethical? some answers from Mahabharat,' *Journal of Human Values* 18 (I) 2012.

Mark W. Muesse. 'Buddhist Spirituality', Centre for Spiritual Growth in Memphis, Tennessee, 2002. Accessed on 13 August 2021 at http://www.explorefaith.org/livingspiritually/following _a_sacred_path/buddhist_spirituality.php

Mazza, Suzane. 'The Best definition of leadership', accessed from http://leadchangegroup.com/ best-definition-leadership/>, on 6 October 2018.

'Military Losses in the 1971 Indo-Pakistani War,' archived from the original on 25 February 2002. retrieved 30 May 2005.

'Operation Pawan. The Battle for Jaffna' Archived 2009-03-30 at the Wayback Machine.

Peri Dinakar. 'Over half of Army personnel under severe stress: Study', *The Hindu*, 8 January 2021. Accessed on 19 June 2021 at https://www.thehindu.com/news/national/over-half-of-army-personnel-under-severe-stress-study/article33528310.ece

Quotes of Swami Vivekananda. Accessed on 13 July 2022 at https://www.goodreads.com/quotes/7174617-talk-to-yourself-at-least-once-in-a-day-otherwise

Randhir Sinh, *The Tribune*. 'The visionary warrior Sagat Singh,' 11 August 2021, https://www.tribuneindia.com/news/features/the-visionary-warrior-sagat-singh-294742

Rao, K.V. Krishna, Gen. (retd.). 'Leadership Challenges at Conceptual Level', *Defence Management*, volume 27, May 2000.

Reave, Laura. 'Spiritual values and practices related to leadership effectiveness,' *The Leadership Quality Journal*, volume 16, issue 5, October 2005.

Riger, M. & Seng, Y. 'Leadership with inner meaning: A contingency theory of leadership based on the worldviews of five religions,' *Leadership Quarterly,* 2005.

Rommel, Ankur, 'Medium, 'Science, Art and Philosophy of War', 29 June 2023.

Russell, R.F., 'The role of values in servant leadership,' *Leadership & Organization Development Journal,* vol. 22, no 2, 2001.

Sadhguru. 'Spirituality is a Certain Way of Being'. Accessed on 10 June 2021 at https://isha.sadhguru.org/yoga/yoga-articles-spirituality/what-is-spirituality/

Sankar, Sidharth & Udhayakumar, C.S., 'Facets of Leadership & Management from Mahabharat,' research gate research paper.

Sant Rajinder Singh Ji Maharaj. 'Science of Spirituality'. Accessed on 15 June 2021 at https://www.sos.org/science-of-spirituality/

Server, Prem. 'Spiritual values in leadership and the effects on organizational performance: A literature review', University of Northern British Columbia, April 2013.

Shardha Batra, *The Times of India.* Speaking Tree, 'Vaak Shakti, the power of creative speech' 15 October 2021.

Sharon Jennis. 'Spirituality for Dummies'. Accessed on 7 May 2021 at https://www.spiritual-happiness.com/sfdch1.html

Singh, A.K. 'Lt. Gen. Hanut Singh — bold commander who led from front in 1971, but was never made Army chief', *The Print,* 13 April 2020.

Singh, I.J. Brig (retd.), 'Leadership Challenges', *Trishul,* vol. X (no 2).

Spencer, Maya. *'What is spirituality? A personal exploration'.* Accessed on 13 February 2023 at https://www.rcpsych.ac.uk/docs/default-source/members/sigs/spirituality-spsig/what-is-spirituality-maya-spencer-x.pdf?sfvrsn=f28df052_2#:~:text=Dr%20Maya%20Spencer,cosmic %20or%20divine%20in%20nature

Spirit of Islam. 'Spirituality in Islam: Towards Global Peace and Spiritual Living', February 2015. Accessed on 21 June 2021 at https://spiritofislam.co.in/ spiritnew/index.php/ari4

Sri Sri Ravi Shankar. *'What Spirituality Can Do For You - What Sri Sri Said',* Japan, 2 April 2017. Accessed on 21 June 2021 at https://www.artofliving.org/ wisdom/wssst/transcript-of-osaka-2-april-2017

Swami Krishnananda. *'The Philosophy of Life'*. Accessed on 21 July 2021 at https://www.swami-krishnananda.org/disc/disc_365.html

Swami Mukundananda. 'Commentary on Bhagavad Gita: Chapter 6, Verse 6'. Accessed on 16 July 2021 at https://www.holy-bhagavad-gita.org/chapter/6/verse/6

The Art of Living. '7 myths about spirituality debunked'. Accessed on 23 February 2023 at https://www.artofliving.org/in-en/wisdom/spirituality/myths-about-spirituality

The Art of Living. 'The essential guide: 8 limbs of yoga by Maharishi Patanjali'. Accessed on 17 July 2021 at https://www.artofliving.org/in-en/yoga/yoga-beginners/ types-of-yoga

http://psychology.iresearchnet.com/industrial-organizational-psychology/leadership-and-management/spirituality-and-leadership-at-work/ Sage, Thousand Oaks, CA.

'Three Indian blunders in the 1971 war,' *Rediff News*, 12 December 2011.

World History Encyclopaedia. *Bhagavad* Gita, https://www.worldhistory.org/Bhagavad_Gita/ Yogapedia, '*Raja yoga*', 10 September 10, 2020. Accessed on 10 July 2021 at https://www.yogapedia.com/definition/5338/raja-yoga

Index